PASSAGE TO VALHALLA

Undaunted Spirits Held High
  Death a Passenger in the Sky
Through dark clouds of Hellish Fires
  Through Beehives of Stinging Fighters

WE TEMPTED FATE – SOME SURVIVED

To Maria
Good Luck & God Bless
Warm Regards
Bill Fili
11-11-06

PASSAGE TO VALHALLA

THE HUMAN SIDE OF AERIAL COMBAT OVER NAZI OCCUPIED EUROPE

by
WILLIAM J. FILI

FILCON PUBLISHERS, MEDIA, PENNSYLVANIA 19063

PASSAGE TO VALHALLA
A true account of aerial warfare

All rights reserved
Copyright 1991 by William J. Fili

This book may not be reproduced in whole or in part, by mimeograph or any other means, without permission of the Publisher.

Filcon Publishers
33 Northgate Village
Media, PA 19063
New tel. Nos. 610-565-5035
Fax 610-565-7382
E-Mail basino@bellatlantic.net
Web Site www.ploiesti.net

Library of Congress Catalog Card No. 91-073148

ISBN 0-9630265-1-8

Printed in the United States of America

First Printing – August, 1991
Second Printing – March, 1993
Third Printing – March, 1999

INTRODUCTION

*Dedicated to the bomber crews and fighter pilots
who flew the fiery skies over Europe
from Schweinfurt to Regensburg to Ploiesti.*

The factual stories of the air battles over Europe will have to be relegated to history. The clear cut and colorful saga of great air victories can only be told by the surviving combatants. Vastly more important, in many respects almost impossible, is to set down in effective prose the story behind the story, the summary of all the intangibles which in the final analysis spells the difference between victory and defeat. Many chapters can never be written or pieced together for the airmen who could have done so are only a memory in some loved one's mind. Those men will never be forgotten by their fellow men who fly. Of the stories that took place in each and every airplane, those bombers that brought caput to Hitler's Nazism, will have to be told by those airmen who traveled the whole gambit in this scenario. Who were they? Where did they grow up? How did they get in the Air Corps? How they met, how they trained to become a fighting team, how they traveled half way around the world to fight in a war, how they survived, — by completing their tour of duty or —by surviving depersonalization in a prisoner of war camp? And how their lives were changed from those experiences? Of the countless examples of unselfish devotion to duty, heroism and courage, high over enemy territory, just as many will never be known.

Command decision and statistics will always be preserved in the archives. Here is the human side of aerial warfare. This story of the air battles of Europe, from Schweinfurt to Regensburg and to Ploiesti will be told through the hearts of one surviving crew. The crew of the B-24 Liberator named "DESTINY DEB". These ten young men were unique only in that they endured equally with the tens of thousands of crew members that flew those bombers and fighters in that war. Their story is a story of the gunners, the navigators, the bombardiers, the pilots who made it possible to bring that war to a speedy conclusion knowing that life expectancy in a bomber over Europe was less than one in three of surviving.

However, we who survived, did accept life's reprieve with humility and eternal gratitude. Those who did not now rest in their rightful place in The Halls at Valhalla.

A special and grateful acknowledgment to my crew buddies who helped me survive the ordeal. To Colonel Gunn who unselfishly pushed aside his own personal safety to implement the greatest rescue mission in the history of Mankind. To Colonel Kraiger and his OSS team who gathered dramatic data and photographs printed in this book and to the 28th Statistical group for it's compilation. To the National Archives, the Aero Space Museum and Tim Cronen for their expertise and help in researching those dusty files.

DEDICATION

The air battles over Nazi occupied Europe were won by Airmen who flew through the best defenses of modern aircraft and flak of the era which a determined enemy could concentrate over his most valuable resources. In the true American tradition and determination, the formations of bombers and escorting fighters of the Allied Air Forces were never turned back by the ferocity of battle.

Some of the bomber crews and escorting pilots did not return. Of all the Airmen who flew those fiery skies against the German War Machine these gave the most, their lives. To them is dedicated this story of their efforts to achieve peace and harmony among nations.

    The day after Pearl Harbor, the people of America found themselves with no Navy, no Army and no Air Force. This did not deter the American spirit of togetherness and the full weight of determination and resources was mustered to bring that war to a speedy conclusion.

    Adult American's went into the factories to produce the greatest fighting force that could be conceived by Mankind. America's youth left high schools and colleges to volunteer to be a part of a fourteen million man fighting force. Young men who had never seen an airplane, a warship or a battle field were determined to do their part. America's Nineteen year old kids, like the author pictured above, learned to fly the mightiest fighter planes, to pilot the huge four engined bombers, to sail the mightiest ships of a two ocean navy and to endure the hardships of the foot soldier in the heat of battle and under the severest weather conditions. They were asked to do a job and responded without hesitation. They put their own lives aside. They did it for America; They did it for America's people.

    In just three and one half years the people of America succeeded in bringing that two ocean war to it's conclusion. Their hopes and dreams were that this war would be the war to end all wars.

ONE

It was a short walk from curbside to the check-in desk for the next leg of my journey. I could not help but admire the immaculate cleanliness, spaciousness and efficiency of this modern 1990 air terminal. I accepted that this was the only way the Swiss could do anything, particularly here at their Zurich airport. Going through customs was rather simple, fast and purposeful. I was directed to go straight to gate #A1 to wait for the transfer bus for Swissair flight #42 to Rome. I didn't realize I was so early for my flight and thought the plane would be sparsely occupied and didn't bother to ask for a seat assignment. Besides, no seat assignments were available.

I decided that I had better exchange my money back into good ole yankee bucks. In the past few hectic days I had accumulated a variety of English, French and Italian currency. There were a few other travelers who had the same idea, and while standing in line, I could not help but be amazed at the linguistic ability of such charming young ladies to converse in the languages that I heard. They were speaking in German, Italian, French and English extremely well. With my turn at the window and as she was counting my money, I asked the lovely lass about her ability to speak in so many languages. She told me that it is not only a Swiss scholastic requirement but it is also a requirement for employment that they speak fluently in four different languages. Oh, how different it is here in America where we have such difficulty in just speaking and understanding the English language. As I left the counter I smiled at her, she returned the pleasant look and just maybe she knew that I was thinking and wishing I was thirty years younger. Resigned that my wish would not be granted I again took a seat in the waiting room.

Airports are usually very decorative and this one was no exception. In waiting for your flight there is somewhat of a hypnotic effect in scanning the same scenery over and over again. Some sort of a jolt is required to bring one's attention to being alert and this happened quite suddenly and from all directions people started to gather at this gate. People with all sorts of attire, apparently from many different cultures and speaking just as many languages. I gave no thought to the time of the year and my travels allowed me to think only in business terms.

The attendant opened the gate and the door to the transfer bus. I stood up and just as quickly as being caught up in my thoughts and mental meanderings I found myself being pushed and shoved out the terminal door and into the bus with little or no effort on my part. Again, I could not help but wonder about so many people from so many places speaking so many languages all going to the same place. Then it dawned on me, it was Wednesday before Palm Sunday and these people were going to the Vatican for the Easter Season with the Pope and at St Peter's Cathedral. Just then the thought entered my mind that the last time I flew by the Vatican City was high above the Italian coast line and the Tyrrhenian sea in the nose turret of a B-24 Liberator bomber. That thought seemed to trigger a switch in my memory bank and a deposit that was made forty six years ago in 1944.

At the airplane the same rush took place through the narrow rear door of this DC-9 jet airplane. Everyone was trying for a window seat or as far forward as possible. I couldn't even get an aisle seat and had to settle for the seat I always dreaded, the center seat of three abreast.

Taxing out and take off was uneventful and followed the prescribed program of the beginnings of most jet flights. The day was beautiful enough to make anyone glad just to be alive. There were scattered clouds and the early morning crispness made the sun seem to shine even brighter. It had the beginnings of a nice smooth flight. With everyone settled and the pilot placing the airplane in a cruise climb the stewardess began serving a light breakfast. Everyone was talking, that is to those who understood each other, they were laughing enjoying the ride and of course a few complaints about someone smoking in the non-smoking section. This required some restraint and argumentative powers of the stewardess to properly resolve successfully.

I didn't want any breakfast as I was just completely overwhelmed by the scenery and the majestic snow capped alps. Off in the distance I could see the Matterhorn peak that borders Switzerland

and Italy. I was so mesmerized at the sheer beauty that I became unaware of where I was or in fact that anyone was even near me. I felt completely alone except for the feeling of "deja vu".

As eerie as it sounds, I was suddenly alone with my thoughts about when I was last over these European Alps. Just as quickly I seemed to be taken back in time, to be exact, February 22, 1944 on a bombing mission with the target being the gigantic Messerschmidt fighter assembly plant near Regensberg, Germany. There seemed to be an eerie silence around me when I heard the sound of machine guns firing at rapid bursts. I could hear voices calling, "fighters at 10:00 o'clock high, get em Bill he's heading straight for us, fighters 4:00 o'clock low, he's yours chief, get em". Then everyone yelling "where the hell are those P-38's that were supposed to be our escort". Another voice yelling, " I see five B-24's going down and count only three chutes so far". It was so real – as if I had been frozen in time!

I jumped convulsively when the stewardess touched my arm as she was trying to place the breakfast tray on the little table where my arms were resting. She startled me so much and I in turn must have scared the hell out of her because I knocked the tray and she half dropped it in my lap. My two seat partners were noticeably disturbed. Fortunately the plastic containers had tight lids or I might have had serious problems. The stewardess' face turned an ashen white and my face must have been fiery red.

We, all four of us, made some attempt at cleaning up what could have been a real mess. The stewardess said, "are you allright sir"? And my two seat mates, a middle aged attractive woman on my right and a young man in his late twenties on my left, silently asked a non verbal question, "what's the matter with this American kook"? I didn't answer them.

I told the stewardess, "Oh, yes, yes, I'm quite allright I guess I was just thinking too intently". I motioned to her that I didn't want any breakfast anyway. She said, "how about a cup of coffee or juice"? I said, "no thank you, I will be alright." And my two fellow travelers were still eyeing me out of the corner of their eyes wondering what will come next.

After the stewardess had left I tried in the usual sneaky way to straighten out my pants and release some of the pressure from my jockey shorts. At the same time I looked around to find if something had happened to cause me to think I heard those machine guns firing. It seemed so real at the time and I am not a person prone to day dreaming. Nothing was apparent or obvious. After a few more minutes everyone including my two side-kicks relaxed and once again I found myself mesmerized at the beauty of those mountains. And once again the noise of flight, the hiss of the high speed air passing over the outside of the airplane, the sound of all those people speaking different languages, all became unnoticeable to me. Once again I was alone with my thoughts and my memories.

I was in my own little world of silence, my own little world of thought and my own little world of the sounds of combat and aerial machine gun fire. This time it seemed more real than before. My eyes were glued on that little window and my head pressing against the head rest as if in retreat. My hands clenched together with white knuckles. The outside brightness could have caused me to believe a real messerschmidt was coming straight at us with sparkle like lights shining through the propeller. But that brightness or anything else could not have caused me to digress in time to those awesome death defying days. Maybe the brightness combined with the snow capped alps could have triggered a switch that opened up my mental vault door to allow me to relive those days as a reminder of how thankful I am to be alive today.

The image of that Messerschmidt 109 seemed as real as it was that day in 1944. Those well trained Luftwaffe pilots were good at their assignments, which was downing bombers and they were cutting us up pretty bad. I did believe the sights and sounds of the ferocity of aerial warfare was a thing of the past and that I had forgotten it forever. How wrong I was. Those memories are still with me and I have no doubt with all the other men who took part in that era.

The unbelievable agonizing sights of bombers with ten strong, healthy wholesome young Americans literally being blown to bits miles above the ground in the European Skies. The torment and the anguish of watching helplessly as men were bailing out of a burning aircraft with their bodies or parachutes or both on fire is indescribable. The straining and reaching out but not being able to reach out far enough to help those men who were falling just to save their lives. In these fast and fiery moments one realizes the value and sacredness of a single human life and that it is worth every effort we can muster to save it from extinction. Some of these men I drank with to a drunken stupor, chased vailed women in the walled cities in North Africa, bunked in the same tents, laughed with and shared some of our most secretive thoughts. These thoughts and real life experiences could never be forgotten.

I probably will never know just how long or how short it will be for me to span the time to relive so many more of those horrifying experiences. In the real anguish of battle an individual does not give a single thought that what he is seeing and experiencing would someday happen to him. But it did happen and did happen unexpectedly. For very shortly it would become my turn to be the helpless one trying to escape from a bomber being blown apart. It was written in stone, or that's the way it seemed, that I was to begin a new and totally different era of my young life. It was inevitable these thoughts and youthful experiences would take me to two particular rooms. Rooms that were to become so much a participant in shaping my life. One room gave me fright, almost a death sentence, with no freedom to fight it off and, from at first, there was no returning and no escape. Another room gave me shelter and protection and finally freedom, a return from limbo and a reprieve to once again see my family and home. Again it was inevitable that my thoughts rekindled the events of my young life as a warrior of the skies. A life shared with thousands of fledgling flyers of that era who didn't have the foggiest idea of the perils and dangers they were preparing to fly into.

As my thoughts and vivid memories of those awesome days seemed to remove me, bodily, from that passenger jet above the Tyrrhenian Sea I began to hear the haunting strains of the theme song of the Army Air Corps: "WE LIVE IN FAME—GO DOWN IN FLAME"

The song was to me and all my daredevil buddies only just that, a song! We all soon learned the awful truth,– the hard way.

TWO

It is the fall of 1943, an azure clear sky is brightened by the seemingly rising sun in the east. Those brilliant rays of sunshine are silently dancing between the many rocks and cliffs of the distant craggy mountain. In following those dancing rays it is not to difficult to spot the magnificent wings of an American bald eagle as he starts his graceful morning respite of soaring down from his home on those mountain tops. For that awesome bird was and still is the inspiration of men who dare to fly uncharted skies and to temp fate for no other reason other than fate is there to be tempted. He picks up speed on his journey as he heads for the home base of the legendary B-24 Liberator bomber at the Davis Monthan Army Air Base in Tucson Arizona. (The B-24 Liberator was and is legendary, being named the Liberator by the British Royal Air Force. A total of 18,280 were built to haul heavy loads of bombs a farther distance and faster than any other bomber of that era. Including the venerable Boeing B-17 Flying Fortress of which about 12,000 were built).

Our American Eagle is heading for the flight line, where lined in neat rows are waiting Liberators, all with an awesome unparalleled mission to accomplish. Approaching, he begins to hear the sounds of military snare drums and hammered dulcimer that are soon drowned out by the cranking sound of mammoth engines as they are backfiring, sputtering and coming to life with a great roar. Directly in his flight path is the smoke from those engines, the white clouds will burn off the residual engine oil in the bottom cylinders and the black smoke from a rich air and fuel mixture that will be promptly corrected by the automatic carburetor, he does not alter his course the slightest in his quest. His dedication of purpose is only too obvious as he dives down to the center bomber heading for it's nose and soars past the astro dome and the plastic bubble of the top turret. He noticed a sign, painted by some wise cracking mechanic on top of the fuselage,

"This Side Up" as he continues through the two huge vertical fins and spots his destination. Off in the distance he sees several buses entering the base gates. He flaps his wings to gain a little altitude, starts his glide down, picking up speed on the way. His graceful flight seemed to be symbolic that particular day as he greets a new and unprecedented gathering of eagles. Perched on the top front of that lead bus as proud as he could be for he is delivering these young eaglets who soon will be quickly transformed into warriors of the open air space and out of the ever protective arms, reach and loving bosom of Mother Earth. As the bus approached the indoctrination building our Eagle cried out as if declaring "with these men I am well pleased" and as anyone would do when they succeed in their mission. Our delivering Eagle flew away never to be seen again by most of those eyes on that base that day for they will pay the eternal price for the sake of mankind.

The young men in those buses were mostly in their late teens or just into their twenties; some were yet to get their first cut from their first razor shave. Yet they did not waver the slightest at the thoughts of what they were about to learn to do, shoot to kill from the heavens. Flying in that B-24 bomber was not their choice as it was made for them. But these young eaglets accepted the assignment with grace, dignity, enthusiasm and, because of their youth, were not completely cognizant of the perils they would be subjected to.

The men in the bus were from all parts of America, rural farms, cities, towns, some left school to help win the war and others felt it was their duty. Behind them was the technical training in airplanes in general, engines and how to keep them running, armaments and how to keep guns from jamming at a crucial moment, How to operate radios normally and in emergencies. The Navigator was trained on how to get from point A to point B in the shortest possible time without getting lost. The Bombardier had to learn how to hit a target that he couldn't even see. And of course the pilots who had to learn not only how to fly the airplane safely but how to earn the faith and confidence of the entire crew. And now they had to put their training to practical use, how to live, eat, sleep and fight a war as a team, with total dependence on each other.

Just as our Eagle flew away we could see the men in the bus. Most were peering out the windows in awestruck excitement at seeing so many giant bombers in one place while a few just sat quietly in meditation. One such man was our central character, Bill Fili, from the Fishtown section of Philadelphia. An airman not yet twenty, wiry, firm jawed, a deep thinker, a maverick mature beyond his years. He too could hear the tones of military snare drums and a hammered dulcimer as the bus rolls to a stop. His eyes are glued to something out the window, the bombers, and he could not help himself as he visualized what is going to happen to most of the men on that bus. He is clearly in deep thought. He couldn't help but to ask, "How many of us, of these guys are going to be expendable?" By contrast, the men around him are in high spirits, jostling for more glimpses of the planes they will be flying in.

Bill grabbed his duffel bag and got in line to alit from the bus and to follow the gang inside. Halfway up the walk someone shouted, "Hey, Billy Fili, God I'm glad to see you." It was Randy Haney, A hill billy from the real hills of Virginia and a real friend who buddied up to Bill, in basic training in Atlantic City, airplane mechanic school in Goldsboro, North Carolina, Glenn L. Martin factory School in Baltimore on the B-26 Martin Marauder and then in gunnery school in Fort Meyers, Florida. That was the first time I ever put my arm around another man's shoulder, it was just not done in those days, but it felt good. Randy was like a brother to me. We had been through so much together. Randy told me he just got in about thirty minutes ago and was returning from the PX.

I picked up my duffel bag and together we went into the office and saw everyone gathering around a bulletin board. We saw the crew assignment lists and the vacancies that had to be filled. I spotted one crew with openings for two mechanic gunners. I said, "Randy, we been together for a long time and we got to know each other pretty damn good didn't we." "We sure did, Bill," Randy replied. I Added, "Randy, why don't we try to go through this whole damn war as a team and sign on the same crew." Neither of us hesitated the slightest and signed our names to the crew of first pilot Lt. Dana V. Varvil. Randy spotted another list, "Hey Bill, look here, we even have our barracks assignment. So let's go over and check in the orderly room and get a good bunk and maybe meet the other crew members, I wrote there names down." I could only say, "good idea, let's go,"

Once in the barracks Randy and I found two lower bunks next to each other. Foot lockers were already placed at each bunk in the aisle. Placing our name tags on our bunks enabled us to seek out the other crew members. I spotted one man I guessed would be our Engineer, only because he seemed older and more wise than most of us fledgling flyers and a man I would want to associate with. He had large work hardened hands as he began unpacking, a ruddy complexion indicative of hard work in the fields and I couldn't help but notice the eagle's claw he placed so gently on his socks. His name tag was yet to be placed but I had to ask, "Are you Bob Culver?" "Yes I am," was a quick response. "Well, I'm Bill Fili, just another member of your crew." I yelled to Randy, "Randy come here a minute" and introduced him to Bob.

I guess my calling to Randy helped the other three crew members to shed their shyness as they walked over and shared themselves en masse. Nothing was said but the feeling we all had that day as we met for the first time was a rare experience that could only happen once in a lifetime. The enthusiasm and cohesiveness that suddenly developed made us all feel more relaxed knowing at least all the non coms on this crew would be able to work together and depend on each other. Our war time family of brothers was off to a good start.

Charlie Kourvelas, a spunky lad of Greek origin from Memphis would be our tail turret gunner. Charlie was only out of high school about a year before joining the Air Corps and leaving his father without his assistance in running the family restaurant. Charlie went to armament school before gunnery school and will be our armour technician. It was easy to see that Charlie would be the one member of our crew that was always looking out for a pretty skirt to chase.

John Foster, for some unknown reason we instinctively nick named him "chief". Chief, raised on a farm outside Denver, went to Armament school before gunnery. Chief had a firm square jaw, always smiling, extremely likable but would never tell us what the hell he was always smiling about. Chief will also be our armour technician.

When Paul Swearingen introduced himself I bit my lip as I almost asked him how old he was. To me he appeared to be about fifteen or sixteen years old. Paul, like Chief, was always smiling, maybe that caused his reddened complexion. Paul went to radio operators school at Scott Army Air Base before gunnery school. We were soon to learn that Paul was much more than an ordinary radio operator. At home he was a ham radio buff and built his own radio system so powerful he could speak to anyone in the world. He soon became the envy of all the crew commanders who tried to pull rank and have him transferred to their crews. But Paul had the last say. The togetherness displayed at our first meeting was sufficient to form an unbreakable bond of friendship.

In sharing each others attributes and claims to fame for the next unrecorded minutes Charlie walked behind Bob's bunk to open a window, got a face full of blowing sand and just as quickly closed it saying, "Don't they have anything but dust and sand down here, gimme gunnery school any day. Instead of broads all we have is sand." I couldn't help but add, " Yeah, Charlie, but look what you'll save on booze. Or you don't drink yet, do you? Neither do I."

Bob told us that he arrived early this morning and found out that we will meet the rest of the crew in the morning with an introduction to the Liberator. We have to be at the engineering office at 7:00 AM tomorrow.

Breakfast enjoyed, bunks prepared for inspection in our absence we headed for the engineering office on the flight line. Bob took the initiative and asked around among the officers there for Lt. Varvil and upon finding him called us all over and completed introductions. All ten of us were noticeably quiet just sizing each up. Lt. Varvil was an extremely good looking man and, a little older than us, maybe about twenty eight, but younger than Bob. He appeared to be a quiet reserved type, a deep thinker and one not prone to fly off the handle at the slightest of provocation rather one who would know how to accept the responsibility of being an aircraft commander.

Lt. Varvil introduced us to our other officers. Lt. Lenus Bahti, Co-Pilot; Lt. Glen Boyle, Navigator; Lt. Edward Bell, Bombardier. We all seemed to take a quick liking to Lt. Bahti and his red smiling face when he said, "son of a buck, looks like we have an intelligent looking crew." Bahti, hailed from the cold northern part of Minnesota and was a tractor/trailer truck driver experienced in driving the rocky mountain hills without too much difficulty. He later told us that he went to cadets and pilot training on a bet and not expecting that he would pass with flying colors as he did. Our navigator Lt. Boyle was just out of college and not being taken to piloting too enthusiastically opted for a course in navigation. Bombardier Lt. Bell appeared not too happy with his assignment and for what reason we were never to find out. Outwardly he would say very little but inwardly we surmised that he wanted to be alone. We accepted his choice knowing that we would not have to depend on him for survival or the operation of the airplane.

Introductions complete, Lt. Varvil invited us out to the flight line and our assigned plane for indoctrination. At the plane the crew chief wouldn't let us go aboard until the engineering officer arrived so we just walked around that huge bucket of aluminum parts.

The engineering officer, a bird Colonel, was much older than any of us, I would guess in his fifties, was extremely gruff in his mannerisms and would tolerate no snide remarks about his bombers belonging to a brothel with all other pregnant prostitutes. We had heard rumors of him blowing his top if anyone asked him, "How does this plane get off the ground?" He started his lecture by saying, "gentlemen, if you're going to fly in this bomber you had better make up your mind this very minute to start liking it, if not you're free to leave right now for another assignment." He hesitated a minute and seeing that none of our crew left he said, "Fine let's get started." His voice and facial expressions changed dramatically as he started his lecture. "This," he said, "is a B-24 Liberator and is and will be for some time to come the work horse of the Army Air Corps. Gentlemen, this is the plane that from all engineering standards cannot possibly get off the ground." Pointing up with his index finger, "That is the famous Davis wing that is also not supposed to create sufficient lift to get a kitty car off the ground. But, Gentlemen, let me tell you. I've lived with these planes from their conception and design in early 1939 until the first plane flew on December 29, 1939 at Lindbergh Field in San Diego. I'm proud to say that no one knows or loves these beasts more than I do. I've flown them just about anywhere, in any kind of weather, I've skipped waves on a bumpy ocean and flown around mountain peaks and I'm here to tell about it. Gentlemen, learn to love this ugly bitch and she will never let you down. And another thing I'm the only one around here that can call her an ugly bitch, don't ever let me hear anyone else say it." He continued his walk around the bomber pointing out the various items that we, by shear necessity, must know inside and out. He continued, "Against flak, you have very little protection, against fighters you will have twin fifties in the tail turret, the top turret and the ball turret. By the time you're heading for that shooting war you will have twin fifties in a nose turret." He inquired "who will be the nose turret gunner'" I answered, " I am sir, Bill Fili." Speaking to me he said, "Sergeant, don't listen to all the tall stories about that nose turret falling out while in flight, it's just not so! There has never been one fall out yet, they are now being used in England. You will also have two fifties in the waist, one at each window."

Passing the other side he stopped at the ball turret and asked, "who's going to drive the ball turret"? Chief said, "I am sir, John Foster." "Sergeant, you will have to depend on your crew mates in the waist to help you in and out. As you can see it retracts up inside during landings." Lt. Bell asked, "what happens if you can't retract it for landing or maybe forget to retract it." The Colonel said pointing to Chief, "he's the one we pick up with a mop and pail, so just don't forget to do anything. Alright all you gunners can get aboard and familiarize yourself with your various positions. You two pilots will join me in the cockpit for familiarization on how to fly a real airplane and both of you will start flying in the morning with your two engineers. The rest of you gunners are scheduled for lectures so check the bulletin boards."

The Colonel reluctantly, or unknowingly, showed us his soft side as he said, "I've seen a lot of crews come through here, some I would have liked to ground, others were so so, but I like what I see here. Lt, Varvil and Lt, Bahti, I think you two have the makings of a great crew I can only wish you the best of luck and God Bless you all." He then climbed into the cockpit, took the right seat, Varvil in the left seat and Bahti standing and listening from behind.

We six non coms must have spent at least two hours before lunch at this warbird. After the lectures and dinner we went to the PX for a round table discussion of our ordeal and getting to know more about each other. We all were enlightened to know that Bob used to do some barn storming with biplanes in his younger day. It sure was a pleasure to know that he knew so much about flying, we could learn from him. Thus we knick named him Pop.

Chief queried, "So whatta you guys think of our officers? Do you think they're gonna be chicken shit?" That Bombardier, what's his name, Bell? I didn't like that smirk on his face when the Colonel told us that I would be mopped up with a broom and dust brush?" Pop changed the subject and said, "Guys, I think out pilot Varvil may not be very experienced now but he is going to learn his way around the sky real fast. I'll take any bets on it. And Bahti is going to right behind Varvil when it comes to ability, we got nothing to worry about or who's flying our airplane. Our worry is going to be who's shooting at us." Randy expressed his opinion, "I think Bell is going to be a loner, which doesn't make any difference cause he isn't going to be shooting any guns." I had to add my two cents. "I agree with everything just said but I hope when and if we have to fly across the Atlantic Ocean our navigator Boyle isn't as nonchalant as he seemed today. He just might have the attitude of "what the hell" if we get there ok, and if we don't so what. I don't think that would set too well with Lt. Varvil." Pop ended the analyzing of our crew by repeating what the Colonel said about us, that should have made us feel real good about ourselves. It did just that. "Besides," Pop added, "I kinda liked the way Varvil nestled his butt into the left seat, he knows what he's doing." Charlie was noticeably quiet but asked, "why do you think Varvil called this crew meeting tomorrow morning at 7:30 AM." Paul quipped in, "I hear these two guys never flew anything bigger than that twin engine trainer called the bamboo bomber or something." Pop came back, "don't you give it another thought, they will be ok in my book." I was not the one to let an in go by unnoticed so I couldn't help but to level a pun at Paul, "don't worry, Paul, they get training wheels for the first couple of flights."

Our morning chores, breakfast, preparing our bunks for daily inspection completed we walked over to the flight line and the little briefing room we were assigned for this crew meeting. We non coms thought it to be unusual but later found out all conscientious first pilots acted in a like manner. The room was small, a few maps on the wall of the tri state area Arizona, New Mexico and Utah, a table in front center and just enough chairs to accommodate a full crew. I was looking up our location on the map when Lt. Varvil entered and promptly took my seat in the last row. Varvil went directly to the front and sat on the edge of the table, his look was all business. "Good morning gentlemen," was his greeting and returned with a like response. I called this meeting to say something, only once. And what I am about to say stays in this room. If it ever gets back to me someone will be looking for another crew mighty fast. We all looked at each other in an exchange of questions, like, ah shit, what's coming next?

Varvil's voice was totally firm for the purpose at hand. Neither loud nor soft, neither harsh nor forgiving, but a straight from the shoulder serious talk with his crew. He started his talk, " Damn soon we'll all be in the middle of a shooting war, a war we did not start and did not want, but rest assured we will be in it. We've got to know, now, just what we can expect from each other." Again we all exchanged glances. "Right now let's drop any ideas of glory and forget about the bombs we're going to drop on the Nazis. Let's forget about saving the world for democracy, unit citations or a hero's welcome at the end of the war. Forget about everything but surviving. Don't get me wrong, we will accept our assignments and fulfill our duty and fight the Nazis with bombs and bullets. But our primary function is to survive, survive to fly another mission, surviving the war, surviving to make it home in one piece and raise a family." Varvil hesitated as he looked everyone of us squarely in the eyes. He continued, "my job is to get your butts home safely before you bleed to death. In our plane, accomplishing the mission is secondary." Again he pauses to let his words sink in. And they did. The sense of feeling at that moment was one of cohesiveness, Varvil had brought these young eaglets to an awareness they never knew. They were instantly transformed into an unbeatable team.

In a more relaxed frame Varvil spoke more softly and added, "that's my half of the bargain. Your half is to do your jobs as if your lives depended on them – as they do, believe me, along with every one of us in this room. What I am adding is, if we ever get shot down, it had better be by flak – and not because some gunner let a Messerschmidt slip through. I don't give a flying damn if your barracks passes inspection or not, or if your hair is too long, but turn in a sloppy gunnery score." Varvil stopped short looking at each and every gunner. He turned to navigator Boyle, "get us lost for no apparent reason;" Turning to Paul, "failure to keep our radios in top notch condition;" and added quite softly, "gentlemen the key to success is the proper performance of the individual tasks. Fail in your duties for no apparent reason I'll be down on you with fang and claw." I could not help but to have a smile on my face and I hope it was taken as complete approval of what was said. I knew right away that we have us a real leader.

"One last thing" Varvil said, "I'm not a party pooper, I like a good time just as much as anyone else, but show up just once on the flightline with a hangover, or overfire your guns, report for a mission when you know your too sick to fly maybe you'll be looking for a new crew. Now I had my say and I want to hear how this sets with all of you." Varvil relaxed and sat completely on the table waiting for some one to say something. For the first time there was stirring in the chairs. We all knew nothing else could be said, we had achieved togetherness. Varvil got to his feet and smiling for the first time said, "Then, gentlemen, we have a pact. And with God's help, some bad aiming by the Nazis, and enough gas we'll land as many times as we take off in our plane."

The momentous day had arrived, we all completed our indoctrination with flying colors with no hitches, we were going to fly as a crew for the first time. Varvil and Bahti had passed their final check rides and Pop received a superb engineering evaluation. Being the second engineer to fill in should Pop get sick I too struggled and passed my engineering evaluation. Preflight complete and all crew members aboard Pop assisted the pilots in starting the engines. Taxing out, take off and climb to about six thousand feet was routine. Being only about 7:45 AM the air was as smooth as glass making our initial team effort a pleasure. This plane did not have a nose turret, a "D" model, but a full plastic nose where I sat alone thoroughly enjoying the scenery. Varvil and Bahti were putting the plane through some maneuvers to get the feel of this big bird. Pop was keeping his eyes on the engines and the gas supply while just behind him Paul was delving into his first love, radios, any kind of radios would make him happy. Us other gunners just enjoyed the ride. Finally after three hours of flying Varvil turned for Davis Monthan Air Base. The landing gear dropped, Randy called in two main gear down and locked, while I checked the nose gear being locked down. Varvil brought the plane in rather hot, too fast, and lands hard, nearly driving the struts up through the wings and taxis to the flight line. Dropping out of the plane we all wanted to check the landing gear struts. I passed Varvil and Bahti as they were looking up into the right wheel well and found the urge to offer a good natured needle, "Shoulda put in a chit for those training wheels — Sirs" As I continued walking away I overheard Bahti say to Varvil, "son of a buck, it really did stay together."

We had our eyes opened that evening when looking at the bulletin board and our flying schedule for the next day. We were scheduled for a six hour long range navigation mission coupled with dropping a few practice bombs. Take off at six in the morning. Our afternoon mission was to be low level gunnery, air to ground, from two to six o'clock. In unison we said, cheez, we gotta fly ten hours tomorrow. Just then the operations officer walked by and said, "you guys had better get some rest because that schedule is for every day for the next two weeks. You're only day off will be Sunday, maybe you'll want to go to church." We just looked at him. As he walked away he turned his head back to us and added, "that shooting war over there isn't going to go away by itself."

The morning flights were enjoyable even with the oxygen masks on our faces for hours at a time, part of our training. The first bomb dropped by our bombardier missed the target by more than five hundred feet. Chief called on the intercom "ball turret to bombardier, looks like your bomb sight is out of focus or something, sir." Bell came back, "keep your snide remarks to yourself." That was when we found out the Lt. Bell lacked a sense of humor.

But those afternoon gunnery training missions were something else. The morning flights were in smooth flying weather. The wind had not picked up because of the low position of the sun. Not so in the afternoon when the sun was at its apex causing the plane to bounce around like a tin can in a hurricane. We were supposed to fly around the hills and mountains and shoot at toy airplanes on the ground as they came into sight. For two weeks each afternoon we would spend three hours shooting at something that went past so fast it was only a blur. But that wasn't the only problem. Being young eagles that have yet to learn how to fly we were constantly up chucking each and every afternoon. I couldn't help but laugh one day on seeing Chief scrambling out of the ball turret making a mad dash to the waist window to perform his daily routine of chucking his lunch. Only this day he faced the wrong direction and what he threw out was blown right back into his face. Varvil and Bahti didn't believe us when we discussed the erratic nature of the rear of our plane. So on one mission Varvil came back to try his luck at shooting at those targets. He stayed long enough to know that he wanted no parts of the waist position and on leaving he said, "I gotta get the hell up in my seat before I get sick too."

Our initial training in a B-24 Liberator was hectic to say the least. In two weeks we learned that the engineering officer who gave us our first lecture on this monster of a plane was right. We did quickly learn to love and believe everything he said. In particular we learned that it does have the capabilities of getting us from point A to point B safely. Only in whispers did we call her an "ugly bitch".

Time really flew by with keeping so busy learning how to fight a shooting war. The operations bulletin board listed our crew as being transferred to Alamogordo, New Mexico where we will be assigned to the new 450th bomb group. But first we were being given a ten day leave. That didn't give me much time at home as it would take three days to go to Philadelphia and three days to return. In those days we could not understand why passenger trains were constantly being side tracked for freight trains. Only later, when we were in that shooting war did we realize that those freight trains were carrying life saving food and ammunition to the Marines on the island of Guadalcanal and to the doughboys in North Africa to keep them from becoming expendable. In leaving Davis Monthan Army Air Base we found ourselves, in just three weeks, transformed from young eaglets to a well honed flying team. We had become as one and learned that each one of us can not and will not let the others down.

THREE

The short visit with our families ended as rapidly as the past year had vanished from our lives. I didn't have to tell my mother, brothers and sisters that I was going over seas to that shooting war, they knew it was inevitable. Randy had taken a train from his hometown of Barboursville, Virginia to Philadelphia where I met him at the station. We were scheduled to leave on the midnight express for Chicago and then onto Alamogordo. But, first we had enough time to go downtown to the USO at the Reyburn Plaza for some dancing and just plain enjoying the nostalgic music of that era.

Being used to the big cities of the north I was shocked to see a town as small as Alamogordo. From my young perspective I could not see more that a dozen houses at one time and they were divided equally on both sides of the hard packed clay street. A GI truck took us to the air base and the sight was not much different than the town. Randy and I just looked at each other wondering if we were in the right place. We could see no bombers or anything else that came close to resembling an airplane. The contractors appeared to be putting the finishing touches on some long strips of concrete that could be used for runways. Off in the distance we could see a few buildings and what looked like new barracks under construction.

The truck that picked us up at the train station stopped at one of the finished buildings and the GI driver said that this is the end of the line. Jumping off we did see the sign on top of the doorway 720th Bomb Squadron, our new home away from home. Randy and I entered and reported to the first sergeant. He looked at us with a puzzled look on his face and said, "what the hell are you guys doing here, you're not scheduled to be here until the fifth of September and here it is only the second. What am I supposed to do with you." I answered, "I don't know Sarge, we're just following orders. Just think, we could have had a few more days at home." Our new first sergeant seemed, at first sight, to be quite gruff and his patience had a short fuse. But after noticing his desk we knew he had to be snowed under with a mountain of paper work in getting his new assignment whipped into some kind of shape. After taking a deep resigned type of breath he added, "Well, over on the other side of that runway you'll find a row of six man tents go on over and take your pick. There won't be any barracks ready for some time to come." That set well with us because all six of us non coms will be together.

The following day the rest of the crew showed up and the only immediate surprise was that our navigator Glen Boyle got married while home and brought his wife, Eleanor an extremely attractive young lady who could be mistaken for a movie star, back with him. It took a few days for him to tell us but Pop Culver also got married while home and that his wife will be joining him in a week or so after she makes some necessary arrangements for the trip. The next two weeks at this newly commissioned Army Air Base was humming with such excitement that we young eaglets had never seen. Getting our flying gear all sized to each man, attending lectures, getting to know our parachute riggers and finally Liberators were beginning to arrive with a full complement of mechanics, specialists and all the other personnel required for such an organization. By the end of September the 450th Bomb Group did resemble a fighting/flying organization. We were going to have a total of sixty two brand new factory fresh B-24 bombers split evenly between four squadrons before leaving for that shooting war we were being trained to participate in. Once assembled our group commander Colonel John Mills, a West Pointer, made it his personal obligation to meet and to get to know each and every man. Colonel Mills was a big man with a kind and gentle nature. A man we all learned to respect not only as our leader but more importantly as a compassionate human being, a trait that surfaced after some heated aerial battles. Only in hindsight and many years later did I realize the awesome responsibility laid on his shoulders. The awesome responsibility of leading more than six hundred healthy young men into aerial battles, battles that only a few may return. Again in hindsight, would we have volunteered for such duty if we knew before hand just what was in store for us?

Some of the first Liberators that arrived were the same training "D" models we were flying at Davis Monthan Air Base. We flew the appropriate long range navigation missions at high altitude, getting used to and enduring the oxygen mask on our faces and to the accompanying extreme cold weather. There were day and night time practice bombing missions intermixed with as many air to ground gunnery missions. Concentration was placed on endurance as we had to prepare for bombing missions lasting anywhere from three to eight hours with more than half the time spent behind the oxygen mask in bitter cold weather. We purposely did not fire any of the guns while on those navigation and bombing missions for the obvious reasons, "what goes up must come down." And those bullets and spent shell casings could harm some innocent people below.

Varvil was scheduled for an instrument night check ride one evening with take off at 2100 hours. The Checkout pilot was a very likable man, Lt. Nicholas Kordich, whom we later learned was a professional civilian pilot and a former daredevil barnstorming pilot. (After the sneak attack on Pearl Harbor by the Japanese our government found that it had no pool of pilots to draw from other than the private pilots who were doing their thing of performing daredevil aerial shows for the enjoyment of the public. These practical men were the nucleus of the massive build up of the American Air Corps. With their flying expertise and dedication to serve, World War II was brought to a speedy conclusion).

We all gathered at the plane except Bahti, Boyle and Bell as their presence was not required for this flight. Pop and I preflighted the plane and found it to be airworthy then we all climbed aboard. Taxing out was, again, rather routine. Pop assisting in running up the engines prior to take off, Varvil calling the tower that he was ready to roll with clearance being given for immediate take off. Rolling down the runway, gaining flying speed and just before reaching the right speed to lift the nose wheel off the ground the unexpected happened and the nose wheel collapsed and the plane started to veer alternately from the right and then to the left. It took all the training and experience he had learned in his short flying life for Varvil to hold the plane in a straight line and on the runway. Meanwhile Lt. Kordich was helping at the controls and calling the tower for the emergency fire trucks. In the rear of the plane we all were thrown forward by the pitch of the fuselage and ended in a heap of human confusion on top of the ball turret, not knowing what the hell happened to the plane. Not thinking, we instinctively, once the plane stopped moving, all scrambled up for the camera hatch to jump out. We didn't realize the tail of the plane was so high and the long drop seemed like an eternity. The sudden jolt when hitting the ground in the darkness led us to believe we landed in hell or some other undesirable place.

Chief and I ran forward to help and to make sure Varvil, Kordich and Pop got out of the plane safely but we found them already out and getting away from the burning plane. The nose had erupted in a small fire that quickly spread to a huge fire-ball when the hydraulic fluid ignited. Just as the fire enveloped the entire nose section the fire trucks arrived. One fireman threw his axe through the plexiglas while another shoved the foam hose in the hole and the fire was smothered in less than an minute. Timing was just right for us that night and a near catastrophe was turned into a small occurrence through the courage of those fireman. Our combat training was so intense that little attention was presented to us of the availability of support personnel such as the fire and rescue teams at any airfield and the dangers they would be subjected to. That small incident served to alert us to need and respect all of the support personnel in any organization. It was a wonderful feeling to know that help would be available on a split-seconds notice should the need arise. On the ride in the truck back to the operations office Lt. Kordich echoed the same observations concerning our crew as did the Engineering Colonel back in Tucson, "You guys are going to be allright, a good crew with good pilots. I know I haven't met your co- pilot yet but if he is like you guys you all will be ok."

Sleep came quite easy that night. When preparing to go to war there is no waste of time and efforts. Lots of overtime was spent by the crews in their training exercises and the ground crews in keeping the planes in an airworthy condition. So to it was incumbent on the contractors to get the facilities built as quickly as possible. We were notified a barracks would be ready for us to occupy within a week. However, since we were not going to be here in Alamogordo much longer we were given, by our first sergeant, the option of staying in the tent or moving, we opted for staying in the tent. We weren't the neatest crew that ever existed, not the sloppiest, but the thought of not being harassed by daily bunk inspections was a blessing in disguise.

There was some leisure time from the constant lectures and training flights and this time was spent either at the PX where I, for one, learned to drink beer even though it was low in alcohol content or time was spent at our tent where we could sun bathe while watching some pilots drive those ever forgiving bombers into the runway. It was meaningless for us to take the time to find out how many washed out.

One day Randy and I were lazying around in front of our tent when Randy noticed a B-24 turning on a downwind leg for his approach to the runway that paralleled our tent. We watched the landing gear coming down. We did not know why this particular plane was an attraction but it was. It continued on downwind, turned on base leg and then onto final approach. It was a clear calm day, practically no wind at all and it appeared this pilot was making the classic approach, meaning a good approach usually results in a perfect smooth landing. For some unknown reason, when about a mile from the end of the runway, the landing gear was retracted up cleanly. I nudged Randy, "Hey, get this, this guy is going to buzz the runway." Randy said, "Yeah, but what's he doing with his flaps all the way down, if he's going to do any buzzing." We both were awestruck in watching him come ever closer and closer to the runway. I interjected, "Boy, this guy must have phenomenal depth perception, look he's down to about a foot and still going." We were shocked at what we saw. That clown made the most beautiful precise belly landing that could be made and just skidded to a stop.

That belly landing was the talk of the PX beer hall that evening, No one had a grand stand seat as did Randy and I but no one would believe us. We learned that there were two pilots being checked out, one instructor pilot, two engineers being checked out and one instructor engineer. It seems the instructor pilot pulled the gear up to check if the pilots and the engineers would perform the required final (Andy) G-U-M-P check of gasoline, undercarriage (landing gear) mixture and props before arriving at the imaginary fence at the end of the runway. This was ok except that the instructor pilot forgot that he had retracted the gear. The conclusion of this saga was that a couple of pilots and a couple of flight engineers had to go back to school.

Our first hair raising experience in training occurred when Varvil and Bahti began to learn to fly in formation. We all had to go with them, even on their first few flights as none of us were accustomed to flying so close to other airplanes. Our flight leader was a young man who just passed his twenty third birthday, 1st Lt. John Giraudo. Blessed with a body that could be compared to a roman gladiator, standing near six feet four inches and a tantalizing boyish smile. Lt. Giraudo could also be described as a hot shot pilot and almost uncontrollable. His superior flying ability was on a par with his flamboyant attitude. Giraudo's flying agility was so natural that most of us had the idea when he was born he must have brought the stork instead of the other way around. I particularly remember him standing in the waist window of the lead plane coaxing Varvil and Bahti to come in closer and we in turn from the waist window would call on the interphone, " Pilot from the waist, don't you think you're close enough. How about calling over to Giraudo and ask him to check on who's flying his airplane." When our training in formation flying was over it became so routine with Varvil and Bahti at the controls we never gave it another thought because they were the best. We used to chide them that they must be getting stage freight and afraid to stick the wingtip in the other planes waist window. Flipping wingtips was a "no-no".

Our days in Alamogordo from the beginning of September to the middle of November were as hectic as could be expected. Every possible preparation for aerial combat was not over looked in our training ritual. The practical side of war, having someone shoot at you, was by sheer necessity delayed until the real thing was forced upon us. What little idle time we had was spent in answering letters from home and just slopping up 3.2 beer at the PX or spending time at the gym conditioning our bodies. As for me I managed a little time for a cute little girl in the PX who took me horse back riding cowboy style on several occasions and for dinner at her families home.

For some unknown reason Colonel Mills took a liking to our crew and flew more than once with us on those long day and night navigation flights. We didn't know it at the time but even the group commander had to keep up his flying skills to be the leader he was.

It was the middle of November when we noticed more and more military police personnel appearing at this air field. We could only guess "our time had come". The entire group was suddenly and without prior notice summoned to the base hanger. Colonel Mills spoke to us and, yes, we guessed right as he explained, all personnel who have their wives or other family members in town will have twenty four hours to say good bye. The base will be sealed off and no one will enter or leave as of 1700 hours tomorrow afternoon. All leaves are cancelled as of that moment and no off duty passes will be issued. Pop and Boyle had to scramble to help their wives obtain train tickets to return home.

Every crew had received their new bomber except our crew and we thought we were going to wind up as an alternate. Our fears were alleviated the following morning when Varvil was notified that he will have to test fly a new plane for Army acceptance that afternoon. A brand spanking new factory fresh Liberator from the Ford Willow Run assembly plant did arrive on the morning of November 18, 1943. Varvil, Bahti and Pop preflighted the plane and then spent two hours in the air checking and double checking the engines, all the flight instruments, control systems and upon landing Varvil signed the acceptance documents and the bomber #42-52142 was ours to fly. It was as exciting as receiving a new toy at Christmas and we savored every minute of it. It was exciting to check out our toys of destruction, that is, until we realized what we are going to have to do. By necessity we had to put those fun thoughts out of our minds and get busy with knowing our new aerial home.

The first group of ten planes left Alamogordo bright and early on November 20, 1943 for the overseas staging area in Herrington, Kansas. We were scheduled to leave on November 23, 1943 and honored that Colonel Mills had decided to fly with us. That caused us non-coms somewhat of a problem in that we would be required by sheer necessity to be on our good behavior at all times. When we arrived in Herrington we found that air base a bee hive of activity. All planes were double checked for any major or minor malfunction, if any were found it was corrected immediately. All guns were removed from the planes and they too were checked. We were issued brand new heavy sheep lined flying gear, new parachutes, a complete new set of uniforms and personal gear such as oxygen masks, electric heated suits and a new forty five caliber pistol still packaged in that oily cosmoline. That was during the day hours. At night we sat, not by choice, through lectures on the do's and don'ts of combat flying. Lectures on survival if and when we would be shot down over enemy territory. We were told that, if we were lucky, we would be among the thirty percent that would finish a tour of duty. (Before being discharged after the war I found some records that indicated the survival rate of my gunnery class. Out of two hundred and fifty men in that class in July 1943 at Fort Meyers, Florida only twenty seven completed their missions.) All the others would either be killed or end up in a prison camp. We were lectured on how to survive in a prison camp, and how to harass the enemy while in that prison camp.

We were told that the enemy would not hesitate to use torture on us if they thought it would be in their best interest. We were lectured on how to survive those tortures if it should come to that. We were told things that seemed to be taken right out of some science fiction book, stole or pledgered off a sound stage in the movie mecca of Hollywood. This information was awfully hard for us to swallow or to accept. The lecturer was an OSS agent. He told us tales of how he infiltrated the enemy lines on more than one occasion and he implored us to listen to him, to heed his advice as he said, "it just might save your life in a perilous situation." A situation that we could never come close to imagine ever being involved. We later learned of the awful truthfulness of his words. Yes, we did learn — the hard way!

The next leg of our overseas journey took us to Morrison Field, near West Palm Beach, Florida. Noticeably absent from our manifest was Colonel Mills as he had received urgent orders to proceed ahead immediately. Assigned to fly with us in his place was navigator Lt. Eagan, another radio operator Robert Bohannon and our crew chief Thomas Cox. Once there, for only three days, we received another physical and had all our equipment double checked and the plane was checked over once again. This was our last chance to change our minds about being on a bomber crew but, no one opted for this out.

The Army Air Corps did their share of planning for the air crews. We were allowed to buy candy, chewing gum, personal toiletries by the carton to take with us. The limit of one carton per item was placed so we would not overload the plane with non essential goods.

The day before we left I found Pop at the PX counter and as I walked up to him said, "Hi, Pop, whats'ya buying" He didn't respond at that moment so I just observed. The girl behind the counter was as pretty as any movie starlet would want to be and the type we young pups only dream about taking home to meet Mom. I guessed she was about nineteen years old. I said, "Pop, I hope you're not trying to make time with this lovely lass, are you." Pop responded, "no, don't be such an idiot." Pop was buying a carton of hershey kisses, chocolate bars, chewing gum and some razor blades. As the young lass was adding up the charges Pop suddenly said, "Oh there is one other thing. Do you have any prophylactics." (In those days it was a bit embarrassing to go into a store to ask for a rubber or condom even if a man was behind the counter). The lass just nodded her head in the affirmative. Pop added, "let me have a box them." The lass left and brought back a packet of three rubbers. Pop said, "this isn't enough, do you have a larger package." Again she nodded in the affirmative but with a little blush on her face. She left and returned with a small box of twenty four rubbers. Pop again said, "Don't you have a box with a larger quantity." The lass's face began getting redder with embarrassment and said, "the next size box is a gross." Pop, with a smile on his face said, "now you're talking honey that's what I want." By this time the lass's face is as red as a jersey tomato. She left the window and returned with the gross of rubbers and while she was wrapping the box Chief walked up to the counter and seeing the lass wrapping the box of rubbers and not knowing what it was said, "Hi Pop, what ya buying a box of cigars." That was the last straw for the young lass, the embarrassment was too much for her as she threw the box of rubbers at Pop and walked away from the counter. An older man came over to Pop to help finish his purchasing. The humor of that little incident was repeated many times during our tour overseas. A supply of those rubbers became as much a part of Pop's battle gear as bombs and bullets each time we took off on a mission. Pop's theory, you never know when you just might need one.

After but only a few days at Morrison Field we finally got our orders to prepare for take-off the following morning, December 3, 1943. During our preflight briefing we were not only warned but were given strict orders we are not to let anyone refuel our plane under any circumstances. We were further advised that there will be occasions where we will be required to hand fill our gas tanks from five gallon cans and through chamois. Pop, Randy and I could only roll our eyes when we heard that, filtering seventeen hundred gallons of high octane gasoline from five gallon cans and through chamois'. I thought maybe the war will be over before we even refueled the plane.

We didn't yet know our destination when our wheels left the runway at about 4:00 AM in the morning. Take off and climb out was routine for the first 30 minutes or so. Suddenly in the darkness we encountered severe air turbulence and the plane began to be tossed around violently and at times seemed, at least to us who were in the rear waist section, to be uncontrollable. It was still very dark and could only guess that we flew into a thunderstorm or a squall line. The unusual and totally unexpected buffeting lasted for at least fifteen minutes. Varvil and Bahti later told us that at one time the plane was standing on it's left wing going straight down to the sea and it was difficult for either pilot to determine if they were fighting each other or fighting the storm. Since our take off heading was in a south easterly direction our course would have put us over the tongue of the ocean, in the Bahamas Island chain, where the Bermuda Triangle stories were spawned. We may have just been the first survivors of the fabled stories of unexplained disappearing ships and planes.

Once out of the storm area, Varvil started to regain that lost altitude, and as he leveled out at eight thousand feet, daylight started to appear to our left, we continued on our southeasterly course. After flying for the briefed prescribed two hours Bahti opened our sealed orders. The next leg of our journey would take us to Waller Field in Trinidad, an island nation off the northern coast of South America seventeen hundred miles away. It finally dawned on me that, in leaving the coast line of the United States I was beginning my worldly education in geography and the many differences in cultures. It was interesting to fly over places and seas that I had only a school day knowledge. To this day it never ceases to amaze me that when flying high enough one can actually see the gulf stream as it flows north and around the oceans. And all those island nations that dot the shallow waters of the Caribbean Sea. The serenity of those moments erased any thoughts of us ten young men going to war completely out of my mind. It was indeed a pleasure trip the balance of the way to Trinidad.

Our orders alerted us to keep a sharp lookout for German submarines along our route as they were operating out of secret bases along the South American coast that so far were undetectable by aerial reconnaissance. Arriving in sight of Waller Field Bahti made initial contact with the control tower and we were cleared for a straight in approach while still about twenty miles out at sea. As the island of Trinidad came closer we were advised by the control tower that a sudden storm had developed and we will have to hold our position in a circular pattern. We had a spectacular view of that storm as it wended it's way across Trinidad. It took only another twenty minutes and we were cleared to land. It became necessary for us to stay at Waller Field an extra day as the weather at our next destination forced the bombers there to stay put and there was no room for the next flight of Liberators to park. Take off from Waller Field was as uneventful as our short stay. The day had, as expected in the winter near the equator, a bright glaring sun and azure skies with nary a cloud in sight.

Again after two hours of flight on a southeast heading Bahti opened our sealed orders. The next leg of our journey will take us to an airstrip on the outskirts of the city of Belem which lies just south of the mouth of the amazon in northeastern Brazil and a little more than twelve hundred miles from Trinidad. We all settled down to sight seeing as we skirted the coast line of South America. Those German submarines could not operate in the shallow waters that extend many miles out to sea and the deep waters off the continental shelf. All we could see was green vegetation and jungle. Approaching the Amazon River we were amazed at the distance we traveled to finally reach the south shore of that estuary. Bahti called on the intercom to advise us we are thirty minutes from Belem, we will circle the field once and land to the south. For the next twenty minutes we in the waist section of the plane peered out the window looking for the airfield, seeing nothing but dense jungle. Suddenly a clearing appeared to have been cut out of that jungle. It had a mile long flat area that looked more like an ironing board than a landing field. Scattered on both sides of this runway were spider web like clearings and revetments for parking bombers. We were still at three thousand feet when turning on downwind leg of our approach and became cognizant of the almost five hundred foot hills on each end of that landing strip. Obviously we will have to slide down the northern one on our final approach, hopefully, to a soft landing. Varvil displayed such masterful dexterity one would swear that he was preparing to land on a load of eggs without breaking the shells. When I asked Varvil about that smooth landing he said, "we did it together, didn't we Len." Len replied, "Son of a buck it was a good one wasn't it."

The "follow me" jeep led us to our revetment. The driver, an American GI, advised we will have to stay at the plane for immediate refueling. I proceeded to check the oil quantity at each engine and noted the quantity needed. I thought it odd that we were not to accept any open cans, only oil from sealed cans were to be put into our oil reservoirs. It took several hours to completely fill our fuel tanks from five gallon cans and through chamois cloths. Some of the local people, working for the Americans, wanted to refuel our plane without our help but orders are orders and we refueled ourselves. The more they insisted on helping the more we refused. It seemed to be an obsession with them and we could not understand why. We did find out why that evening.

After refueling and closing up the big bird as best we could MP's were stationed to guard all the planes. We non coms left for some chow and a place to sleep. While eating we started a conversation with an American GI mechanic who had quite a tale to tell. Yesterday a C-54 returned to this air field, after only a half hour flight, with a seized engine that stopped so abruptly the propeller left the engine nose and kept right on screwing forward into the air. He said that was not the first time it happened. That C-54 engineer had let the locals help put oil in the engine oil tanks while he was putting the fuel in his gas tanks as we had just done. He did not notice the local had slipped about a quart of water into the oil tank. When the engine was started and the oil began to circulate the water was vaporized away from the heated oil in the crankcase. It took just about thirty minutes of flying time for the water to build up a head of steam in the oil tank. The resultant pressure blew off the filler cap and siphoned out all of the oil in the tank. The sudden eruption starved the engine of oil and "voila" one more seized engine. I had to ask one question, "who taught them to do that." The mechanic just shrugged his shoulders negatively. He told us that these people were not being willfully destructive they just wanted a job. Changing engines require a lot of man hours. He told us that a job was so precious in that region of South America that a man just might kill his brother to get his job. (Twenty years later I found a book that was titled "Fate is the Hunter" by Ernest Gahn. It is a book about a pilot named Dan Roman who blazed the very trails that we were now flying. I found it interesting to read in the book about a similar incident of putting water in the oil tank as was described to us that December day of 1943. I reflected that, just maybe, Dan Roman or alias Ernest Gahn was at that Belem air field the same time as we were. Ernest Gahn also wrote the books, "Island In the Sky" and "The High and The Mighty". "Fate is the Hunter" is a must read for all pilots, airmen and aviation enthusiasts everywhere.)

Two nights in Belem was about all the monotony we could take. Absolutely nothing to do, not even to take a stroll in the jungle nearby. To play the part of Jungle Jim petting those snakes, crocodiles or any other jungle animal was just not my cup of tea. Even their beer was awful tasting, to all of us except Len Bahti. If it was called "beer" Bahti would drink it.

Surprise of surprises came pleasantly the next morning while at briefing for the next leg of our journey. We were finally told where our next stop would be, Natal, Brazil, about a thousand miles away and still on a southeast heading. Boy, did I have my eyes opened to what I did not know about the geographic locations of countries and continents. In my mind North America was just that North of South America. I was shocked to learn that North America is west of South America and in order to get where we were we had to fly on an almost straight southeast course. Next time I go to school it would be prudent for me to pay closer attention to the subject being taught.

The air field at Natal was more attractive as air fields go. I could see more than one runway with repair hangers on the area perimeter. Once again there was a bee-hive of activity. Although we supervised the refueling of our plane it wasn't necessary for us to keep a watch on every little drop of oil and gasoline. American GIs were there to help with our every need. It was a little more relaxing to find a decent PX and the beer, according to Bahti, was much, much better. Just about every crewman bought South American leather goods of some sort, mostly in the form of cowboy boots. Much to the dismay of one crew, who bought a South American spider monkey, they lost their radios half way across the Atlantic Ocean when the monkey chewed through a bundle of electric wires. Our wait in Natal was less than forty eight hours. We were scheduled to be on our way to the dark continent of Africa and the city of Dakar early the second morning. Briefing at three o'clock in the morning could hardly be received with much enthusiasm with eyes and senses only coming to life. The S-2 officer encouraged our span of attention when he spoke of the German submarines spotted about three hundred miles from the Brazilian coast. He also advised there would be a good chance of more subs being off the coast of Africa and that they would be out of their fueling range in the center of the Atlantic Ocean. His advice was "just turn away from them if you spot any. They have forty millimeter guns and cannons on their decks and you will only be at less than ten thousand feet." This would be the longest leg of our journey to that European war, a little more than two thousand miles. An engineering officer finished the briefing on the need to monitor our fuel supply very closely and be ever cognizant of your engine power settings. He cautioned us to keep in mind that RPMs eat up fuel and suggested lower RPMs with higher manifold pressures to conserve as much fuel as possible while monitoring the cylinder head temperature.

As with the last five take offs this sixth one was routine and uneventful and could have been downright boring if we weren't aware of where we were heading. Siting in the nose turret with the plane on a northeast heading I was dozing off now and then catching a few winks of sleep. I was brought to my senses suddenly by a gleaming beautiful and bright sunrise as those life giving rays penetrated through my eyelids. The azure sky, sunlight and blue waters below was a once in a life time sight. I looked at my watch and found that we were in the air for only two and a half hours with possibly another seven or eight hours to go.

I opened the doors to the turret and heard voices from behind me. Boyle and Lt. Eagan were apparently doing their thing in navigating us across the Atlantic Ocean as charts were spread all over the compartment, even on the floor. It looked like one of them was using the sextant for a fix of just where we were at that moment. I sat there listening to them for a period of time and heard both of them say, at different times, "no, the reading says we are here." They each took turns at using the sextant again. I must have watched them for about thirty minutes and could not determine who was right and just where the hell we were.

I climbed out of the turret to go up to the cockpit. In squeezing past those two navigators I could not help but to add a smart remark, "Sirs, if you need any help just call me on the intercom, I'll be up in the cockpit." I guess that didn't set too well with Lt. Eagan as he just gave me a cold blank stare. In the cockpit, I stood between Varvil and Bahti for several minutes before speaking. "Lts are we still on course for Dakar?" Bahti looked around and said, "Bill, we're right on course" I responded, "then why are those two navigators arguing about where we are." Bahti just smiled with that ever present smiling red face of his and shrugged his shoulders.

I got tired standing between those two pilots and went back to the waist section to start a conversation with Randy and Chief. Paul was playing with his radio and doing some ditty-dum-dum-ditty tinkling with the short wave set. Charlie was asleep in his tail turret. Randy and Chief asked together, "How's things up in the front office?" I couldn't help but to add a little intrigue to my answer. "Well, I'm going to put my bets on Varvil and Bahti getting us to where we're going. We could be lost right now because those two navigators have been up in the nose arguing for the last hour as to who was right concerning our position, and whether we are on time, and do we have enough gas." Both gave me a worried look at which point I couldn't hold back a laugh. I then added, "Well, don't worry, Boyle may have a "don't give a damn" attitude, but he'll get us there on time and before we run out of gas." I guess I shouldn't have said anything about enough gas as that caused another puzzled look on both their faces. They soon calmed their concerns and I climbed up on the command deck over the wing and fell into a sound sleep for a few hours. Varvil and Bahti were spelling each other in cat naps as they both would want to be alert should the need arise.

When I awoke I felt completely refreshed and after a few sips of water and a few words with Paul, Charlie and Randy, I went up to the cockpit. Just as I got there Bahti said, "I think I see the coast line of Africa." "Yeah, but is it Dakar," I said. "It had better be" was Bahti's response. Pop added, "it sure had better be because I expanded our gas to it's limit, I doubt if these engines will run on fumes alone." Bahti then called "Pilot to Navigator, is that Dakar coming up on the horizon," Boyle's lack luster response, "I don't know, let me check on it." Pop got on the intercom, " Navigator, you had better make sure it is Dakar so we can make a straight in approach cause I ain't guaranteeing we have enough gas to make a "go around" let alone fly up or down this coast to try to find the airport."

Paul was on the radio doing some fixing on his own and told Varvil and Bahti he fixes the airport straight ahead. Varvil said, "I sure hope so, Bahti, try to contact the tower." The smile on Bahti's face was enough to know that we were cleared straight in. Then Boyle got on the intercom saying, "I don't know what you guys were worried about, I told you before we left Natal I would take you to Dakar on a straight line." The closer we got the darker the terrain became. No wonder they call it the dark continent. About five miles out I went back to the waist section with the rest of the crew. Only Varvil, Bahti, Pop and Paul were in the cockpit area. The end of the runway was only a few miles from the coast line and we braced for a landing.

The speed of that bomber on final approach and the split second before touch down didn't leave us much time to examine the terrain or the runway. We got the most startling shock of our lives when the planes wheels touched the runway, it sounded like the plane was falling apart. The skin seemed to be rippling, the control cables to the rudders and elevators were vibrating with an eerie high pitched sound. Everyone scrambled to find something to hold onto to protect themselves if and when our plane does fall apart. We all continued to grip what ever we could find until the plane slowed sufficiently for us to look out the window to find out just what had happened. Our concerns were unfounded as we had landed for the first time on a steel matted runway. In hindsight it sure would have been nice to have been fore warned of the noise and vibration that type of runway matting would make when we were briefed for this, our first ocean crossing.

After pushing our hearts back down into position, where it should be, we just observed Varvil as he wended his way through the maze of taxiways in back of the follow me jeep. Bahti called back to us and said, "Close all the hatches, windows and don't open the bomb bay doors. The tower just advised that our plane had to be decontaminated." Shortly, after parking the plane at the far end of a long line of Liberators, a jeep drove up and a GI climbed aboard through the camera hatch with a couple of aerosol bombs. He went through the plane spraying DDT all over us and the planes interior. For what? We never did find out! But years later we were to find out that spraying of DDT in our faces and in our breathable air in such a confined area was the worse thing they could have done. At the time we didn't know any better.

Our first visual contact with Darkest Africa gave us a few surprises. Being forewarned we prepared ourselves for a few more.

Crews of the 450th

On the following pages, (before chapter four) are the names of the air crews of the 450th (H) Bombardment Group that left Alamogordo beginning on November 20, 1943 to become part of the Fifteenth United States Air Force based in Italy. There were eight other alternate crews without bombers that filled in when a crew member was injured or sick. It might be well to note here that of the sixty two air crews that left Alamogordo only about twelve completed their missions and returned home safely. The other fifty crews were either killed in aerial combat or survived as best they could in a prisoner of war camp somewhere in Nazi occupied Europe.

720th BOMBARDMENT SQUADRON

B-24 Liberator #42-52142
Col. John S, Mills Gp. Cmdr.
Lt. Dana V. Varvil P
Lt. Lenus A. Bahti CP
Lt. Glen E. Boyle Nav.
Lt. Edward W. Bell B
Sgt. Robert Culver E
Sgt. Paul Swearingen R
Sgt. William J. Fili AE
Sgt. Randolph F. Haney G
Sgt. John C. Foster AG
Sgt. Charles P. Kourvelas
Lt. Jerome R. Goldvard Gp. N.
Sgt Robert J. Bohannon R
Sgt. Thomas S. Cox C. Cf.

B-24 Liberator #42-64443
Lt. John C. Giraud
Lt. Stanley A. White CP
Lt. Franklin A. Sherrill N
Lt. Edward J. Pomerville B
Sgt. William C. Brown E
Sgt. Vernon L. Johnson, Jr. R
Sgt. John Manak AE
Sgt. John H. Rerardon AG
Sgt. Charles F. Barr G
Sgt. Russell C. Privateer AG
Lt. Jerome P. Bowes III B
Sgt. Harry Bistritsky R
Sgt. Jesse W. Alexander C.CF.
Sgt. Bruce G. Selby

B-24 Liberator #42-7728
Lt. Ernest F. John P
Lt. Jorgen JJ Augustenborg CP
Lt. Lawrence J. Smith N
Lt. Harold E. Gladstone B
Sgt. Robert E. Beshore E
Sgt. Donald VanDeusen R
Sgt. Joseph Bernstein AE

Sgt. Richard E. McCorkle AG
Sgt. Norman J. Kirkland G
Sgt. Raymond H. Strautman AG
Lt. Harold A. Felder CP
Sgt. Francis H. Smith R
Sgt. Herbert R. Taylor C.CF
Sgt. Donald B. Schanel Eng.CK

B-24 Liberator #42-52119
Lt. Edmund A. Ley P
Lt. Winston C. Watson CP
Lt. John E. Malarkey N
Lt. Albert S. Teed B
Sgt. Walter O. Cannon E
Sgt. William W. McDonald R
Sgt. Arlie L. Griffin AE

Sgt. John Mason, Jr. AG
Sgt. Edward F. Herrrman G
Sgt. Clarron F. Frymire AG
Sgt. Alfred R. Russo R
Sgt. Oscar C. Barnhill G
Sgt. Anthony Kulchistzky G
Sgt. Bill McLaughlin C.CF.

B-24 Liberator #42-7742
Lt. Dalton W. Smith P
Lt. Frank W. Molina CP
Lt. Thomas F. Hart N
Lt. Arlie L. Brown B
Sgt. Ryan D. Harper B
Sgt. Maurice W. Moore G
Sgt. Richard S. Mancuso C.CF

Sgt. Edwin F. Grzywe R
Sgt. Robert L. Morgan AE
Sgt. Carl A. Moon, Jr. AG
Sgt. Cyril G. Heineman G
Sgt. Eugene M. Compton AG
Sgt. Ralph K. Gauker RM
Lt. James G. Wright Asst. Opts

B-24 Liberator #41-28612
Capt. Clark J. Wicks Sq. CO
Lt. Monroe Sacks CP
Lt. Robert L. Brown N
Lt. Rolland R. Carr B
M/Sgt. Jack M. Board Li. CF.
Sur.Jack W. Ryne Com. O
M/Sgt. Norman W. Huber Insp.

Lt. Max L. Williams, Jr. Eng.O
Sgt. Solomon Wasserman AG
Lt. Harley W. Rhodehmel Ar.O
Sgt. Joseph Flanagan Grp. S-4
Capt. Alfred W. Wagner Flt.
Capt. Verne A. Weber S-2 O
Sgt. Frank Grrgurich C.CF

B-24 Liberator #42—7735
Lt. Nicholas P. Kordich P
Lt. William H. Cooper CP
Lt. William A. Jones N
Lt. Norvin C. Grieve B
Sgt. James A. Baker AG
Sgt. Raymond R. Morrison R
Sgt. David W. Bartley AE

Sgt. Willis W. Fletcher Jr. AG
Sgt. Eugene C. Flolo G
Sgt. Solomon E. Lubin AG
Lt. John A. Botrem
Sgt. William D. Batho E
Sgt. John R. Kenne Flt. CF
Sgt. Harry W. Scott C.CF

B-24 Liberator #42-7743
Lt. Ronald R. Whitehead P
Lt. James M. Bibb, Jr. CP
Lt. Joseph W. Brown N.
Lt. Thomas K. Lowen B
Sgt. Joseph L. Goodman E
Sgt. John M. Sternberg R
Sgt. Chester J. Kraska AE

Sgt. Paul G. Young AG
Sgt. Jack W. Means G
Sgt. Donald R. Amundson AG
Sgt. Russell J. Hecht G
Sgt. Wallace C. Hopkins G
Sgt. Withold A. Plentis Flt.CF
Sgt. John F. O'brien C.CF.

B-24 Liberator #42-52148
Lt. Gerald M. French
Lt. Richard S. Cummings CP
Lt. John L. Polce N
Flt OF. James D. Cumming B
Sgt. John L. Ward E
Sgt. James A. Wood R
Sgt. Stanley J. Johnson AE

Sgt. Charles C. Felchner G
Sgt. Howard J. Verduin AG
Sgt. John Starkovich E
Sgt. Kenneth C. Finnigan G
Sgt. Dillard D. Centers C.CF
M/Sgt. Elwyn D. Roberts AG
Sgt. Leonard Shaw Elec.

B-24 Liberator #42-7748
Lt. Frank C. Marpe P
F/O Warner T. Walls CP
Lt. Joseph J. Joyce N
Lt. Lawrence B. Guthrie B
Cpl. Joe W. Dunn E
Sgt. Francis A. Matan R
Cpl. Earl E. Boren, Jr. AE

Sgt. Marion D. Anderson AG
Sgt. John J. O'hara G
Sgt. Jay R. Adair AG
Sgt. Leo M. LaRivee R
Sgt. Samuel Kosanovic Flt.CF.
Lt. Hartley C. Dewey P
Sgt. Michael A. Rechichar C.CF

B-24 Liberator #42-7697
Lt. Reaford C. McCraw P
Lt. John S. Fulks, Jr. CP
Lt. William R. Taylor N
Lt. Ernest D. Connors B
Sgt. Dominique Juneau G
Sgt. Charles R. Flanagan R
Sgt. Harold J. Violett AG

Sgt. William H. Britton AG
Cpl. John F. Barnacle G
Sgt. Thomas W. Netherton AG
Lt. Dave Counts B
Sgt. Paul C. Elrod E
Sgt. Harry M. Stoy, Jr. C.CF.
Sgt. Nolan H. Lemond, Sq. Com.

B-24 Liberator #42-52162
Lt. Robert W. Edwards P
Lt. Robert L. Farmer CP
Lt. Harry L. Lamb N
Lt. Thomas H. Allen B
Sgt. Joseph D. Baz R
Sgt. Jack Schoonover E
Sgt. William J. Signs G

Capt. Thomas W. Jackson Gp.S-4
Sgt. Frank Gentile G
Sgt. Michael Dellario G
Sgt. Melvin L. Openshaw AG
Lt. Francis L.J. Kitson P
Lt. John W. Ward, Jr. CP
Sgt. Homer B. Wilson, C.CF

B-24 Liberator # 41-29247
Lt. William R. Cranston P
Lt. Keith G. Bush CP
Lt. Joseph J. Oravec N
Lt. Louis Amster B
Sgt. Angelo T. Ferry R
Sgt. Leo H. LaFountain AG
Pvt. Aubrey H. Geiger,Jr. AG
Sgt. Richard L. Heinlen G
Sgt. Kenneth M. Chambers AG
Lt. Eugene A. Williams CP
Sgt. Herbert F. Johnson G
Sgt. Burdette L. Cain C.CF.
Sgt. Chester O. Leatherberry
Sgt. Albert L. Thompson E

B-24 Liberator #41-28598
Lt. Donald F. Wagner P
Lt. Donald R. Bechtell CP
Lt. Elvyn G. Hopper N
Lt. Richard E. Brannon B
Sgt. Stephen W. Kusmirak E
Sgt. Lloyd K. Kittleson R
Sgt. Robert A. Peterson AE
Sgt. Edward L. Clapporrd AG
Sgt. Lawrence R. Miller G
Sgt. Charles C. Fasolas AG
Lt. Lewis D. Hannah N
Lt. Ralph G. Hodgson P
Sgt. Merle A. Evans C.CF.
Sgt. Stephen Radkoff Gp. Insp.

B-24 Liberator #42-52124
Lt. Paul B. Cantrell P
Lt. Elmer Adrian CP
Lt. Donald De Kraker N
Lt. Lawrence H. miles B
Sgt. Scott M. Aylesworth E
Sgt. Jack R. Moe R
Sgt. Victor J. Monkus, Jr. AE
Sgt. Harley O. Tedford, Jr. AG
Sgt. Howard R. Barkley G
Sgt. Charles J. Boynton AG
Lt. Richard F. Hackel N
Sgt. Cliff W. Knappenberger E
Sgt. Samuel H. Kerr C.CF.
Capt. Henry C. Macqueen Gp.Ops

B-24 Liberator # 42-644458
Lt. Harry T. Stebbing, Jr. P
Lt. Charles E. Cunningham CP
Lt. John D. Adeimy N
Lt. Arthur D. Park B
Cpl. Joseph A. Mandanyohl AG
Sgt. Stanley L. Kristol R
Sgt. William J. Haight AG
Pvt. Joseph J. Heffernan G
Sgt. Julio Castro AG
Lt. Sidney W. Hodgson P
Sgt. Ralph Heyman E
Sgt. Glen W. Ester C.CF.
M/Sgt. Ralph J. Mason, ARM.CF.
Sgt. Hugh A. Meely E

721st BOMBARDMENT SQUADRON

B-24 Liberator #41-28592
Major R. R. Gideon Dep. Cmdr
Lt. Thomas M. Haggerton CP
Lt. Luther J. Thompson N
Lt. Francis A. Hager B
Sgt. Stanley W. Ezell E
Cpl. Michael Mozier AE
Sgt. Huron R. Boliva R
Sgt. Anthony Domagala C.CF
Sgt. Adolphus J. VonDette AG
Sgt. David L. Almado Arm.
Sgt. Nicholas J. Sciarrotta AM
Lt. Richard C. Davis Gp.Arm.OF
Lt. Holly G. Ponder CP
M/Sgt. Thurston A. Doriety F.C

B-24 Liberator # 41-29224
 Capt. G.T. Cooley Sq. Ops Of.
 Lt. Edmund H. Wolcott P
 Lt. Victor K. Meeker N
 Lt. Robert H. Leebody B
 Sgt. William N. Flanagan E
 Sgt. James R. McGown AE
 Sgt. John V. Goldthwaite R

 Sgt. Benjamin F. Runyan AG
 Sgt. Robert C. Fisher Arm.Sp.
 Sgt. J.R. Frank Asst. Arm. Sp.
 Capt. Paul W. Osincup Flt.Sur.
 Lt. Herbert S. Huff CP
 Sgt. Robert S. Bulkley AG
 Sgt. Edwin E. Nelson C.CF.

B-24 Liberator #41-29222
 F/O Elmer J. Hartman P
 Lt. Joseph C. Penn CP
 Lt. Richard J. Pratt N
 Lt. Robert W. Lilley B
 Sgt. Merle L. Morine E
 Sgt. Harold R. Askins AE
 Sgt. Aldo J. Ciliotta R

 Sgt. George L. Bronson AG
 Sgt. William L. Broughton Arm.
 Sgt. William G. Kleeman Arm.
 Lt. Verne A. Nelson Sq.Arm.Off
 Sgt. Jessie C. Cummings Arm.
 Sgt. Vincent M. Genna C.CF.
 Sgt. Lester C. Massey R. Main

B-24 Liberator #41-28622
 Lt. Wade H. Williford P
 Lt. Erving J. Weilert CP
 Lt. Frederick A. Burns N
 Lt. Robert M. Wagoner B
 Sgt. Ray H. Wingate E
 Sgt. Elmer E. Hinnenkamp AE
 Sgt. Eugene A. Lloyd R

 Sgt. William E. Larecy AG
 Sgt. Herbert A. Levene ARM.
 Sgt. Jack Matau Asst. Arm.
 Lt. Gordon J. Salinger P
 Sgt. Clarence L. Baird Inst.Sp
 Sgt. Earl S. Carson Flt. CF.
 Sgt. Waymon A. Bell Mech.

B-24 Liberator #42-64455
 Lt. Harvey E. Helmberger P
 Lt. Russell E. Boggs CP
 Lt. Julian D. Fleming N
 Lt. William J. Heiser B
 Sgt. Hugh E. Cameron E
 Sgt. Alvah W. Snitehurst AE
 Sgt. Joseph C. Darby, Jr. R

 Sgt. Willie H. Tate AG
 Sgt. Glenn W. Pinter Arm.
 Sgt. Connie J. Jones Asst.Arm
 Lt. Charles S. Bowman S-2 Off
 Lt. Albert C. Kirsnis CP
 Sgt. Clarence W. Anderson C.CF
 Sgt. Howard W. Morgan Supply

B-24 Liberator #41-29212
 Lt. William A. Clarke P
 Lt. Lloyd R. Bishop CP
 Lt. Raymond L. Malloy N
 Lt. Theodore W. Schunk B
 Sgt. Daniel G. Chaplain E
 Sgt. Wilford A. Lafond AE
 Sgt Russell E. Gilmore AG

 Sgt. Carlton H. Negus Fl.CF.
 Sgt. Lyle R. Drager Arm.
 Sgt. Leon C. Scatterfield Arm.
 Lt. Russell C. Jackson Wea'r
 Sgt. Wayne H. Farquhar C.CF.
 Sgt. James W. Moore Arm. CF.
 Sgt. William J. Mccarthy R

B-24 Liberator #41-29188
Lt. Jack W. Graham P
Lt. Harry D. Feltenstein CP
Lt. Hugo J. Paggi N
Lt. Samuel E. Artzer B
Sgt. Charles S. Vorhies E
Sgt. Maynard J. Lawson AE
Sgt. Ralph L. Pippins R

Lt. Henry C. Kaecker Gp.B.
Cpl. Ernest R. Hamrie AG
Sgt. Thomas R. Ternillo Arm.
Lt. Charles W. Robinson Eng.Of
Sgt. J.D. (10) Moore Arm.
Sgt. Wilbert J. Eggerss C.CF
Sgt. Omri P. Manring C.CF

B-24 Liberator #42-52112
Lt. Thomas A. Scott P
F/O George Stanley CP
Lt. Leonard Robbins N
F/O Joseph.J. Basamania B
Sgt. Joseph R Bury E
Sgt. Lawrence J. Hoover AE
Pvt Agatino Rigano R

Sgt. James T. Driscoll Tur Sp.
Sgt. Tilman J. Thompson AG
Pvt. Louis Grande Ast. Arm.
Sgt. Jesse N. Bradley Asst.Arm
Sgt. Francis A. Loguercio Insp
Sgt. Richey E. Nelson AG
Lt. Borden S. Chronister Photo

B-24 Liberator #42-7746
Lt. Abner D. Hervey P
Lt. Leroy D. Tate CP
Lt. Bernard Wasserman N
Lt. Stanley I. Gottlieb B
Sgt. Charles T. Wernett E
Sgt. Frank R. Collinge AE
Sgt. Benjamin A. Stock R

Sgt. John O. Brown AG
Sgt. William W. Shergold Arm.
Sgt. Frederick A. Lauer Arm.
Sgt. Eugene Martin C.Cf
Sgt. Byron K. Beard Arm.
Sgt. Leo J. Heier BSM
Sgt. John C. Murphy R

B-24 Liberator #42-6448
Lt. Joseph P. Gallagher P
Lt. Edgar J. Hall CP
Lt. Maynard I. Wayne N
Lt. John B. Kantner B
Sgt. Raymond F. Welty E
Sgt. SamuelBelgio AE
Sgt. Corbett E. Robinson AE

Sgt. Stephen Malarik R
Sgt. Thomas J. Isgrigg AG
Sgt. Thomas R. Lindeland Jr AR
Sgt. Charles H. Durritt AR
Sgt. Lester J. Witherspoon Mec
Sgt. Edwin Hoime AE
Sgt. Samuel E. Armstrong Arm.

B-24 Liberator #41-28604
Lt. William E. Reno Jr. P
F/O Harold J. Houghton CP
Lt. Louis J. Prentice N
Lt. Jack M. Montgomery B
Sgt. Henry N. Erickson E
Sgt. Harry A. Kandarian AE
Sgt. Armond E. Miller R

Sgt. Roger W. Goodson Ag
Sgt Arthur H. Mainard Arm.
Sgt. Claude D. Day Arm.
Sgt. Robert O. Sisting InstSp
Sgt. Carl N. Herocki AG
Lt. Joseph A. King Com. Off.
Lt. Arthur L. Campa S-2 Off.

B-24 Liberator #42-64446
Lt. Robert L. Waste P
Lt. Harold J. Ayme CP
Lt. Lawrence H. Kravetz N
Lt. Bruce C. Lindsay B
Sgt. Stanley J. Dryla E
Sgt. J.L.Chain AE
Sgt. Robert E. Ludwig R

Sgt. Jerrie Curreri AE
Sgt. Richard A. Purcell AssT R
Sgt. Oklahoma V. Carroll Arm
Sgt. Bruce W. Mahar, Arm.
Sgt. Frederick Downtain APMech
Sgt. Robert E. Monohan E
Sgt. Roy Meyer Jr. Com. CF

B-24 Liberator #42-52109
Lt. Howard L. Anderson P
Lt. Joseph S. Henchman CP
F/O Lawrence Levinson N
Lt. George W. Murray B
Sgt. Charles A. Shafer E
Sgt. Fred L. Walsh AE
Sgt. William J. Ford R

Sgt. Robert Acosta AR
Sgt. Edward W. Molenda Arm
Sgt. Byron H. Nelson Asst Arm
Lt. Merle W. Emch CP
Lt. Arthur D. White N
Lt. James T. Morris Jr. B
Sgt. Harols C. Johncour APMech

B-24 Liberator #41-28227
Capt. Howard A. Davis P
Lt. Leonard D. Scott CP
Lt. Olin L. Reynolds N
F/O Andrew Poggi B
Sgt. Walter U. Borneman E
Sgt. Joseph A. Perry AE
Sgt. William R. Bristol R

Sgt. Ralph S. Stephenson AR
Sgt. Harmon L. Small Arm.
Sgt. Clifford E. Nagle Arm.
Lt. Raymond E. Barthelmy Sq.N.
Lt. Chester S. Kingsman Sq.B
M/Sgt. William H. Holman L. CF
Lt. Earl G. Anderson, Jr. CP

B-24 Liberator #41-28618
Lt. Frederick H. Wandell P
Lt. Tilmen A. Morken CP
Lt. Edward H. Lovvorn N
Lt. William C. Goldberg B
Sgt. Kenneth E. Ziehlke E
Sgt. John J. Palmich AE
Sgt. John R. Demyan R

Sgt. Albert H. Brose AR
Sgt. Henry B. Price Arm.
Sgt. Robert L. Snyder Asst.Arm
Lt. Warren C. Blim Ops Off.
M/Sgt. Paul B. Gillum AP Insp.
Sgt. JB (10) Tandy E
Sgt. Clarence L. Ashmore APMec

B-24 Liberator #41-29255
Lt. William P. Cannon P
Lt. Ralph E. Peck CP
Lt. John L. Miotchell N
Lt. Joseph F. Gavin B
Sgt. Roy B. Hansen E
Sgt. Henry C. Urech AE
Sgt. James E. Flynn R

Sgt. Charles H. Powell AR
Sgt. Jack H. Tracey Arm.
Sgt. James Carder Asst. Arm.
Lt. Leslie J. Paul P
Lt. Goerge W. Lamoreaux N
F/O Patrick J. McGinnity B
Sgt. Herman C. Peitz C.CF.

722nd BOMBARDMENT SQUADRON

B-24 Liberator #42-52088
F/O Gerald E. Weathermon P
Lt. Ross E. Howe CP
Lt. Courtney D. Shanken N
Lt. Louis Siegel B
Sgt. Woodrow W. Tatnman E
Sgt. Anthony J. Vola R
Sgt. Charles R. White AE
Sgt. Harold J. Saperstein AR
Sgt. John T. Atteberry G
Sgt. Ray E. Ault AG
Sgt. Gerald P. Meritt C.CF.
Lt. Mathew B. O'hara Comm. Off
Sgt. Paul D. Boaz G
Pvt. Joseph L. Lanoir AG

B-24 Liberator #41-28603
F/O Francis S. Rzatkowski P
F/O Francis J. Morrissey CP
Lt. Harry E. Parr, Jr. N
Lt. John W. Taylor B
Sgt. Herbert N. Wilch E
Sgt. Raymond W. Flora R
Lt. Charles Coyle N
Sgt. Dee R. Jones, JR. AE
Sgt. Benedict L. Klinshaw AR.
Sgt. George G. Grad G
Sgt. William J. Booth AG
Sgt. Claude W. McKee C.Cf.
Sgt. John F. Robertson, Insp.
Lt. Albert R. Strathie B

B-24 Liberator #43-52152
F/O J.C. Word P
Lt. Lauman E. Shain CP
Lt. Earl Shanken N
Lt. Allen C. Hart B
Sgt. Gilbert W. Hatfield E
Sgt. Morris Spector R
Sgt. Harry M. Beightel AE
Sgt. James G. Shirley AR
Sgt. Stanley B. West G
Sgt. Loyd Whitley AG
PFC. Frederick G. Miller C.CF.
Lt. Harold C. Phillips OpsOff
Lt. Charles P. Lehman Bomb Off
Sgt. Edward J. Sullivan E

B-24 Liberator #42-7753
F/O Hobert R. Maddux P
Lt. Robert W. Poore CP
Lt. Frank M. Ryan N
Lt. Vernon J. Tipton B
Sgt. Harold C. Vlass E
Sgt. Richard J. VanRoden R
Sgt. Harold D. Bosserman AE
Sgt. Thomas J. Ryan AR
Sgt. Edwin F. Vrla G
Pfc. James A. Forti AG
Sgt. Edwin J. Dernak C.Cf.
Sgt. Edwin R. Upchurch Inst Sp
Lt. Howard A Fox Comm. Off.
Sgt. Thomas F. Gamble R

B-24 Liberator #42-52141
Lt. Walter J. Sharff P
Lt. Marion D. Medley CP
Lt. Henry A. Mazzuchelli N
Lt. William H. Glavin B
Sgt. Francis W. Geiser E
Sgt. John P. Conner R
Sgt. Charles R. Warren AE
Sgt. Baltizai C. Balazic AR
Sgt. Walter J. Kostro G
Sgt. Glen K. Platt AG
Sgt. Donald G. Hines C. CF.
Sgt. Roy M. Gaertig AE
Sgt. Adam E. Wood AR
Sgt. Michael F. Garby Ops Clk.

B-24 Liberator #42-7714
 Maj. William L. Orrris Sq.CO
 Lt. Robert O. Burnham Ops OFF
 Lt. Albert E. Aubin Sq.N
 Lt. William J. Brohm, III B
 M/Sgt. Herbert B. Chester L CF
 Sgt. Paul R. Drury R
 Sgt. Glen G. Hovey AE
 Sgt. Andrew A. Anzo AR
 Sgt. Louis D. Springer G
 Sgt George E. Shatzer AG
 F/O Walter P. Vanderkamp P
 Lt. Phillip Kraus CP
 Sgt. Vito A. Berardi AE
 Sgt. August L. Musich E

B-24 Liberator #41-29221
 Lt. Clarence B. Caldwell P
 Lt. Albert Kahan CP
 Lt. Harlan S. Place N
 Lt. James F. Gleason B
 Sgt. Morris B. Clark E
 Sgt. Bouford L. Lowrance R
 Sgt. Johnie C. Taylor AE
 Sgt. Leon Levis AR
 Sgt. James D. Stansell G
 Sgt. Robert A. Lanier AG
 Sgt. Stanley J. Gerdes C. CF.
 Sgt. John H. Brown Flt. CF.
 Sgt. James D. Macy BSM
 Lt. James M,. Ryan CP

B-24 Liberator #42-7740
 Lt. Bernard J. Gillespie P
 Lt. Tommy F. Bruner CP
 Lt. John J. Ryczek N
 Lt. Harold L. Cooke B
 Sgt. David J. Martin E
 Sgt. Jack M. Perkins R
 Sgt. William Brazzle AE
 Lt. Richard F. Kava N
 Sgt. Lucious W. McClellan AR
 Sgt. Arthur R. Vance G
 Sgt. Thomas W. bishop AG
 Sgt. Clyde W. Sullen C. CF.
 Sgt. Lawrence H. Seider T/Su.
 Sgt. John T. Dandurand Tur.Sp.

B-24 Liberator #41-29252
 Lt. Joseph D. Anderson P
 Lt. Albert W. Cox CP
 Lt. John P. Dowiak N
 Lt. Michael Grofik B
 Sgt. William A. Beck E
 Sgt. Victor N. Heinselman R
 Sgt. Aubrey A. Clark AE
 Sgt. Carl W. Thomas AR
 Sgt. George B. Sanders G
 Sgt. Roy Caudill AG
 Sgt. John D. Kubas C. Cf.
 Sgt. John E. Meadows Elec. Sp.
 Lt. Charles W. Vogel Stat.Off
 Lt. James D. Harrison B

B-24 Liberator #42-7731
 Lt. John McLaughlin P
 F/O Clyde O. Primrose CP
 Lt. George L. Decker N
 Lt. Carl G. Walker B
 Sgt. Anthony J. Kosak E
 Sgt. Lowell E. Root R
 Sgt. Roy D. Maxwell AE
 Sgt. Albert Slinkard AR
 Sgt. Melvin Fouer G
 Sgt. James H. Reese AG
 Sgt. Russell S. Lyon C.Cf.
 Cpl. Juan R. Stout Welder & SM
 Pfc. Robert E. Glenn E
 Sgt. John A. Lockwood R

B-24 Liberator #42-52096
Lt. Dewitt C. Dawkins, Jr. P
Lt. Edward W. Schleier CP
Lt. Edward F. Garrett N
Lt. Edwin Gross B
Sgt. Max E. McClaskie E
Sgt. Carl Graziano R
Sgt. Howard Barnett AE
Sgt. Norman A. Kath AR
Pfc. Walter L. Crotty G
Sgt. Harry V. Haver Jr. AG
Sgt. Howard L. Badger C. CF.
Lt. Albert T. Leonhard Arm. O
Sgt. John J. Visosky AE
Sgt. Theodore H. Erickson AR

B-24 Liberator #42-52085
Lt. William B. King, Jr. P
Lt. James C. Stripp CP
Lt. Zane P. Laurini N
Lt. Henry A. Gottfried B
Sgt. Theodore R. Hospedar E
Pfc. James R. Hogan AE
Sgt. Rodman Z. Reade AR
Sgt. John J. Geeghan R
Sgt. Leonard J. Ward G
Sgt. Alexander Witkowski,Jr AG
Sgt. James E. Riddle C. CF.
Lt. Herman H. Zowader Eng. Off
Lt. Robert B. Johnson S-2 Off
Lt. Frank A. Brusek P

B-24 Liberator #42-52144
Lt. Horace G. Ferry P
Lt. William W. Sisserson CP
Lt. Gerald L. Meyers N
Lt. Raymond K. Jennings B
Sgt. Loran V. Rodman E
Sgt. William G. Smith R
Sgt. Guy R. Walters AE
Sgt. Donald J. Timmerwilke AG
Sgt. Lloyd W. McLaughlin G
Sgt. Fred B. Kemp AG
Sgt. Alexander V. Wilkins C.CF
Sgt. William J. Dupre Flt. Cf.
Lt. William R. Wright,Jr CP
Lt. Frederick W. Wheary N

B-24 Liberator #42-7760
Lt. Willis R. Retzlaff P
Lt. William A. Parrish CP
Lt. Edward J. Nisiobinicki N
Lt. J.C. McClure B
Sgt. Alcide J. Champagne E
Sgt. Hugo L. Greinert R
Sgt. Walter S. Johnson AE
Sgt. Melvin C. Hellem AR
Sgt. Richard H. Cosgrove G
Sgt. Emil N. Beaman AG
Cpl. Adolph A. Eberle C.Cf.
Sgt. Edward L. Reynolds Li.CF.
Sgt. John A. Blazczak G
Sgt. Eugene Digiovanni AG

B-24 Liberator #42-52122
Lt. William A. Notle P
F/O Frank M. Painter,Jr CP
Lt. Neil E. Simmons B
Lt. William Wisbrod N
Sgt. Carl O. Beebee C.Cf.
Sgt. Ronald G. Linkous R
Sgt. Richard L. Weaver AE
Sgt. Herbert J. Wood AR
Sgt. Alphonso S. Dominski G
Sgt. Russell Archibald AG
Sgt. Robert VanSandt AE
Sgt. Sherald R. Bird Prop. SP.
Cpl. Carl E. Hiller Rad. Sp.
Lt. Robert V. Schafranky P

723rd BOMBARDMENT SQUADRON

B-24 Liberator #42-52161
Lt. Sigurd J. Nilsson P
Lt. La June Wilk CP
Lt. Clarence W. Smith Sq. N
Capt. William A. Miller CO
Maj. George L. Thorpe GpSur
Lt. Chester A. Richman Sq.B
M/Sgt Philip Stuart Sq.Li Cf
Sgt. James R. Ish E
Sgt. Lycurgus Bratton AE
Sgt. Robert J. Waldrop R
Sgt. Stanley Kyriakos
Sgt. William D. Rogers G
Cpl. Clyde C. Hubbell AG
Sgt. John A. Jones C.Cf.

B-24 Liberator #42-52090
F/O Robert J. Clay P
Lt. Robert A. McGregor CP
Lt. Bertell A. MacDonald N
Lt. Edmund C. Hale B
Sgt. Harold J. Gamache E
Sgt. Alphonse Lanteigne R
Sgt. John E. Marinangeli AE
Sgt. John H. Briggs Jr. AG
Sgt. Milton S. Feffer G
Sgt. Sidney Rulnick AG
Sgt. Paul G. Schultz C.Cf.
Sgt. Stephen Rutkowski Elec.
Sgt. Livio L. Miller R
Lt. Charles Molitor B

B-24 Liberator #42-52143
Lt. John F. Wells P
Lt. Bert O. Baker CP
Lt. David Waterman N
Lt. Ronald J. Kaulfuss B
Sgt. Silvio P. Farina Jr. E
Sgt. William J. Ballentine R
Cpl Wilburn D. Mangrum AE
Sgt. John P. Luna AR
Sgt. Nick Lepovich G
Sgt. William E. Duda AG
Lt. Joseph P. Orley N
Sgt. Joseph B. Mason C. Cf.
Sgt. Anthony J. Sica Inst Sp.
Sgt. Glenn Harper G

B-24 Liberator #41-29228
Lt. Richard M. Whitney P
Lt. Patrick A. Barbati CP
Lt. Edward C. Roberts Jr. N
Lt. William C. Flock B
Sgt. James B. Shaw E
Sgt. John O. Squires R
Sgt. Lawrence J. O'Connor AE
Sgt. Robert C. McGarvey AR
Sgt. Charles E. Allen G
Pvt. BVernard E. Bernard AG
Lt. William Conklin P
Lt. William Buksa B
Sgt. Frank D. Hoza A Li. Cf.
Sgt. Alexander E. Esposito CCF

B-24 Liberator #42-7710
Lt. Ralph R. Rickey P
Lt. Alexander Sinila CP
Lt. Edward A. Wojcoski N
F/O Anthony Santamango B
Sgt. Peter J. Venezia
Sgt. Luis A. Vasquez R
Sgt. Rocco J. Mitchell AE
Sgt. Zelford Mathis AR
Sgt. Joseph C. Portuges G
Sgt. William Rossman AG
Lt. James H. Isbell P
Lt. Calvin H. Brown N
Sgt. John A. Evans E
Sgt. Walter J. Robertson C.Cf.

B-24 Liberator #42-7724
Lt. Ira J. Holloman P
Lt. John F. Wick CpP
Lt. Michael Kyak N
Lt. William A. Conradis B
Sgt. John J. Cook E
Sgt. Noble L. Wilson AE
Sgt. Othie L. Perdue AR

Sgt. Earl R. Brown R
Sgt. Thomas C. Postle G
Sgt. Cyrus B. Butts AG
Sgt. Irby N. Sullivan C.Cf.
Sgt. Lawrence L. McClain E
Cpl. Herman Goodyke R
Sgt. Bert H. Ashton AG

B-24 Liberator #42-52095
Lt. John H. Lane P
Lt. Robert G. Zink CP
Lt. Dale F. Robertson N
Lt. Chris E. Dalgish B
Sgt. Leroy F. Adams E
Sgt. John B. Tierney R
Sgt. James Keleshian AE

Sgt. William R. Campbell R
Sgt. Edward J. Mackafee G
Sgt. Vernon B. Hasley AG
Lt. Robert H. Gernand Ops Off.
Lt. George H. Andrews Arm. O.
M/Sgt. Floyd W. Fair A. Li. Cf
Cpl. Robert B. Patton C.Cf.

B-24 Liberator #41-28579
Lt. Edward Loomis P
Lt. Theodore Tautfest CP
Lt. John L. Vernon N
Lt. Robert F. Long B
Sgt. Leo J. Dombrowski E
Sgt. James M. Fox R
Sgt. Allen O. Byers AE

Sgt. J. C. Ward AR
Sgt John M. Florip G
Sgt. Earl W. Ringland AG
Lt. Luke C. Quinn Int. Off.
M/Sgt. Harry D. Cobbledick Arm
Sgt. William T. Roach C.Cf.
Lt. Ralph Schultz N

B-24 Liberator #42-52163
Lt. James C. Courtright P
Lt. Leonard M. Zeitler CP
Lt. Edward T. Pickard N
Lt. Charles L. Coates B
Sgt. Walter E. Spees E
Sgt. Selwyn L. Palmer R
Sgt. William J. Larbig AE

Sgt. Henry A. Stenvik AR
Sgt. Ralph L. Wilgy G
Sgt. Alfred Nielsen AG
Sgt. Charles E. Ingersoll
Sgt. James A. Higgins C.Cf.
Pfc. William Harrelson AG
Sgt. Paul E. Hunt AG

B-24 Liberator #42-52164
Lt. Harry L. Kellman P
Lt. Carl Huber CP
Lt. Robert L. Keller N
F/O Samuel C. Bailen B
Sgt. Ronald Boucher G
Sgt. John Lombardo AG
Lt. Nicholas W. Kaltenbach

Sgt. George A. Franz E
Sgt. Frank S. Campbell R
Sgt. John L. Pevey AE
Sgt. Edward L. Fedor AR
Lt. Quintin R. Voigt Eng.Off.
Sgt. Raymond L. Cook Ops Clk.
Sgt. Louis J. Noto C. CF.

B-24 Liberator #41-29226
Lt. Phillip H. Scanlon P
Lt. Glenn M. Davis CP
Lt. George C. Stong Jr. N
Lt. Donald A. Forbes B
Sgt. Kenneth C. King AE
Sgt. Sidney J. Levin AR
Sgt. Frank J. Dzurik G

Sgt. William J. Heinegger AG
Sgt. John H. Grogan E
Sgt. Orin D. Swift R
Lt. Edward J. Makowski B
Sgt. Charles W. Merrill AR
Sgt. John E. Sullivan AE
Sgt. Edward B. Cushing Jr. C CF

B-24 Liberator #41-29213
Lt. Louis J. Samsa P
Lt. James R. Green CP
Lt. Leonard R. Getuan N
Lt. Franklin J. Bublitz B
Sgt. Robert A. Breneman E
Sgt. Raplh E. Vorhees R
Sgt. Edward L. Papierniak AE

Sgt. Frederick A. Uphoff AR
Sgt. Lyle L. Hanson G
Sgt. Thomas K. Newman AG
Lt. Hodgson T. Jackson CP
Sgt. Henry L. Greenough C. Cf.
Sgt. John H. Hohman Arm
Sgt. Emerson E. Lee R

B-24 Liberator #41-28620
Lt. Richard C. Hefner P
Lt. James C. Lombardi CP
Lt. Martin Gelman N
Lt. George B. Snachez B
Sgt. Charles B. McVeigh E
Sgt. Edward F. Opitz R
Sgt. Vernon F. Akin

Sgt. John F. Waters AR
Sgt. Clarence A. Tillison G
Sgt. James D. Six AG
M/Sgt. Oliver Williamson Insp.
Sgt. Peter P. Pietroski AE
Sgt. Clare A. Easily C. Cf.
Sgt. Buriel A. Johnson Bomshi.

B-24 Liberator #42-64454
Lt. Francis V. Lael P
Lt. Jack C. Morris CP
Lt. Johnnie M. Walters N
Lt. Eugene F. Hagenson B
Sgt. Russell H. Preihs R
Sgt. Syril J. Chadwell AE
Cpl. Lawrence E. Good C. Cf.

Pvt. Richard B. Sellers AR
Sgt. Thomas E. Devlin G
Sgt. John A. Mytych AG
Lt. Thomas B. Miller A.Ops Off
M/Sgt. John G. Valk Comm Man
M/Sgt. Robert H. Ford Ops Clk
Sgt. William W. Turrentine E

B-24 Liberator #42-7752
Lt. Leland H. Henerson P
Lt. Robert Jeff Thomas CP
Lt. John A. Dickerman N
Lt. Frank D. DiGiovanni B
Sgt. James P. Vaughn E
Sgt. John J. Deinhardt AE
Sgt. Robert F. Hahn AR

Sgt. Stanley Montgomery G
Sgt. James R. Gallagher AG
Lt. Robert J. Thomas CP
M/Sgt. Louis E. Fink C.Cf.
Sgt. Edwin R. Williams Eng.Clk
Sgt. Virgil H. Hutchinson AG
Sgt. Clarence M. Wentzel R

VARVIL'S CHARGES
ALAMOGORDO, NEW MEXICO OCTOBER 29, 1943

Standing L to R - Bob,Pop, Culver, Engineer & Top Turret; John Foster, Ball Turret; Edward Bell, Bombardier; Glenn Boyle, Navigator; Lenus Bahti, Co-Pilot; Dana V. Varvil, Pilot and Aircraft Commander.
Kneeling L to R - Randy Haney, Waist Gunner; Paul Swearingen, Radio Operator and Waist Gunner; Author Bill Fili, Assistant Engineer and Nose Turret: Charles Kourvelas, Tail Turret.

FOUR

While we were waiting for almost a half hour for the decontamination to be administered, the heat inside the plane became intense, almost unbearable. It then dawned on us we were at the hottest part of Planet Earth, the Equator. After the DDT spraying we left the plane to find the outside temperature was not much lower. The slight ocean breeze made it more tolerable. All of us were standing in front of the plane, those that smoked lit up and the others simply surveyed the surroundings. Just ahead of us in the line of bombers was Lt. John Giraudo's plane and crew, just behind us was Lt. Nick Kordich with his crew.

I couldn't help myself and the need to wonder around our plane alone with the thoughts I had at seeing all those awesome bombers lined up in neat rows as far as my peripheral vision could see. There must have been at least three hundred, four engine Liberators, at that Dakar airfield that day. Each one capable of delivering twelve five hundred pound bombs on any selected target. And those numbers were repeated at least once every month. It really began to dawn on me, we're going off to war. It was a frightening thought to be sure. I could not help but ask the unanswerable question at the time, "Where the hell did all these bombers come from? Why are so many needed?" Some were replacement crews and planes heading to England and the 8th Air Force. The others, including us, are heading in a different direction, where, as yet we don't know. "Are we going to blow the whole continent of Europe off the map?" The logistics of putting such a plan into effect had to be mind-boggling. To provide the landing fields, to have sufficient supplies of high octane gasoline on hand at all times, to have food, sleeping facilities, spare parts and repair facilities on hand on split seconds notice. All these things and so many more were completely out of comprehension for my young mind.

In looking back on our travels thus far it had been purely an American endeavor. The training, the gathering of planes and guns, the travel over foreign lands and wide oceans was but an excursion. Now, here in Dakar on the western African coast, the reality is beginning to drive itself home into our minds. These rows of bombers were for no other purpose than to rain destruction on the enemy. The perimeter of this airfield was ringed by guards from the Senegal tribes of that region. They were a unique race of people. All standing at least seven feet tall. When standing at attention with their rifles by their sides those rifles were as tall as they were. To make things more awesome the bayonets on those rifles towered at least two feet above their heads. It would be easy to estimate that, with a seven foot rifle capped by a two foot bayonet, they could spear at least three of us from a distance of six feet. Later Randy and I managed a closer view of their bayonets. They were square with one side curved inward. According to learned information we found that the curved side served for raking, creating a suction cup, extracting the insides of anything it entered. How horrible it would be to be disentrailed and such a thought insisted we be quite happy they were on our side.

Again up to this point we did not have the pleasure or the experience of meeting any of the Allies that we were to fly and fight alongside of. Dakar was the western most city of Colonial French West Africa and the airport facilities were constructed by the American Corps of Engineers as the Free French Armies did not have the man power or the equipment.

My attention was brought back to the present when an engineering captain arrived with a jeep and informed us of just what we had to do. Basically the same scenario of refueling before we leave the plane, but with one added refinement, we are not to leave our plane unattended. At least one crew member must be there at all times and armed. The captain took all the officers with him to the BOQ or at least that what they call officers quarters in the states. All six of us nom coms helped with the refueling and drew straws for the guard shifts. Paul and Charlie drew first shift from six PM to midnight and Randy and I volunteered for the grave yard shift Midnight to six AM. Pop suggested that Paul and Charlie flag down a jeep to take them in to the mess hall for something to eat and secure some bunks for the night. Refueling finished, Pop and Chief stood guard while Randy and I went to eat. After chow I found Bahti at the make shift PX and as expected he had a frothy mug of beer in his hand. When he saw me he just grinned, smacked his lips and said, "Boy, this is good beer. The bartender told me it's made from peanuts." I could not help but say to myself, "boy, this guy sure likes his beer. He better get his full now because there may not be any such thing where we're going and I hope it's not to see St. Pete."

After eating chow and taking a cat nap Randy and I took a jeep ride out to the plane shortly before Midnight to relieve Paul and Charlie. We decided on two hour shifts and Randy volunteered for the first and I went to lay down on the cockpit floor for some more cat napping. Even though we were at the Equator it was still chilly in the evenings, probably from the ocean breezes, and did require a blanket.

It was about an hour into my trip, I guess about three AM, and standing just under my nose turret I could not help but to notice the night sky that was full of stars, I had never seen so many before. Those stars were bright enough to allow me to see the ominous rows of bombers. Their olive drab color only added to the dreadedness of their upcoming missions and the thought of darkest Africa added another dimension of dread. My mind was forever wondering about what is in store for us and how long will it be for us to make the return trip.

Being alone with thoughts and mental meanderings one could be startled into reality by all sorts of disturbances and this place and time was no exception. I was brought back to reality by a slight scuffle behind me that forced my body to stiffen to some degree, in fact I was frozen in my shoes and they wouldn't move either. There was an involuntary question posed to me, "Shall I turn around or shall I run like hell and then turn around while pulling out my brand new forty five pistol. I decided not to pull out my forty five as I just might shoot my toes or foot off. Discretion is the better part of valor and decided to slowly turn around and when I did I wish I didn't, if that makes any sense. Darkest Africa gave me the darkest scare of my life. Standing in back of me with less than six inches between us was one of those

Senegalese soldiers standing there, frozen at attention, the whites of his eyes were steadfast straight ahead. So tall was he that I had to lean my head back to look straight up at his face and further to see the end of that disentrailing bayonet. I did let out a "Whew" at the thought of what he would have done if I was the enemy. We were later informed just how these humongous soldiers did decide who was friend of foe. If they were not sure who you were they would grab you by the throat collar, pick you up off the ground and shake your body. If they heard your dog tags rattle you were a friend, if they heard nothing you might have found out what it's like to be disentrailed with that square bayonet. Mentally, I called out for divine guidance, "Christ, will you please tell me what I'm to do now." He didn't answer me. I don't know how long I stared up at his face and he in turn didn't waver one iota, just looking straight forward at attention as he was trained to do. I slowly calmed my nervous system, being convinced he meant no harm to me else he would have done so even before I heard his first shuffle. It became apparent that he was no dummy either as that shuffle was to alert me of his presence. Still somewhat frightened out of my wits, I once again, asked divine providence for guidance. "Christ, please tell me what to do?" Still no answer.

Then a single alternative dawned on me. I knew he couldn't speak my language so I reached into my shirt pocket for a pack of cigarettes, offered one to him. Then struck a match and lit it for him. He put the cigarette between his lips and continued his brace at attention while staring straight ahead and puffing on the cigarette. Ah shit, I still didn't know what else to do so I placed the whole pack of smokes in his right hand hoping that he then will go away. He placed the pack into his pants pocket and reached for my arm in a gentle way. Not knowing his intentions I retreated somewhat and he quickly retrenched to his attention position. By instinct I started to reach for my pistol and he put up his hand in a sign language of meaning "no harm". Apparently he knew what he wanted to do, but I didn't and that was the problem. He motioned for me to go inside the bomber and with a circular motion of his hand and pointing to his chest. I got the message that he would guard my plane for me while I got some sleep. He was quite adamant in that he would let no one near this plane for the rest of that night. Indeed darkest Africa does have some unbelievable surprises.

Climbing up through the nose wheel and onto the flight deck, I crawled over Randy and woke him up. Half asleep Randy demanded, "What the hell are you doing here? You're supposed to be guarding the plane." "Shut up Randy", I replied. "I was chased up here by one of those Senegalese. If you don't believe me go out and see for yourself." I related to him the whole scenario and ended with how we got our own special guard. Randy's initial reaction was that I had "lost my marbles." He believed me only after he climbed up in the nose turret and peered out in the darkness and saw our guard standing just off to the right side. There was room on that deck for only one man so I sat in the pilot's seat for some shut eye.

At sunrise, Randy and I were awakened by pebbles bouncing off the side of the plane. Bleary eyed, we peered out the cockpit window and saw the rest of our crew about thirty feet off to the left. Evidently, that pack of cigarettes given to that Senegalese Guard had been precisely what he wanted and disposed him to prevent anyone from entering that plane without my permission. Or had that gift of cigarettes been just another survival gesture? I called out the window and advised all of them to behave or I'll have my man Friday take care of them. Randy and I quickly crawled out through the nose wheel and I walked over to the guard patted him on the back, he in turn bowed and walked away never to be seen again. Varvil commented to Randy and I, "I could be upset at your not being outside guarding our plane if I hadn't seen this with my own eyes." I added, "Sir, you too would have been scared to death as I was last night when he snuck up on me." Varvil, could only smile when he said, "I sure would like to have taken a picture of your face when you first saw that Senegalese soldier. Anyway, you and Randy better hustle up to the mess hall for breakfast because we're going to take off in less than two hours." Randy said, "where we going this time Sir?" Varvil said, "never mind, I tell you when you get back, just get going."

Our belly's full of powdered scrambled eggs and spam, preflight of the plane and engines completed we all climbed aboard for the next leg of our journey. Take off and setting course in a cruise climb was normal. Standing between the two pilots I asked Bahti, "Where we headed now?" Bahti responded, "Marrakech." I now know as much as I knew before I asked and that is nothing. I never heard of Marrakech or of it's existence. I may have just as well been told I was heading for Valhalla for all I knew. Anyway I went up into the nose section where those two navigators were still doing their thing of trying to get us from point A to point B without getting lost. I struck up a mini conversation with Boyle while Eagan was using the sextant. Pointing to the charts Boyle explained that we have to be extremely careful as we have to go through the Kasserine Pass in the Atlas Mountain range just south of Marrakech. If the weather gets cloudy it could be a trick to make sure we don't hit the peaks. They go up to fourteen thousand feet and we can't be over twelve thousand feet without oxygen. He added that we would have to go to fifteen thousand feet if we were to clear the highest peak. On a lighter note Boyle was relating some facts about the place we were heading. It's a desert vacation wonderland for the sheiks and their harems and one of those fabled cities that had an ancient walled city in the center. Sort of a Miami Beach in the middle of the Sahara Desert. I thanked Boyle for the lesson in geography and told him I would be up in the nose turret keeping a look out for those peaks and added, "If you hear me yell you had better make instant arrangements to alter our course."

Fortunately for us the weather stayed rather clear when we approached those peaks. I noticed far off to the west that clouds were getting closer and might seal off the visual contact needed for proper clearance for us and the planes that were behind us. I now know why take off from Dakar was at three minute intervals, providing separation when going through the pass. Those ominous looking clouds proved to be a disaster for one of the other bombers and the crew that took off after we did.

We didn't learn until a few days after new years of 1944 that Lt. Nicholas Kordich and his crew did not make it all the way through the Pass and their bomber crashed into the western peak. At the same time a group of Bedouins (a nomadic tribe of Arabs) were crossing the mountain pass on foot and heard the crash. In looking for survivors they found only the tail turret gunner who was asleep in the turret at the time of the crash and his turret with him inside was thrown clear of the wreckage. The Bedouins carried him down the mountain and dropped him off at a French Foreign Legion outpost. It is sad to report what the crash search party found. Before the Bedouins left the crash site they removed all the clothing from the bodies of the dead crew men and took whatever valuables they could find. In hindsight it might be possible to accept their behavior since their very existence in the harsh environs of the desert, searching for food and water, is not an easy task.

Landing in Marrakech was an eye opener. There was a never ending stream of airplanes - fighters - bombers - transports - either landing or taking off. Planes with every conceivable insignia and from as many nations. Apparently the desert war with Rommel's Nazis did not reach this far west and was confined to the North, along the Africa Coastline, and as far east as western Egypt. Serious problems arose among the Allies since the Free French wanted control of the air field and the communications tower. In clearing planes for landing with pilots who speak a different language could be trying at times. Accidents were bound to happen and it was hard to accept as a normal occurrence of a French P-38 landing on top of a B-24 Liberator that was on its landing roll. Or to see two planes landing on the same runway but in opposite directions. Seeing this I just had to turn away and wait for the explosion. Somehow or someway they managed to pass each other on the runway and didn't even scratch a wingtip. Those pilot's sure must have had God or his representative as their co-pilot. All but a few of our groups planes had landed that day December 10, 1943. As mentioned before Lt. Kordich didn't make it and Lt. Giraudo got lost and somehow found himself over the airfield in Casablanca, an unexplainable occurrence of this nasty war.

It was late afternoon when Colonel Mills summoned all crew members to an area of the ramp. Standing on a truck he began a speech of the do's and don'ts while here in Marrakech. Do get some rest, take care of your bomber, be careful of what you buy from the local people in the way of food and most of all stay away from the women. And "don't" go into the walled city (Medina) looking for vailed French women. He advised us to go to the USO building on the main boulevard and no where else.

Well, we have been living a life of "eat, drink and be merry for tomorrow we may die" and this guy tells us not to look for women. Secretly I think he was telling us where they were. When evening came and we arrived at the USO building we found it was a converted palace of sorts. Outside were long lines of horse drawn carriages all wanting to take us to where, as the driver tells it, all the virgin french women were. Without exception all the cabbies were eager to barter with the price of an incursion into the forbidden walled Medina.

All six of us non-coms were standing in front of the USO when Pop spoke first. Not to us, but to a cabbie, and began bartering the price. After some haggling, Pop agreed on two cabs for the six of us, but first, he passed out the treasures he bought at the PX back in Florida, saying, "you guys had better take some of these rubbers." I just had to ask, "Pop why do we need these rubbers if we're going to have virgin french women?" I got a blank stare from everyone except Paul who asked, "what do you mean Bill?" Pop added, "just make sure you use them and stop asking why." It was a leisurely ride to the Medina, down a wide boulevard that was lined on both sides with orange trees that still had an ample supply of fruit on the branches.

Arriving at the main entrance to the Medina the driver turned to the right. Pop hollered, "where you going, that's the entrance back there?" The driver said, "it will be easier to go in the side door." He put his finger to his lips as in a whisper as if saying "trust me." About two hundred yards from the main gate the driver started hollering some sort of gibberish, unintelligible to us foreigners, and a gate opened up for him to drive the carriage inside. Once inside he drove to a fashionable, clean looking residence, he stopped and beckoned us to go inside which we did. It was quite nice with fashionable furniture and colorful drapes on the walls and windows. We were greeted by what I suppose was the madam of the house, she escorted us to a large room, clapped her hands and from all sides lovely young ladies appeared, each in a silky shear negligee. All of them seemed quite young. The madam, with hand gestures, beckoned us to select our choice of lady. Pop, with a silly smile on his face, asked the madam which one was the virgin. The madam just looked at Pop and winked at him and said, "take your pick." With all selections made and couples pared off we were then motioned by the madam to go to their rooms which was in different directions. Of course we had paid the cabbie our twenty dollars each before we left the USO building.

Were we all naive young men at the time, that is, all except Pop? Just as we left the main room there was a commotion at the front door and the cabbie came running in shouting that the MP's are coming and we can't get caught there! He quickly ran toward the rear door while motioning us to follow him, he kept saying "quickly, quickly" and then putting in hands together as if praying and again saying "quickly, quickly". Once outside we had no choice but to follow him through some of the weirdest back alleys I would ever want to see. It was straight out of the tales of Arabian Nights and at any moment we could expect Sinbad to come and rescue us. Running through those alleys and watching every step we took because the center of those alleys were the city sewer lines and only God could know what we might step in along the way. We received cold blank stares from men clothed in long black robes, walked in black leather boots and with long curved sabers hanging from their sides, under their robes. I thought at any moment we might be robbed or gored with one of those razor sharp curved swords. Our cabbie finally led us to a wooden door cut in the Medina wall. And outside was our carriage but with a different driver. All six of us jumped into that single cab for the hurried ride back to the USO. We didn't talk to each other very much except with a quizzical smirk on our faces. None of us wanted to admit that we had been taken or that we could have been so gullible to believe our cabbie when he shouted, "the MP's were going to raid the place". A twenty dollar lesson in lost love making and we didn't even get to unbuckle our belts or drop our zippers.

Once at the USO we all headed to the latrine which doubled as a pro-station and it was filled to capacity with Americas Don Juan lovers just paying the price of spreading wild oats on these foreign lands. A lesson well learned and a quiet ride back to the base for a good nights sleep in preparation for the next leg of our journey.

With the sight of all those soldiers dressed in different uniforms, speaking different languages and making use of different guns, tanks and airplanes, foreigners who are our Allies, this war is rapidly coming ever closer to us. The ominous nature of our journey is gradually sinking into our minds. We are being conditioned for the ultimate, "TO FIGHT IN A WAR."

Only the pilots were briefed on the next leg of our journey and Bahti came on the intercom after take off to tell us that we were heading for an air field on the south side of Tunis, on the northern African Coast. This flight was a little different than those of the past as we were to fly with other planes of the group in a loose formation to conserve fuel. Looking down over the terrain we were flying over we could see nothing but desolation called the Sahara Desert. Nothing but brown and reddish rock and sand. In passing Boyle on my way to the nose turret I glanced at the chart and saw that Tunis was not far away, maybe only six or seven hundred miles, and would be the shortest flight we had made so far. Only three or four hours away.

Later Bahti briefed us on the progress of the war and what we were expected to do. The Army landed at Salerno in Southern Italy in late September and have finally pushed up the eastern side of Italy to the Plains of Foggia where the terrain was flat and that the Army Corps of Engineer's were cutting out runways for these big birds to land. I called up to Bahti and asked, "You mean we're going to Italy." He responded, "No it looks like we are going to operate from North Africa near the City of Tunis."

About three hours flying time Varvil came on the intercom to tell us we have been diverted to another airfield. It seemed the Nazis were counter attacking somewhere in the Mediterranean Sea near the Island of Pantelleria and it would not be advisable for so many unarmed bombers to be in that area. We were diverted to a place called Chatteaudun De Romel. Varvil started to descend for a landing and while still in the nose turret I kept a look out for an airfield and could see none. I couldn't help but think, "where the hell is he taking us." I left my turret and went back to the waist section just as the wheels touched down on the ground. We all looked out the waist windows to see where we were and all we could see was desert and then desert dust. We quickly closed the waist windows before we started to choke to death. We finally came to a stop and the engines were cut off. When the dust settled and the windows were opened we saw nothing but desert and rows of army tents. We were in a no man's land for who in their right mind would want to be anywhere near such desolation. Outside the plane, Varvil said, "let's hope we don't have to stay here too long." The army truck took us to the mess tent for chow and then to the supply tent for assignment to a tent and check out some blankets. At the supply tent I asked the clerk, "what the hell are you handing out blankets here in the middle of the Sahara Desert for." He just grinned while handing me four blankets and said. "you'll find out." Leaving the supply tent I could not help but to think they sent all the looney tunes to this out of the way place just to keep their minds occupied. Needless to say, I had a closed mind to this asinine stupid place to land bombers, feed and bunk the crews and for no reason at all. Only with experience did I learn there was a valid reason for everything in this mind altering war.

The sun went down faster than we novice travelers could expect and the air suddenly started to get chilly. We all retrenched to inside the tents. We had no lights except our flash lights but managed to spread out the blankets on the standard army cots. After meaningless conversation we laid down on our cots for some shut eye. I placed one blanket on my cot, thinking I would not need more. It wasn't long before I had to put another blanket on top of me. And again it wasn't long before I placed another on me and finally reached for the fourth blanket and folded all four in such a manner that I had four layers of blanket under and over me and I was still shivering. I thought I was coming down with chills and fever and asked Randy, "Hey, Randy, are you cold." Randy said, "Shut up, I'm freezing my ass off and talking lets some heat out of my mouth." Laying there shivering and shaking brought back the look on that supply clerk's face when I asked about so many blankets here in the desert. Apparently he knew what he was doing.

We woke up as the first morning rays of sunshine began to filter through the seams and doorway of that tent. Just as fast as the temperature went down last night, it came back up and we had to shed those blankets because we started to sweat. At the mess tent, standing in line for chow, I spotted the supply clerk at a nearby table. Our eyes met and he had that shitty smirk on his face. I could do nothing but laugh at my own stupidity. I send him a silent apology.

Chatteaudun was without a doubt a place to stay away from and a place anyone would want to leave behind if only just to forget that it ever existed. We had rush orders just after breakfast to gather our belongings and get to our plane and prepare for immediate take off. Varvil advised we will be in the air for only about thirty minutes and our destination will be Tunis. After take off I hurried to my nose turret for the first glimpse of the Mediterranean Sea and where fierce battles were recently fought. Arriving at Tunis I could see, what I guessed were thousands of ships in the harbor and a sea of army encampments all over the area. Hundreds of bombers, fighters and transport planes were scattered all around the perimeter of the airfield.

After parking the plane we were given the usual greeting by the engineering officer and told to refuel the plane before leaving it and post our own sentry at all times. The war was now a reality as we observed the bombed out buildings and the bomb craters in the area as the service truck took us to the mess hall. No fighting was within ear shot but the usual bee hive of activity was evident on the way back to our plane. This was the reality of war with so many nations taking part in the effort. French, British, Australians, South Africans, Canadians and so many others were doing their part, supposedly to achieve a lasting peace and do away with all diabolic tyrants.

Randy and I were at the plane that first evening and struck up a conversation with the British anti aircraft gun personnel that were close by our revetment. Just as the conversation began I noticed several men in French uniforms being marched ahead of two men with their rifles pointed at them. When they were abreast of us I could not help but to notice that the men with the rifles had a big "P" painted on the back of their fatigues. The British hollered to them in Italian and they responded. That Tommy began to laugh hysterically. The men with the "P" were Italian war prisoners and the others were Frenchman. It seemed the P.O.W's caught the Frenchmen stealing gasoline out of the American planes and were escorting them to the MP's.

Our conversation with those "tommys" lasted for hours, and only ended when they were relieved and we were talked out. We learned they were in the African campaign for more than two years, they were fighting in a war even before I joined the Air Corps. I inquired about the news reels I saw before coming here and the long lines of Italian prisoners of war that surrendered by the thousands and wondered why so many gave up fighting so easily. Those "tommys" just laughed as they said, "You would give up too if you saw what they didn't see." I had to ask, "What do you mean if I saw what they didn't see?" Then we were told an unbelievable scenario that evidently shocked the Italians into submission.

The British had at their beck and call a certain group of scouts who had the ability to silently infiltrate the enemy lines and even to get into the middle of a scouting party without the enemy realizing it. They were so crafty they would sneak up on a scouting party at night without being heard or noticed. The scenario went like this. The Italians, at night, would place a sentry as the others slept. And they always slept in rows. Now the scout would creep up to the men sleeping without being noticed by the sentry and choose the man sleeping in the middle of the row and either slit his throat or just cut his head off. The next morning the other men would find that bloody mess. One of the "tommys" added, "Well, Yank, where would you want to sleep if you were in that group, besides the Italians aren't fighters, they're all bloody lovers." Walking the few feet back to our plane I said to Randy, "I guess we made a good choice in going to war in an airplane. Cheez, those guys really must be conditioned to war, how easy it was for them to tell us that story." Later that night Varvil came out to see us and said, "Colonel Mills just gave orders for us to get ready to take off on a moments notice sometime in the morning. I asked, "where we going this time?" He replied, "I really don't know right now, I guess we'll know tomorrow."

Another morning arrived with the bright rays of sunshine and an azure sky. Maybe there is an omen somewhere in the many azure sky's we experienced on our journey to war. With preflight completed, the plane and her engines finely tuned, all onboard were set for what we were lead to believe would be the final leg of our excursion. The overnight delay at ChatteauDun was caused by a few Nazi submarines that were lobbing some shells into Tunis but were chased or destroyed by the Allied naval ships in the area.

Take-off from Tunis was straight out over the blue waters of the Mediterranean on a northeast direction. We were going to our destination, our new home and base of operations, as a group, thirty two planes today and the rest of them tomorrow. Colonel Mills was in command and piloting the lead plane and selected our crew to fly on his left wing. We were going to the town of Manduria, in the heel of the Italian Boot. When Bahti told us the name of the place I thought he meant that we were going to China and Manchuria and told him so. Bahti came back and said, "Hey Fili, why don't you clean your ears out and listen to what I said, Manduria, in southern Italy." I replied, "OK, I'll take your word for it." The flight in formation was uneventful and being in the number three slot we would be the first to land at our new home.

Flying around in that traffic pattern my mind again wondered about the awesomeness of what we are doing. It had been only two and a half months since the invasion of Italy at Salerno and already the southern third of the Italian boot is under Allied control. In that time the ground forces had to oust the Germans, build the air fields, install the pipe lines to provide at least one hundred thousand gallons of high octane gasoline each day for each air field, secure the ports to provide food, ammunition and bombs for delivery by the bombers, then multiply these needs by twenty or thirty, the number of air fields, and you end up with logistical problems that could turn into a nightmare. But it had to be done since the world was at war.

It was December 20, 1943 that our plane was the first to touch down at the Manduria air field in the rain and found what was later to be described as Lake Manduria. It was situated in the center of the Italian heel, the city itself was about five miles to the south. The place where Hannibal watered his elephants after crossing the Alps to conquer the Italian Peninsula. Just four miles to the north of this Field was the city of Oria that was built on a rocky hill. It dates back to the glory days of the Roman Empire and was protected from attack by a walled castle in it's center that now overlooks the new conquerors and their sinister looking aerial war machines.

Manduria Army Air Base, as we named it, had but a single runway and the bombers were disbursed on either side. The unmarked revetments were assigned to who ever got there first and being first Varvil had selected an area that appeared to have less mud. We came to southern Italy at the worst time of the year, weather wise that is. It was the wet and damp time of the year and good only for the olive groves. Our ground crews had not arrived as they were still on the high seas somewhere between here and America. This air field was a former fighter base for the Italian air force and had but one hanger and several dilapidated and dirty barracks. We did not know then and didn't ask why but our squadron, the 720th, was assigned the barracks. The other squadrons were assigned tent areas until appropriate facilities could be constructed. The rest of the day was spent in getting our gear into the barracks, with an attempt to clean it up to make it liveable and to secure the plane. Since the infantry was still on alert and guarding the perimeter of the field, there was no need to schedule guard duty. That first night was spent moving around the bunks from the dripping rain water as the roof leaked like a sieve. The next two days everyone pitched in to patch the leaks and to make the insides compatible with our civilian lifestyles.

Christmas Day 1943 and my first Christmas away from home could have made us all homesick if we weren't kept busy with setting up shop. I don't know how they did it but the cooks whipped up a fantastic Christmas dinner complete with all the trimmings, cranberry sauce and even pumpkin pie. While standing in line to get my share a big fellow walked past me to the head of the line. Everyone shouted, "hey, the rear of the line is back here," The big fellow turned and started to walk to the rear when we all noticed that it was Colonel Mills. Everyone apologized to the Colonel and wanted to him to go ahead but Colonel Mills, being the man that he is, insisted on waiting his turn. Our admiration for the Colonel only increased in intensity.

Finally about the sixth of January 1944 the weather started to change and the 450th Bomb Group was scheduled to prepare for it's first combat mission in a few days. We were jubilant, in a naive way, at the thought of finally getting to do what we were trained to do. Our anxiety soon mellowed and became apprehensive to say the least with each succeeding mission.

(While in Dakar we were privileged to witness the culmination of a historical meeting. We were preparing to leave when we noticed a convoy of limousines, heavily guarded by MP's in the front, sides and rear, and wondered what was happening. That convoy was escorting President Roosevelt to the Naval ships in the harbor for his trip back to the United States after his famous meeting with Winston Churchill in Casablanca. We all stood at attention and saluted our Commander in Chief as he passed by.

When we landed at Chateaudun we were greeted by our Air Force Commander General of the Army "Hap" Arnold who informed all the pilots of their destination in Italy.)

Manduria Air Base, December 1943

FIVE

If there was a way to send a message to Hitler, Goering and his other partners in worldly crime that Varvil's crew was here we would have done so. It also would have been an exercise in stupid futility. But we were determined to do our job to the best of our God given ability. The next two weeks were confined to making a homestead, going to war time and survival lectures and keeping our big bird ready and willing to fly and fight on a moments notice. We had many area indoctrination and familiarization flights so all crew members would know where they were at all times should we have to bail out to save our lives. I wanted to go on as many of these flights as I could because Varvil gave me my first lessons in flying. Most fledgling pilots start out in small planes like the ancient but venerable Piper Cub. Not me, I had to start out learning to fly in the biggest bomber that was ever built in this or any preceding eras.

Late in the afternoon of January 7, 1944 we were advised the 450th will fly on our first mission tomorrow and all passes were cancelled. Our ground crews had not yet arrived and thus we had to load our own bombs and all the fifty caliber machine gun bullets for ten machine guns. The bombs were delivered around dusk and Charlie, being the armament specialist signed the receipt. Pop delegated both Charlie and Chief to supervise the loading and fusing of the bombs. We had no external power and had to hand crank twelve five hundred pound bombs (three tons of bombs) up into the bomb bay and latch them in place. Even though we took turns at cranking we all had tired sore muscles by the time we were done. Each man took charge of loading the bullets in his own gun or turret. Fueling was completed earlier.

I guess it was about midnight when our loading was completed and we all returned to the barracks for a not so hot shower but we did have clean sheets on our cots. Sleep came easy. Pop reminded us all that briefing would be at eight o'clock.

For some unknown reason during the night briefing was changed to seven o'clock and our bombardier Ed Bell was supposed to tell us non coms. Well, the CQ came in and woke us up at six thirty AM and we took our time dressing and going to breakfast. We all arrived at the briefing room at seven forty five am and found the briefing room empty. Just then Varvil showed up mad as a chicken with a fox in the hen house. "Where the hell have you guys been?" was Varvil's question. We didn't know from nothing and puzzled at his being uptight. He continued, "Why weren't you at briefing?" Pop related our understanding of the briefing time and no one told us of any changes. "Didn't Bell come to you're barracks to tell of the change?" asked Varvil. Pop said, "no sir, he didn't." I could see Varvil's lips move as he said to himself, " why that lazy son of a bitch." Varvil then added, " Bell didn't even show up for the bombardier's briefing" I could then understand why Varvil was so furious at us when he told us Colonel Mills had selected our crew to lead the 450th bomb group on it's very first mission and he was going to fly with us. This was a sought after honor and would have propelled Varvil to a position of flight leader and speed up a deserved promotion to Captain. Both positions he could have easily filled. To say that Colonel Mills was pissed off when his driver took him to our airplane and he found no one there could be a gross understatement. The Colonel sped to another plane and bumped the co pilot.

The bombers that flew that first mission encountered no opposition from fighters or flak, it was a milk run. But a lot of flak was received from Captain Wicks the 720th squadron commander who called all of Varvil's crew into his office and proceeded to berate Varvil for not properly disciplining his crew. Varvil didn't deserve such treatment and we non coms could not do or say anything to support him. Lt. Bell did not offer any excuses or to own up to the fact that it was his fault. Wicks, in completing his admonishment, told Varvil that it will be a cold day in hell before you all fly together again. To this day we never found out why, but Captain Wicks had an intense dislike for Varvil and his crew. In hindsight, perhaps the dislike stemmed from the fact that Colonel Mills attitude toward Varvil was just the opposite. The Colonel thought we were a well trained and disciplined crew. But, Wicks was adamant and we stayed on the ground for most of January 1944. During which time he tried his best to split us up as a crew but thankful for Air Corps regulations we had the right to remain the crew we were trained to be.

In sitting out those first few missions we had time to think and to analyze this war and how relatively easy the first four missions seemed to be. No casualties and only a few minor holes were in the skin of a few planes, not sufficient to take them out of service. We were beginning to think this war was going to be a piece of cake and we will complete our fifty missions and be home in no time at all.

But the day of reckoning and the awful truth that war is hell surfaced unexpectedly. January 24, 1944, Varvil's crew sat out another mission and, as we were becoming accustomed to doing, we sat at the end of the runway to wait for our friends and buddies to return. When they did return it was less one bomber and it's crew. It was the fifth mission of the 720th squadron to destroy the fighter base at Mostar, Yugoslavia. The crew that did not return was piloted by 2nd Lt. Ronald R. Whitehead, his bomber was brought down by flak. A few weeks later Two gunners were rescued by the Partisans in Yugoslavia and returned to Manduria by way of the island of Vis. A small island off the western coast of Yugoslavia that was being secured by the British just for rescuing downed flyers.

The two gunners brought with them a heart warming story of true heroism. Lt. Whitehead, himself wounded, stayed with the bomber to keep it flying to enable all the others to bail out and save their lives. It is not known if he had time to bail out and went down with the bomber, it exploded when it hit the ground. "No greater love hath no man than to forsake his life for his friends."

Later that afternoon Captain Wicks called a meeting of all the bomber crews in front of the orderly room. He talked about Lt. Whitehead and his crew being shot down. He added a few words about how easily it could happen to any or all of us. Instead of expressing regrets and sorrow for Lt. Whitehead and his crew Captain Wicks said, "I'm more worried about them catching venereal disease than being safe and alive." The silence among all us crew members was deafening except for the silent words everyone sent to Captain Wicks, (it can be said with confidence those words were not of the complimentary variety.) Everyone knew that Lt. Whitehead's crew were the epitome of the human race and not ones who went out on drinking sprees or looking for women of the night. They even refused a sight seeing trip to the Medina and the vailed women while we were in Marrakech.

Everyone in the 720th squadron somehow and someway felt sorry for Captain Wicks for not being able to enjoy the respect and friendship of his subordinates and we never knew why. On a later mission in early February 1944 Wicks was leading the 720th over a target area that encountered only light but accurate flak. A lucky shot from the ground exploded just under his cockpit and a piece of shrapnel went through the half inch thick armour plate behind the pilot's seat and into the spine of Captain Wicks. The co pilot flew the bomber home and upon entering the flight pattern ordered the shooting of red flares on his downwind approach indicating wounded on board and landed the plane to a complete stop at the end of the runway. The medics had a difficult time in removing Wicks from the pilot's seat. He died soon after arriving at the Bari General Hospital.

On March 17, 1944 Lt. Reaford C. McCraw and his crew were shot down by flak over Austria. In September 1990 a reunion of the 450th bomb group was held in Orlando, Florida and attended by one of Lt. McCraw's surviving crew. This one crew member is still trying to have the Air Force bestow, posthumously, an appropriate medal to Lt. McCraw, who went down with his ship, and his unselfish devotion to duty.

From the first mission on January 8, 1944 to January 27, 1944 the 450th lost five of it's original sixty two crews and bombers.

After scanning the next days flight schedule every day for the last three weeks we finally found our names on the list and we would finally fly as a crew for the first time tomorrow. This time we did not have to load any bombs or belts of bullets as the full compliment of ground personnel had arrived on January 15, 1944. We took every precaution we could to make sure no one or anything would screw things up for us this time.

For the first time we were able to sit in on the mission briefing, to know where we were going to drop bombs, if we were going to encounter fighters or flak opposition and just how a crew is briefed on survival and rescue in the event our plane gets shot out of the sky. This being our first mission we had not experienced the need to visit the latrine just after being told where we are going. A phenomenon we watched but never knew why. At the plane we began the ritual of helping each other in making certain our equipment is on properly, that we have all the necessary paraphernalia, parachute, oxygen mask, flak vest and of course Pop had his ever present supply of rubbers with him. Our crew chief, Tom Cox, promoted to inspector, was transferred to the air depot in Bari. Our new crew chief, Sam Grybel, made sure our plane was air worthy and would bring us back home safely. Everything and everyone was in place when the green flares were fired from the control tower, the signal to start the engines. We were heading to bomb the Italian railroad marshalling yards at Ferrara in northern Italy.

Take off at thirty second intervals with twelve five hundred pound bombs was uneventful even though this was the first time we took off at maximum gross weight. It took every inch of that runway to get our monster up in the air. Varvil began maneuvering into formation in the fourth slot, just under the lead plane of the high right group of six planes piloted by Lt. Frank Marpe. I was standing between my two pilots and asked Bahti why he held the plane down so long. He just looked at me with wide opened eyes and said, "this plane is a ground lover and just didn't want to go up." I added, "maybe it's telling us something, like it's more scared than we are, or maybe, is this trip necessary?" Bahti said, "Fili, get the hell out of here, go up into your turret and stop asking foolish questions."

Once in the air we all settled down to enjoy the flight. The air was as smooth glass, a few scattered clouds hanging around, the blue waters of the Adriatic Sea was inviting and none of us had the slightest sense of what we are about to do. Near the northern end of the Adriatic Marpe started to turn left to the coastal town of Rovigo the initial point to commence the bomb run on a heading of about 240 degrees. Sitting in my nose turret there was nothing that could escape my vision. All the planes started to open their bomb bay doors and after a few more seconds Bell came on the intercom saying "Bombs away." The big bird took a leap upward after unloading three ton of bombs. Marpe then turned the flight formation to the left and out over the Adriatic Sea where no flak guns could shoot at us. I thought to myself, "this is war, this is how bombing is accomplished?" In the same instance I had to ask myself "why is my heart beating so rapidly and why are my hands sweating inside my electric heated gloves, they aren't cold?" My inner sense was telling me to stop being so nonchalant and start taking this ride in a bomber serious. Apparently I was not listening to my own little voices .

On the return route to Manduria and about half way down the Italian boot I looked over to the west and spotted what looked like black puffs of smoke. I asked Varvil what he thought they were. He answered, "they look like flak bursts." They seemed so fascinating to me I had to ask him to alter our course to get a better look at them. Before Varvil could respond Charlie roared on the intercom, "Tail to Pilot, don't you listen to that frigen nutso in the nose, I don't want to get any closer!" Varvil came back, "Fili you're a stupid idiot, you'll get your fill of black flak puffs soon enough so don't be too anxious to get near these few."

I took his advice and settled down to sight seeing. The spur of the Italian boot came into view as we started our descent and were able to remove our oxygen masks. The sight of that spur would be the telling point, of future missions, that we are out of harms way and back in Allied territory.

Varvil did his usual toe dance down the runway, landing without the slightest of a jar. It wasn't too long before we gunners had some difficulty determining who landed the plane Varvil, or Bahti, they both became experts. Our crew chief Sam, as expected, was waiting patiently for our return and was delighted to know that we had no write ups for him to repair. The truck to take us to operations and debriefing arrived as we emerged from the plane.

This day was to be another first for us. For after each mission the Red Cross girls were handing out coffee and donuts and the medics were handing out two ounces of whiskey to each man. The coffee and donuts we ate right away but the two ounces of whiskey we took back to the barracks and just slowly sipped it to make it last longer. There was a lot of pros and cons about this two ounces of whiskey for each crew member on their return from a mission. Some unknown writer was spreading gossip that the air corps was keeping the airmen inebriated in order to get them to fly combat. Nothing was farther from the truth. We crew members were always and at all times in complete control of our faculties. Besides no one ever forced us to take and drink that two ounces of whiskey. But for us crew members it was welcomed with enthusiasm, for enjoyment and the greatest relaxer we could be given. There wasn't a post mission briefing since no Nazis fighters came up and no flak guns were fired to challenge us. Only the bombardiers were required to stay at headquarters to answer any questions asked by the Group intelligence officers.

After stowing my flying gear and cleaning up my body, I walked over to the orderly room to scan the next days mission schedule. Sure enough Varvil and his charges were once again going to fly. We all had a secret thought Captain Wicks was told by higher authority to lay off Varvil and to forget the past.

We were scheduled to hit the railroad marshalling yards at Siena, again in northern Italy. The mission briefing and the flight was a carbon copy of the previous days attempt at fighting a war with the exception that no flak bursts were visible anywhere. The two ounces of whiskey was enjoyed just as much. Having just past my twentieth birthday a few weeks ago while in Tunis on December 17, 1943, I laid on my bunk sipping my whiskey and sent a mental note to the Liquor Control Board back in Pennsylvania, "Hey guys, I'm not twenty one years old yet but try to stop me."

Another stop at the orderly room and another schedule for flying tomorrow and, yes, we were listed. Looks like somehow we're going to make up for lost time, three days in a row. Varvil stopped at the barracks that evening to see us for no special reason other than just to chat for a few minutes. Secretly I guessed he wanted to make sure that his charges weren't having second thoughts about flying combat. He did leave with us, notwithstanding the fact that our first two missions may have been milk runs, a word of caution for us not to become complacent and not to expect the same to continue.

The same morning routine, being woke up by the CQ, breakfast, briefing and gathering at our bomber to prepare our own individual paraphernalia for combat. The target today was the airdrome at Udine in northeast Italy, about forty miles due north of Trieste. The green flares from the control tower told us to get moving. The weather was getting warmer and didn't help Varvil and Bahti a bit in getting our monster off the ground in any shorter distance. Once again every inch of the runway was required and this time I think we took the tops off some of the olive trees on the northern end of our airfield. Climb out and getting into formation again was routine as was the trip up the center of the Adriatic Sea. During this time I was given an easy assignment in counting the ships north of the Italian spur and report the sightings and numbers at the post briefing meeting.

Reaching the northern end of the Adriatic, climbing up to altitude, donning our oxygen masks, charging our guns and making ready for an aerial battle was again almost routine. The sky had scattered cumulus clouds below which could be termed two tenths overcast. Off in the distance I saw our target and called Nose to pilot, "Target in sight at about two o'clock." Bell responded, "I have it in sight." Getting closer to the target I would be the first to spot the black mushroom like clouds caused by the exploding flak shells. The closer we got to the target and the dangers ahead swiftly brought me to my senses and the ever present need for self preservation. I could not help but think of that asinine desire of mine a few days ago of wanting to get closer to those flak explosions. Looking at so many of those mushrooms just ahead of us I began to wonder how the hell are we going to get through them?

The formation turned right on an easterly heading direct to the target. The steady unwavering direction would last for at least ten minutes during which time any deviation from the selected heading could not to be tolerated or the bombs would miss the target. And during this time the ground gunners could get a fix on our direction and altitude to set the fuse on their flak shells. They in turn would fire hoping for a direct hit. Another first for us and on this bomb run our plane started to bounce around as if in rough and turbulent air. But the air was smooth. I called nose to pilot, "any troubles with the plane, why is it jumping around like it is?" Bahti answered, "Nose, there's nothing the matter with our plane, just those gunners on the ground seem to have our altitude pinned down and are getting their shells to explode too close to us." I came back, "then let's get the hell out of here before they get any closer," Randy called, "waist to nose, you wanted to get close to flak, well here it is, I'm glad you have to see it before I do." Randy added, "hey Fili, you have to watch where we're going then hope and pray that we get through. Back here we see where we were and know we made it through." I asked Randy, "do you wanta trade places?" "Not on your life," was Randy's response. Just then Bell came on the intercom and said, "bombs away!" And the formation began it's rallying right turn in a descending attitude to pick up speed and headed for the safe confines above the Adriatic Sea.

It didn't take too long to go from twenty thousand feet, our bombing altitude, (that's four miles above the ground) to thirteen thousand feet and we were able to remove our oxygen masks. Boyle called on the intercom, "hey, Fili, are you all right, I'm going to open your turret doors." He opened them and pushed a cigarette between my lips, one between his lips and struck a match and lit both of them while saying, "boy, that was an experience wasn't it." I just took a few long drags of that cigarette and said, "it sure was." (the nose section was the only place smoking was allowed in our ugly bitch's insides.) Boyle then asked, "do you wanta see some more flak?" "No thank you" was my swift reply.

The two hours to our base was uneventful with Varvil and Bahti taking turns at flying what I thought was an extremely tight formation. We were so close we could almost read the lips of the others guys in the wing plane. Another tip toe landing lead us to believe that Varvil and Bahti were trying to out do each other. I was back with the guys in the waist when we landed and while taxing in I noticed the right aileron was hanging almost straight down. After parking, Pop shutting down the engines I jumped out of the bomb bay to examine the aileron and sure enough I found that the cables were not even connected. I Called Bahti over to show him and asked him if he had known of having only one aileron would he have flown such a tight formation. Bahti called Varvil over to show him and said, "son of a buck look what we didn't have." Varvil only smiled and said, "Lenus, let's be more careful, and stay away from those flak guns."

Besides telling Sam Grybel of the severed cable both Varvil and Bahti asked him to check on the elevator trim tab, it seems to be sticking at high altitude. Sam rose to the call and installed a new aileron cable that same night and did a thorough test of the trim tab and found it to be in good working order. Sam also found six small flak holes in the fuselage and had the sheet metal specialist repair them.

Once again the post mission coffee and donuts was enjoyed still not as much as that two ounces of whiskey. As the medic was measuring my share I begged him to tilt his hand a little more, he just shook his head no, however the distraction gave me a few more drops in my cup. Stowing our gear, cleaning up, chow and a trip to the bulletin board brought smiles to our faces. We have a day off tomorrow.

To keep our minds occupied and busy During the past month I had purchased a motorcycle from an itinerant Italian for fifty bucks as did Charlie and Paul with their pooled money. So this day off we planned on going to the port city of Taranto to try to buy a few steaks from some of the sailors that were in the port. On the way my cycle quit running and had to be towed all the way back to our base. It wasn't too long after that towing episode that I found another Italian that wanted the cycle more than I did and sold it to him for a hundred dollars. We never did get those fresh steaks.

February was a busy month for the 450th bomb group with most of the missions being confined to railroad marshalling yards and German air fields yards in northern Italy, Bulgaria and Yugoslavia. The ground crews were kept busy and did a superb job repairing holes in the planes and in general keeping the big birds in tip top flying condition. But the elevator trim tab on our plane kept freezing up at high altitude and Sam was getting frustrated at not being able to pin point the problem. It got so severe that Sam grounded the plane. And on a day that once again Colonel Mills was going to fly with us. The Colonel arrived at our revetment hopped out of his jeep gave some instructions to his driver and said "let's go men." Sam, standing on top of the right wing said to the Colonel, "Colonel, I put a red X on this plane for a jamming elevator trim at high altitude and I need time to find out why." Colonel Mills replied, "Corporal, I'm ordering you to remove that red X!" Sam stood his ground and said, "no disrespect sir, I can't do that." (Air corps regulations required affirmative action to be taken whenever a Red X was placed on a plane and required an inspectors approval.) At this point the Colonel got in his jeep and went to fly in another plane.

When the Colonel left I looked at Randy and Bahti and said, "Guys, looks like we're going to be on the shit list again." Bahti, while shaking his head could only say, "son of a buck." It would have been impossible for any of us to realize the pressure and the anguish of seeing so many of his men either killed or shot out of the skies a commander is constantly subjected to. That night after another mission with only moderate flak encounter, Colonel Mills sent for our crew chief. The Colonel thanked Sam for standing his ground because he was right and promoted him to staff sergeant. When we heard this we were ecstatic with joy. Our respect for Colonel Mills increased ten fold because of this and so many other leadership situations that occurred during our short stay together.

February 16, 1944, we were scheduled to fly a mission to bomb the railroad marshalling yards at Pontassieve, Italy and everything was proceeding as planned with one exception. All of the pilots were complaining about the need to use so much of the runway for take off. Fifteenth Air Force Headquarters in Bari was aware of this and after lengthy tests issued a directive to load all Liberators with only ten five hundred pound bombs instead of the usual twelve. There was a decided sigh of relief from all the pilots since warmer weather and thinner air was rapidly approaching.

Pop had asked me to take over as engineer for take off on this mission as he wanted to make some adjustments to his turret. On the take off roll and just as Varvil picked the wheels off the ground I noticed out of the corner of my eye that some fellow made a mad dash out on to the runway just after we passed where he was standing. There was no reason for me or anyone else to be concerned by his actions at this time. Climb out and settling into formation was again routine, Pop had completed his adjustments to his turret and I went up to the nose turret and began my own preparations for combat: Check my turret before entering, donning my flack vest and steel helmet, checking my electric heated flying suit and place my parachute in it's usual handy place in the unlikely event that I just might have to use it. Everything checked out perfectly but the whereabouts of my parachute. I began to hit the panic button. I didn't dare ask Boyle or anyone else if they saw my parachute, that was always the individuals problem and responsibility. Then it dawned on me, that fellow who ran out onto the runway just after we passed him must have been going to retrieve my parachute that fell out of the nose wheel well. I remember placing it inside from the open nose wheel doors and had every intention of going up to the nose before takeoff to put it in my turret for safe keeping as I had always done. For the life of me I do not know why I forgot to take care of this vital life supporting apparatus. I could only ask myself, "what the hell am I going to do now?" If I tell Varvil he would have to abort the mission and all the crew will lose credit for the mission making their stay overseas that much longer. If I tell Boyle he surely will have to tell Varvil. This isn't the same problem that Boyle had on our second mission that, fortunately for him, was a milk run when he accidently popped open his parachute while over the target. Paul told us later of how comical Boyle was in his frantic attempts at trying to repack it in such cramped quarters. He finally decided to roll it up in his arms, hug it as tight he would a million dollars and then jump out if that became necessary. But I had no parachute to hug!

I decided to say nothing and climbed into my turret and looked for divine guidance (something I seem to be doing a lot of these days since we left the States) and prayed, "Christ, I need you now, please let this be another milk run." The route to Pontassieve took us over the instep of the Italian foot, the Tyrrhenian Sea and over the Island of Capri. As we approached Capri I was spell bound by the number of ships off to our left. It was an armada of war ships, landing ships and freighters. I was mesmerized at the sight of so many ships that stretched out as far as I could see. I called to Varvil and Bahti and asked if they saw the ships and they too were surprised and did not know what they were or what they were doing there. I couldn't see any wake from any of them to determine their direction of travel. The speed of our formation quickly took us out of visual range and for the moment out of mind.

With Capri and the naval armada out of sight I looked to the right and spotted the City of Rome. Looking farther eastward I could make out the dome of the Basilica of St. Peter's Cathedral in the Vatican City. I could only think, "God, don't allow us to drop any bombs near there."

The farther north we flew the thicker the clouds became and at times completely obscured the sea and the Italian coast line. The formation leader turned inland and could find no holes in the clouds and targets of opportunity were sought after. No flak was sent up probably so we would not know where the weather protected target was. We continued our right turn for about ten minutes, then left and looking at the Sun I surmised that were heading in a southerly direction and home. I looked up to the heavens and said, "thank you Lord, for this milk run." When we were in sight of Rome and the Vatican City I just had to bless myself and send a thank you to that heavenly place if indeed it does exist.

I thought I was going to get away with the sloppy care of my life protecting parachute. But on the truck back to headquarters for our donuts, coffee and whiskey Varvil spotted my gear and noticed something missing. He just stared at me for a few moments and suddenly shouted, "Fili, where's your parachute I don't see it." I guess I wanted to be smart and say "neither do I." But discretion is the better part of valor and this was not the time to be a wise ass. I simply said I don't know. Varvil added that he heard on the radio just after take off someone had to run out on the runway to remove a parachute and asked me, "was that your's." I had to own up and say "I think so." "What the hell were you going to do if we got hit with flak or fighters and had to bail out" asked Varvil. My only explanation was, "Sir, I didn't want the crew to be mad at me for losing a mission credit if you had to turn back for such a stupid mistake, I'm sorry." "Well, you would have placed the others in jeopardy by forcing them to help you, - did you think of that?" Varvil asked. "No sir, I did not" I replied. Varvil added, "Fili, we'll discuss this further later." Back in the barracks I talked to Randy and told him that I was afraid that what I did was grounds to have me removed from the crew. Randy replied, "I don't think he'll go that far." I added, "I sure hope he don't."

I put my stupidity on the back burner for the time being and asked Randy and Chief it they saw all those ships near the Island of Capri. They saw them and also wondered what they were doing out there. Paul came over to us and added, "Did you notice that captain at post briefing had a silly grin on his face when we told him about all those ships. I'll bet he knows what they were or are going to do and wouldn't tell us. They must be our's or they would have shot at us when we were on top of them." Pop joined the conversation and added, "yeah, but if they were German they might not have shot at us just to make us think they were friendly." Back from chow and sitting on my bunk I could not help to wonder when and how Varvil was going to lower the boom on me.

Another check of tomorrow's flight schedule found Varvil and his kids part of another show. At briefing the curtain was still down on the wall map. We had no idea of where we were going but the S-2 officers were huddled in the far right corner of the room. For the first time the group S-2 officer, a major, walked to the small stage and started to raise the curtain. We were puzzled as the string didn't seem to go much farther than Naples. The Major started his talk by asking us to recall seeing all those ships just off the island of Capri. Then he added in a tone that told us of his excitement:

"Today, gentlemen, we, the 450th bomb group are going to lead an invasion on the Anzio Beach that is only forty miles south of Rome." One could expect roaring hurrah's or sounds of jubilation but there was only noticeable stirring in the chairs. To lead an invasion meant that we would be the first to get shot at. We would be the enemy's target of opportunity. For myself, I could not help but to think about my lead position in the nose turret and the muscles in my stomach began to tighten up. I told myself to stop being selfish in thinking about me and pay attention to this briefing. Again I didn't really listen to my inner voices.

I looked around that room and saw the looks on everyone's face when they heard the major speak. Those looks were of apprehension, of concern, of the seriousness of our involvement. And yet they were looks that said, "finally we're going to do something significant to bring this war to an end." The major continued, "We don't want anyone to become complacent because the travel distance from here to there is quite short compared to the time you are used to traveling. I cannot emphasize too strongly this is not going to be another milk run.

The targets you will be assigned to hit are heavily fortified and will be vigorously defended. We don't expect the Germans to commit their fighters to the defense of Anzio however they have been known to do the unexpected. So all you gunners had better keep your fingers near your triggers just in case. They do have formidable anti aircraft batteries with many experienced gunners who know how to set their fuses for maximum damage from the exploding shells. Your targets for today will be the storage warehouses and motor pools about four miles from the shore line. Other groups will be targeting bridges and railroads. We have intelligence reports that the Germans have installed one of their forty foot "Big Bertha" railroad cannons in this area. Those guns are capable of lobbing shells fifty miles out to sea. And We don't want the Doughboys in the landing party to be jeopardized any more than they will be before they hit the beaches. Let's hope we can put that monster out of commission once and for all.

For the first time I experienced the need to take my place in the long line to visit the latrine after briefing and to take care of that uneasy feeling in my intestines. These briefings are becoming the ideal laxative and I am not suggesting one go find a war to achieve such an experience.

At the group operations office and climbing onto the truck to take us to our plane I had hoped that Varvil would overlook my error of yesterday and the intensity of today's mission would cause him to put me on the back burner. That was not to be my luck. On the way out Varvil asked me, "Fili, what do you think I should do to chastise you?" I answered with some sheepishness, " Sir I don't know." When we all disembarked from the truck and standing together Varvil said, " Fili, from this moment on, and that goes for every mission we take off on, when everyone is aboard the plane and we are taxing out, you are to go through the plane, just make sure you don't fall through the bomb bay doors, you are to ask every man where his gear and parachute is and then report to me in the cockpit of your findings. And do this before we take off. If you fail once you'll be off this crew faster than a daddy rabbit hopped on and off a mommy rabbit. Do you get the message." I replied in the only way I knew how "yes sir." To myself I was relieved that I am still on the crew. I looked over to Randy and Chief and saw a silly grin on their faces. Paul, Charlie and Chief were laughing as they walked to the tail of the plane.

Our flight direction was much the same as yesterday, over the instep of the Italian foot and out over the Tyrrhenian Sea, only this time about forty miles farther out to sea. On turning back toward Anzio we could see the armada of ships. Paul called on the intercom telling us to switch to the communications channel to hear a BBC shortwave broadcast from London. We were shocked to hear the commentator reporting the details of this invasion by the Allies. He was describing how the men were landing on the beaches while the bombers were flying overhead dropping bombs and blasting away at the entrenched German Army. I called Paul on the intercom and asked, "Hey, Paul is this a real broadcast?" His response was, "it sure is." I added, "how can that be. That guy is saying the men are landing on the beaches and we can see the landing boats with their wakes just circling around waiting for us to drop our bombs to make sure we don't have any of them misdirected and maybe land on them. They haven't hit the beaches yet! Who the hell side is this guy on, something awful screwy is going on?" Bahti came on the intercom and said, "I know how you guys feel and I feel the same way but cut the chatter and keep a sharp look out for fighters, they may just try to sneak some in on us. Besides we're starting our bomb run." From my nose turret my eyes were glued to the terrain just behind the shore line looking for a glimpse of the ack ack guns that, without a doubt, will be firing at us. It wasn't long before I saw the flashes of light and then the black mushrooms. I called to everyone to tell them that it looks like they're going to throw everything up at us even the kitchen sink.

We started flying through the flak and once again our big bird started to bounce around in the smooth air. This time it was more severe, we knew why and said many silent prayers that those mushrooms don't get any closer. From my vantage point I kept ducking and flinching each time one of those mushrooms appeared in my cone of vision. At times I didn't know which way to flinch since they were in front and sides simultaneously. I probably would have gone stark raving mad if my head didn't pivot on my shoulders.

Some of the shells did come so close I could hear the sound as it whisked past my turret and see the trajectory as the speed of the shell parted the air waves. This was war in all of it's death dealing ferocity and instinctively called again on the intercom, "let's get the hell out of here, guys, tempting fate is just not one of my better traits." Finally, after bombs away, the formation turned left to return to the safe confines of the open sea.

Instead of continuing left and then south to return to Manduria the formation leader headed back to Anzio to make another run at the target. In those hectic days radio silence was a sacred trust but when that leader turned to go over the target a second time our silence was broken with chorused shoutings, "What's that frigen man doing, taking us over the target again, we dropped our bombs, there's nothing else we can do?" He didn't even change altitude when crossing the coastline, those radar controlled guns were going to be more accurate than before and we, yes, we bounced all the more. The inevitable happened and one of those shells tossed our right wing upward and continued right through leaving a hole about a foot in diameter. Off to our left I could see one plane diving out of formation, possibly out of control, I didn't see any parachutes.

(later information told us that the lead planes camera malfunctioned during the bomb drop and the leader took the formation over the target after the camera was repaired. We could not understand why a photo recon P-38 was not dispatched for picture taking instead of jeopardizing the entire formation that resulted in the loss of one bomber and it's crew and damage to more than a half dozen planes. The pilots of our group were the only ones privy to any more information. We gunners were not to be told of any reasons or why the need for this double jeopardy, or why did not just the lead plane go on this second trip?

Another hair raising mission ended with the usual coffee and donuts and two ounces of whiskey. By this time Paul and Charlie had accumulated about a fifth of the stuff, they didn't like it. Pop, Randy, Chief and I tried as best we could to coax them to at least sell it to us but they were adamant in keeping it for a more useful purpose someday. Pop added, after what happened today he thought they ought to help out their crew buddies. That didn't prevail either so we had to be content with just our own two ounces.

Operations posted a memo that a warm front is settling down on northern Italy and we will not be flying for a few days. It wasn't much of a vacation as it rained most of the time.

By the time our mission to Anzio was completed Varvil's charges had twelve missions of experience under our belts. We were ready and willing to accept any mission that would be asked of us. It was nice to look forward to a few days of R and R. For only God knew what was in store for us.

It was during this time of inactivity that we gunners became aware of one of the Italian kitchen helpers and wondered why he was always around during briefing. Randy and I mentioned this to our squadron intelligence sergeant who in turn gave the information to the group S-2 officer. They had an MP keep an eye on the man and at the appropriate time followed him to his home in Oria. When he left they went into the home and found a radio transmitter with German markings on it. Subsequently they arrested him and placed him in a prisoner of war camp with the rest of the Germans. When we heard of this we told our S-2 sergeant to turn him over to us and we would take him on a mission with us and somehow he just might fall out of the plane over the Adriatic Sea. We knew we couldn't do it but the thought was another form of therapy in satisfying our ego.

SIX

Scanning the bulletin board on the night of February 21, 1944 and finding our crew listed for tomorrows mission was a welcome relief from the dull mundane life of the past week in sometimes sunny, but mostly muddy, Italy. The last four days were spent dodging raindrops going to and from the mess hall and then cleaning the mud off our GI boots.

It was a happy-go-lucky group of airmen that gathered in the briefing room about 7:00 AM on the morning of February 22, 1944. That nonchalance quickly dissipated when the S-2 officer mounted the stage and raised the curtain over the map of Europe. The red string would take us on the same flight path as our previous two trips over the Tyrrhenian Sea and then started north. We thought we were going back to Anzio. Somehow, although not intentional, the raising of that curtain always seemed to be handled extremely slow. Maybe our minds wanted the string to stop before it took us over any danger zone.

Today was going to be different. The string continued on up and up and up. It got to the alps and the Brenner Pass and we thought we were going to try to knock out the anti aircraft guns on those high mountains. No such luck and the string continued on up through Austria and into the heart of Germany. This was to be our first bombing mission in the core of the German Homeland. We didn't have to be told, we knew in our guts the Germans would be overly zealous in protecting their country. We were now going to engage the enemy on his own soil and where the fighting would get down-right nasty with each ticking second with death dealing ferocity. When the curtain stopped at the top everyone just stared.

The briefing officer started his dialogue. "Gentlemen, the 450th is going to Germany for the first time together with every flyable bomber and fighter in the Fifteenth and Eight Air Forces. Today's mission is the beginning of an all out attempt to destroy the biggest deterrent in bringing this war to an end, the German

Luftwaffe, and blow it out of the sky once and for all time. The Eight Air Force from England will be striking airfields, aircraft factories and assembly plants in the north while the Fifteenth will be concentrating on these facilities in the south of Germany. It will be our longest mission to date. Our target for today will be Regensburg, where more than forty percent of the Messerschmidt fighters are produced and assembled. The target is close to eight hundred and fifty miles away and most of the time, except for flying over the Tyrrhenian Sea, you will be over enemy territory. You can expect long air battles with an unknown number of fighters to be sent up against you. We realize flying over the Tyrrhenian Sea to Regensberg is the longer route but it is being used as a diversionary tactic hoping that the German fighter command will be confused and delay in sending up the fighter planes until they can guess which target we are aiming for"

Our silence was again deafening as the mission briefing continued. "You have to remember there are fighter bases all along your route when landfall is made about twenty five miles east of Genoa. From then on you will be on oxygen with your target still about four hundred miles away. That translates to about two hours of flying time to the target and two hours from the target. Four hours of possible attacks from German fighters with their most experienced pilots in those cockpits. Including the pilots from the elite FW-190 Goering Yellow nose squadrons. It is possible that you will be attacked by the same fighters more than once after they land to refuel and reload ammunition because of the those bases along your flight path. You gunners will have to conserve your ammunition, shoot in short bursts and try to make sure your target is within range with a better chance of hitting a bulls eye. You don't want to be caught short of ammunition, if you lose an engine and have to fall out of formation making you a sitting duck for any aggressive enemy fighter pilot." At this point everyone was looking at everyone else and no doubt asking, "what the hell is a nice guy like me doing here?" And getting no answers.

"There is one satisfying fact that I can offer," added the S-2 officer, "You will be escorted by two groups P-38s to and from the target once you make land fall in northern Italy. The massive sigh of relief could be heard almost as one big gust of wind circulating around that briefing room.

If all of the information we were told thus far wasn't scaring the hell out of us the weather officer had to put some more icing on the cake. "The warm front that came down from the north, giving us all those rain showers for the past five days was pushed out to the Mediterranean Sea by a massive cold front that invaded northern Europe." The weather officer continued, "Besides being the longest mission to date, today's mission will be the coldest. That Arctic cold front dumped a lot of snow on Germany and the Alpine Mountains you will be crossing. Gentlemen, it will be cold today! You waist, tail and ball gunners will feel it the most so make doubly sure your electric heated gear is in tip top working order. It could be expected for you to want to close your waist windows but you will have to keep them open to scan for any possible fighter attacks. I wish I could end my part here with a lighter touch and more encouragement but I cannot except to say, Good luck to you all."

There wasn't much talking on the way out of the briefing room that morning or as we filed out to the latrine to take care of that doggone queazy feeling in our intestines. The filing into the equipment room to check out our parachutes and flak vests was equally as quiet. At the plane we acted as nonchalant as we could but the prospects of such a ride that we are about to take was only too apparent on our faces. No, we never considered opting out as being sick, it was just unthinkable. The few minutes while waiting for the flares to be shot from the control tower was spent is mundane talk about anything that came into our minds except this mission.

While taxing out for take off I accomplished my assigned project of checking on everyone's equipment and reporting to Varvil that all crew members are prepared properly for this flight. Take off and climb out was normal with Varvil sliding our bomber into the number seven slot of the lead center flight. As we turned north over the Tyrrhenian Sea the formation leader, (time has erased his name) tried to climb the formation over a huge wide spread and high cloud bank. As a result we flew directly into it. It was so thick we couldn't see the planes above or beside us. How Varvil and Bahti managed to extricate us out of that nasty situation could only be described as a masterful piece of pilotage. When we broke through the cloud top I saw our formation scattered all over the sky, we all made it through without colliding into each other.

I guess it could be said that the nose turret gunner was the eyes of the crew having a clear peripheral vision of better than two hundred and twenty degrees. But from my point of view it at times was allowing me to see too much of things I didn't want to see. Like all those black mushroom flak bursts that were too close for comfort to this nice little kids ass.

Through a break in the clouds I could see Anzio and wondered how the Doughboys were making out and if we really did knock out Big Bertha for them. Although I couldn't see it through the clouds I waited a few minutes past Anzio till we were abreast of Rome and the Vatican. I couldn't help but to look in that direction and to say a silent prayer for all of us. If there was anything such as a guardian angel I sure hope they are riding our shoulders this day.

As we made land fall in Northern Italy Varvil called on the intercom advising, "keep a sharp look out for fighters and report any sightings." We were at our bombing altitude of twenty one thousand feet, on oxygen and getting nervous by the second. The high European Alps came into sight and we knew that Germany and Regensburg was on the other side. We skirted the Brenner Pass and those high gun emplacements. In scanning the skies I looked to the northwest and caught a glimpse of the Matterhorn peak, that separates Italy from Switzerland, majestically rising above the clouds. I couldn't help but notice all that snow of the past two days. I opened the turret door to get a peak at the temperature gauge and saw the hand hitting the peg at sixty degrees below zero. I asked Boyle, "is that gauge broke or is it for real?" His reply, "It's for real." "No wonder my feet and finger tips were almost numb," was my response.

Once pass the Alps the queazy feeling in our stomachs became more queazy by the second. Off to the west and too close for comfort we could see the well defended city of Munich. A little farther west and in clear sight, as the clouds had broken up to about three tenths cover, was Lake Constance that bordered Switzerland and Germany. Boyle came on the intercom and suggested, "anyone want to go to Switzerland and sit out the war, there it is in clear sight." Charlie answered, "can we take a vote on it." He no sooner stopped talking about Switzerland when a bomber from the lower right flight broke formation and headed for that haven. Whether he had engine trouble or any other malfunction we were never to know. Nor do we know if that bomber really did make it to Switzerland because just as he broke out of his formation it seemed the whole German Air Force hit us. To say those fighter pilots were aggressive would be an understatement. They were like bees that suddenly came out of their hive to attack their predators from all directions. And we were the predators and we didn't like it. All we could see were these little planes darting in and out of our formations and each time they took at least one bomber with them.

The Luftwaffe was using a new battle tactic. They knew we flew in echelons of about eighteen bombers The center of the echelon had six or seven bombers, the high right group with six bombers and the lower left with six bombers. There were two echelons, we were in the second. Their battle plan was to concentrate on surprise. The initial attack focused on hitting all the formations from every conceivable direction simultaneously in an attempt to confuse the gunners seeing so many fighters at one time and take out as many bombers on the first two attacks. They succeeded to the extent they did take out three bombers but did not confuse the gunners.

From my turret and watching the initial attack on our front echelon, I saw the lead bomber pull out of formation and start down out of control in a wide flat spin. I had to turn my attention to the fighters coming in on us. Paul and Randy in the waist were calling out ME-109s and FW-190s all over the place. Charlie spotted two ME-210s staying just out of range. At the same instant I saw the biggest black puff of smoke ahead of our formation and Bahti called to Charlie to keep an eye on those ME-210s because they just shot a rocket through the formation. The lead plane also saw the rocket explode and changed course. We knew that the rocket launcher needed a two minute steady target to be very effective.

After those first two passes the German pilots changed to attacking both sides of both echelons. It was on these outside bombers they had their most success since there were fewer guns shooting back at them. We left Manduria with forty two bombers and thirteen had returned to base for various malfunctions. Of the twenty nine that approached the target area not all of them returned. I saw four bombers go down out of the lead echelon. A few parachutes came out. One bomber was totally in flames, two others were enveloped in smoke. The agony and the trauma of trying to reach out to help your fellow airmen save their lives is indescribable when they are falling to earth without a parachute or their bodies and parachute on fire. Or to watch helplessly as the bomber is going straight down in a spin, on fire and with ten fellow human beings onboard. That first air battle over Germany lasted at least thirty minutes before we reached our initial point to make our bomb run. Once on the bomb run the fighters broke off the attack and headed for their bases for refueling and more ammunition. It was a reprieve of sorts and now all we had to do was to sweat out the flak guns, hoping that they weren't as good as those fighter pilots were at downing bombers. Once again I went into my ducking and flinching act as those shells were coming too close for comfort, if comfort is the proper word to use.

The flak run lasted for about ten minutes, five before and five after we dropped the bombs on the target. Those fighters again took up their aggressive attack and downing more bombers. The bombers that were damaged by flak over the target and had to fall out of the formation were sitting ducks for the fighters who jumped on them like a falcon on a field mouse. Radio silence was broken long before reaching the target with all the pilots calling for our fighter escort and why the hell aren't they going after the Luftwaffe. The aerial battle on the return route lasted for at least another twenty minutes and was broke off when we reached the northern slopes of the Alps at the same time our fighter escort showed up. Where were they, we never did find out? But we lost more bombers and crews than we could imagine and blamed it on the screw up in the timing of the escorting P-38s.

The return route was by the shortest route and the safe confines down the Adriatic Sea to Manduria. Passing the southern end of the alps our formation speeded the pace by dropping down to a lower altitude and by the time we reached the coast of the northern end of the Adriatic Sea we were able to remove our oxygen masks and breath normally. Boyle again opened the doors of my turret and shoved a cigarette between my lips and his lips lighting them both. He just stared at me as if he wanted to say something. He finally said, "This is my last mission, I ain't going up in any of these frigin bombers again, not when we're supposed to have so many fighters for an escort and they don't show up." My answer was, "me too."

For some unexplainable reason our flight down the Adriatic to the Italian boot spur seemed to take only a few minutes and the approach to Manduria over the olive groves was a welcome sight. I wanted to stay in my nose turret as long as I could to savor the euphoria of seeing the end of another mission. It dawned on me the flight leader was preparing to buzz the field, the sign of a successful mission. Flying downwind and looking to my left as we paralleled the runway I felt an unusual degree of excitement and wished I had a movie camera with me. Looking forward from my vantage point I could see nothing but big bombers in front of me and on both sides. These seven bombers were flying wing tip to wing tip. Turning on final approach the flight leader began his descent when we were over Manduria about three miles from the end of the runway. Suddenly there was an eerie silence as three of our engines conked out from, as we found out later, fuel starvation. I scrambled out of my turret, scratched the floor panels in a panic attempt to get away from the nose of the ship. I didn't want this kid's body to be splattered all over the Italian ground or to be the first statistic if we crashed. I managed to get to the flight deck just as the wheels touched the ground. Varvil just rolled the plane down the runway, maintaining enough speed to let it roll off the end with enough space for the other planes to land and get by. Being tail end Charlie has it's benefits but being able to economize on fuel is not one of them. We weren't the only plane to run out of gas that day. One of the bombers from another squadron wasn't as fortunate as we were and belly landed in an olive grove killing one of it's crew members when the ball turret tore lose from it's frame and fell on top of him.

As we sat on the end of the runway waiting for a tugger to pull us to our parking revetment I couldn't help but to notice the speed that Lt. Giraudo was taxing past us. Watching him go by I had to wonder where the hell he was going when all of sudden his plane came to an abrupt halt and the tail was sticking up in the air. Later, looking over his plane, we found that his nose wheel found the only hole on the entire field and dismembered it from it's axle. It had to be embarrassing for Giraudo to be admonished so heavily by Colonel Mills that evening.

Another hair raising episode of a bunch of kids trying to survive this asinine war. The Red Cross girls were there with the usual coffee and donuts but most of us opted first to the medic for that two ounces of whiskey and drank it right away. Not far from the Red Cross table were standing Colonel Mills, Lt. Colonel Gideon Deputy Group Commander and General Spaatz Commander of the Mediterranean Allied Air Forces. My attention was drawn to a little pilot, (little in size only for a bomber pilot) who was walking very briskly up to where Colonel Mills was standing. With his whiskey cup in his left hand and upon reaching two inches in front of the Colonel stood at attention, saluted, bent his head straight back to look up into Colonel Mills eyes and raising his right hand with his index finger pointing straight at the Colonel's face shouted, "Colonel if that screw up happens again I ain't flying and neither is anyone else" and briskly walked away. The Colonel was aware of the man's frustration but that knowing was not reciprocal. No one could know the personal torment and anguish Colonel Mills was suffering at the loss of so many of his men he knew so well. I was close enough to detect the trauma Colonel Mills had in holding back the tears he knew would come before he could sleep that night.

Not much talking was done at debriefing except for the multitude of complaints of the escort not showing up to help fight off those German fighter pilots. We were not offered any consolation by the S-2 officer other than "today was one of the coldest days on record for that section of Europe." One tail gunner had to have his hands pried off the turret control quadrant due to frost bite. The fellow lost all of his left hand except the index finger and thumb. Half a dozen other gunners had to be hospitalized with frost bite.

Although some intelligence reports indicate only four bombers were lost on this mission in the target area it was not all encompassing. It should have gone further to report the fighter escort failed to make the assigned rendezvous, contributing to so many bombers that did not return to Manduria, or the stragglers that had to leave the formation because of damage to the plane, engine loss or other malfunctions. At least two bombers were seen losing altitude on approaching the northern edge of the Alps where several parachutes were seen opening. It was never discovered if they made it back or landed in a high glacier and are entombed there for all eternity. In all the 450th lost ten bombers and their crews on it's first mission over Germany. It became quite evident the number of original crews of the 450th was dwindling very fast, too fast. Silently we all said, "I wonder when our turn is coming."

If there is any consolation on performing your duty with precision the 450th had the opportunity to pat it's self on the back. That evening Berlin Sally came on the radio and singled out the 450th and that it was the group the Luftwaffe is out to get. She called us the white tailed Liberators (Colonel Mills had the tops of the rudders painted white) and she knew we were based in Manduria. Her ending statement was "We're waiting for you boys, so come on up and get your surprises." Just as Berlin Sally signed off Chief came in the barracks to give us the good news that we were scheduled to fly again tomorrow. Randy threw something at him saying, "thanks a lot, pal."

For some unexplainable reason we never had any trouble sleeping soundly before or after any of our missions. I guess we can send some compliments to our inner minds that seem to close off the traumas of everyday aerial combat and keep us from going stark raving mad. There was some satisfaction in knowing we could shoot back at the enemy fighters but there was no consolation knowing we could do nothing to save ourselves when flying into those thick clouds of black mushrooms and without the foggiest idea if we will come out the other side or if some gunner on the ground is going to get a lucky shot and blow us out of the skies. Trying to figure life's extension while going through those clouds of mushrooms could only lead to a term in a straight jacket or a mission to the funny farm.

Briefing was extremely quiet the next morning and no one stirred in their seats when the curtain was raised. Again it seemed so slow going up and up and up. And, yes, once again we are going into the very bowels of the enemy. The target for today will be the ball bearing factories and engine assembly plants at Steyr, Austria only about seven hundred and fifty miles from Manduria. This time we will not be taking the long way around but straight up the Adriatic to the target area passing just to the west of Zagreb, Yugoslavia. Like yesterday we were briefed on ample escort to and from the target. In unison the gunners responded, "we'll believe it when we see them."

The flight up the Adriatic and across Yugoslavia was uneventful except for some inaccurate flak from the Zagreb area and none was encountered from the Graz area since we were to far to the west. Our escort did show up this time and although the Luftwaffe was up in force they did not have the easy pickings of yesterday at Regensberg. The four bombers we did lose over Steyr were downed by flak over the target area. None were seen from our vantage point in the formation. The P-38s made some "brownie points" with us in keeping those enemy fighters away. I guess it was their way of apologizing for their goof up yesterday. The flight back to base was a welcomed relief. At briefing and two more ounces of whiskey we were told that the weather over Germany would be solid overcast tomorrow and we had a day off.

We were looking forward to sleeping in tomorrow and have breakfast at our leisure. But, expectations usually don't pan out. Colonel Mills called a meeting of all the air crews at the base operations office at nine o'clock. There he repeated that the 450th has Axis Sally biting at the bit along with all the other Heinies in Germany. The Colonel added, "She called us the white tailed liberators (soon to be knick named "Cottontails" by some unknown briefing officer) who go hopping around their skies. Well, we're going to paint more white on them and make them yell louder until they holler uncle." With that a roaring crescendo of approval came from the lips of all the crews. Colonel Mills ended with, "you guys are great and I'm proud to serve with you." I think he knew how proud we were to serve with him. We did enjoy an Italian sunny day for a change.

After evening chow Randy, Chief and I were standing outside our barracks as Paul and Charlie arrived back from Oria with their laundry. We did not know at the time they struck up an acquaintance with a woman who had a twelve year old daughter.

The deal made was that the mother would do their laundry if they would teach her daughter to speak English. As it turned out the relationship became intense, approaching that of family life. The woman began to consider Paul and Charlie as her sons since they spent so much time at her home. It then became obvious to us why they both were taking food into town with them. Paul said, "on the way we scanned the bulletin board and we're flying again tomorrow."

The morning of the twenty fifth of February was not to be much different than the past couple of days. The mission map took us up into the intestines of Germany and the city of Regensburg once again. And once again we began our ritual of visiting the latrine after briefing, picking up our parachutes and other life saving paraphernalia. Take off and flying up the Adriatic was routine as was crossing the alps out of the range of any anti aircraft guns except at the target. And once again we were hitting the Messerschmidt aircraft factory and getting the hell shot out of us. Our escort was on time and did a superb job of keeping those Heinie fighter pilots away until we dropped the bombs. The P-38s were all over the sky above and beside the formations concentrating on the lead bombers.

The German fighter command saw this and ordered an attack on the rear echelons of bombers. A quick call was made and the P-38s drove them off and picked us up when we rallied after the target. We were flying in number four slot of the high right flight with Lt. Giraudo in the number three slot. Giraudo caught some flak, had to feather an engine and fell out of formation. He managed to stay close enough to keep the German fighters away. By the time we got to the alps he could stay with us no longer and dropped down and in back of the safety net of other bombers. It wasn't long before the whole crew had to bail out, were captured and spent the balance of the war in a German prison camp. On a subsequent bombing mission over Germany Lt. Bob Gernand, the operations officer of the 723rd Bomb Squadron, was shot down and ended up in the same prison camp with Giraudo.

(Lt. John Giraudo stayed in the Air Force after the war. Flew F-86 fighters in the Korean war and was again shot down and ended up in a Chinese prison camp. After two, one hundred mission, tours of duty flying various jet fighters in Vietnam Lt.

Giraudo retired as a Major General after thirty seven years of distinguished military service. In September 1990 at Orlando, Florida, Bill Fili enjoyed a memorable reunion with John Giraudo and recounted those youthful exploits.)

Getting closer to home but still over enemy territory about one hundred miles south of Zagreb, Yugoslavia, the crew of Lt. Edwards had a hard decision to make. His left waist gunner Frank Gentile was hit in the chest by a twenty millimeter shell. The projectile was slowed by his flak vest and was deflected upward and went through his left shoulder. They knew Gentile wouldn't be alive for the two hours it would take to reach Manduria since Gentile was unconscious, Edwards made the decision to put his parachute on, tie a static line to his rip cord and drop him out the bomb bay in the hopes that the Germans would pick him up and administer the necessary medical attention. Upon landing and reporting this incident Lt. Edwards could only hope, pray and wait for some news from the International Red Cross

If it can be called fortunate losing only four crews and their bombers on this mission, then we were fortunate. But for the crews that did not make it back and either paid the eternal price, their very lives, or ended up in a prisoner of war camp it was something else. Approaching Manduria I again stayed in my turret for the thrill of being in the front of a fantastic buzz job. For the life of me I still to this day cannot understand why things don't go as planned. The lead pilot forgot that he had bombers behind and lower than he was. Sitting in my turret I shouted, "nose to pilot, aren't we getting too low, there's nothing on either side of this bird but bombers and tents on the ground and that idiot is still coming down, let's get the frig out of here." I couldn't help myself, but at this point I had to put my hands over my eyes and start praying. If Varvil pulls the plane up we will be in the other planes propwash and possibly flip over and he can't go down. But Varvil, the pilot he was, extricated us out of that near catastrophe. It was a heart-pounding close call with the pearly gates and I decided right then and there I was not going to sit in my turret on any more buzz jobs. Coffee, donuts and that precious nerve-settling two ounces of whiskey was the only prescription we needed. At debriefing we were told the Fifteenth

Air Force is sitting down for a while as so many men have severe frost bite on their cheeks, hands and feet from the unusual cold weather. He received no objections from us. It never dawned on us that we were doing our part to bring this war to a conclusion.

It might be well to note here that by all reports, the last week in February 1944 was to be the beginning of the end of the German Luftwaffe as an effective fighting force. This was a unique campaign made possible only by the superior equipment and productive capacity of the United States of America and above all, by the shear determination, courage and resourcefulness of a group of intrepid airmen who would die before allowing an enemy to defeat him. There had to be close to one thousand bombers over Germany on each of these last three bombing days. The air battles over those European Skies were carried on principally by fleets of American four engine bombers, each with ten dedicated airmen, penetrating deep inside the enemy territory and bringing the attack to the heart of the German war machine striking relentlessly and destroying it's most vital installations. Of all those airmen that flew those missions they can be proud of the fact that never once were they turned back or retreated from the ferocity of battle. After that second heart-pounding trip to Regensburg the 450th sat down for the next six days.

On February 27 after lunch I stopped to see Doc Wagner. He wasn't in, so I asked the medic for some aspirin for a splitting headache. Instead of an aspirin he shoved a thermometer in my mouth. He looked at it several times and kept popping it back in my mouth. He sent another medic to get Doc. Wagner. When he arrived he looked at my mouth piece and with usual medical term said "Hmmm" and he too put it back in my mouth. He then had one of the medics go with me to my barracks to get my toilet items, I was being sent to the general hospital in Bari. Doc. Wagner told me I had a good case of walking pneumonia. I spent the next eight days in that Hospital.

After being discharged from the Hospital I arrived at the base only to find my crew out on a mission. I walked over to the operations office just in time to hear the ops officer tell all the others the mission was scrubbed. Varvil's charges returned and I sure was glad they didn't get one mission up one me. Randy related what the mission was. At briefing the crews were told that the Supreme Headquarters Allied Expeditionary Forces, SHAEF, had learned that the German seat of Government was moved from Berlin to Brieskow-Finkenheerd, about thirty miles southeast of Berlin. The plan was to meet the move with a surprise bombing raid that would destroy the headquarters buildings as they were being set up. SHAEF decided that it would be more of a surprise if the Fifteenth Air Force would make the attack even though it was completely out of range being almost twelve hundred miles from the nearest base in southern Italy.

To overcome this disadvantage the navy was sending a fleet of destroyers up the Adriatic Sea to pick up the crews after they ditched their bombers when they ran out of fuel. It was expected only the lead bomber might be able to make it back to it's base. Fortunately, after leaving Manduria and flying north for about an hour, all of the 15th's formations were recalled and the mission cancelled. Apparently some one somewhere was a little smarter than those planners in SHAEF and convinced the Brass it was too costly in lives and bombers and the mission had less than a thirty percent chance of being successful.

Once again Pop, Varvil and Bahti complained to Sam about the elevator trim tab sticking at high altitude. We all worked on it to discover the problem and each time we thought we had it licked it would again stick on the next mission.

March 17, 1944, we were again going up into the German Heartland to drop some bombs on an aircraft assembly plant at the Schwechat airdrome. It was a hazy day and from my vantage point I could barely make out the ground and the airdrome let alone see the buildings in the target area. The Germans didn't send up much flak probably in an attempt to hide the location of the target area. On leaving the target area I called Bahti and asked, "how's that trim tab." His answer was a disgusting, "still the same, stiff as hell."

On landing and picking up our whiskey, coffee and donuts we found out we did get credit for two missions today and now have reached the half way point of our tour of duty with twenty four missions to our credit. More surprising to us as we walked away from the medics we were told that Doc Wagner wanted to see us. Varvil said he would find out what he wants and let us know. At this point in time, and not a discussable item, we now have less than half of the original crews in our squadron. Our flight surgeon was sending us on a weeks' vacation of R and R in Santa Cesarea. It was a Mediterranean seashore resort honed out of lava rock and situated on the very bottom of the Italian heel

To say that we enjoyed ourselves with nothing to do but take mineral baths, eat and sleep for seven whole days was another understatement. I soaked in solid marble bath tubs that were more than two thousand years old, filled with the same spring water from the same mountains traversed by the Caesars of ancient Rome. I could very well have been in the same bath tub used by Hercules after he slaughtered the giants. Or bathed in the same marble bath tub used by Mark Anthony and Cleopatra on one of their clandestine meetings. In seven days we came close to putting the war completely out of our minds.

Varvil's crew new B-24 Liberator

AUTHOR'S REVISIONS FOR THE SECOND PRINTING

During the week of February 22, 1944 there emerged the biggest and bloodiest air battles of that European war. In the annals of aviation history it was called "BIG WEEK" by the Allied writers. But unknown until recent years some Luftwaffe pilots called it the "WEEK OF WHITE DEATH". This term developed because of the great number of bombers and fighters that were shot down. Men, on both sides, were parachuting out of their planes to save their lives and many landed in some of the most treacherous terrain in the Alpine Mountain Range. Due to the massive snow storm in central Europe on February 20, 1944 it became impossible for any rescue team to reach them. Many are still entombed in those high Alpine glaciers. Another monument to man's inhumanity to Mankind.

On a lighter note, the author, traveling on the air show circuit in 1992 promoting his book and talking about that European air war, became aware of how so little information is available to the general public. At one air show, in Reading, Pennsylvania, a man approached the author's display of model world war II airplanes and started a conversation. He focused his talk about the week of February 22, 1944 and asked if he was a participant. The author answered "Yes". At this point the man reached over and touched the model of an ME-109 and said, "I was in one of those". It was a surprise for both men who enjoyed reliving their youthful experiences. More importantly they learned, even though they were on opposite sides in the 1940's, they now have parallel objectives in life. Both are trying to convince anyone who will listen to them, "War Is Not An Inevitable Way Of Life". Their conversation ended in a warm sincere handshake appropriate for two warriors of the skies.

On page 105 the aborted mission that took eighteen Liberator Bombers over the City of Trieste, Lt. Ley was mentioned as one of the pilot's in command. Lt. Ley was wounded on a previous mission and was not on this flight and did not go down with his crew. Who the pilot in command was is not known. Lt. Ley completed his missions with another crew. He later retired to Florida where he passed on in 1988 to take his place in Valhalla.

SEVEN

The personnel carrier to take us back to our base at Manduria arrived about ten in the morning of March 23 1944. The ride back was unlike the ride to Santa Cesarea in the rain and was pleasant enough despite the ruts and pot holes in the road. Another azure morning sky kept our minds off what we were returning to. It was a pleasure to take notice of the living styles of the people in that area, a style that hasn't changed much in the past two thousand years. It was only too obvious they were extremely happy in doing what they do best, grow a few vegetables and tend the olive groves that seem to grow between the lava rock formations.

We arrived at the orderly room just in time for noon time chow. First though, we had to report to the first sergeant, where we were given a pleasant surprise. The first sergeant presented each one of us with a gold framed blue citation ribbon. While we were on "R and R" the 450th was awarded a Presidential Unit Citation for it's leadership and pin point bombing accuracy on Regensburg Germany and Steyr Austria. As we were leaving he said, "by the way guys, you all are on the flying list for tomorrow, welcome back." "Thanks a lot sarge," was our unison reply. After lunch at our barracks we were greeted with some more news that was not so pleasant. Two more of our crews, who bunked in the next barracks were shot down near Graz, Austria. It was on our minds but none of us wanted to count how many of our original crews were left. It might give us an indication of when our turn was coming, something that just could not be faced. Performing our duty as instructed without question was the best therapy, a saner approach and a quicker way to complete our tour of missions and that related to the ultimate mission, a trip home.

As I left the orderly room with the rest of the guys I ran into Jim Campbell who was the group public relations master mind and he wanted to tell me about Johnny Oaks a waist gunner on

Lt. Grammy's crew. (These names are fictitious only because time has erased their real identities. I am hoping that they are still with the human race and not in Valhalla.) When we came off the Regensburg target on February 25, 1944, Lt. Grammy's plane had one one hundred pound bomb hung up and straddled in the bomb bay. It lay between the bomb rack and the outside beam. The bomb was fused as the spinner was disengaged by the wind when the bomb bay doors were opened. The slightest jar could explode the bomb. If they waited until they got to a lower altitude and an oxygen mask was not needed then they would risk hitting bumpy air and that could set the bomb off. It had to be dislodged while still at high altitude. No one on the crew wanted to go out to the bomb bay with a three minute portable oxygen bottle to remove that bomb. No one except Johnny Oaks, a likeable young man, just nineteen years old who weighed about one hundred and forty pounds soaking wet.

But Johnny, without any hesitation and without saying anything to anyone, simply put on the portable oxygen mask, and without his chest type parachute as it would be in his way climbed around the ball turret went out into the bomb bay. He straddled the open door, endured the freezing air blowing in his face and with nothing between his crotch but open air space and the alpine peaks two miles below. He meticulously picked up that one hundred pound bomb turned it around sufficiently so that when he dropped it it would not hit the sides of the bomb bay, and succeeded. By the time he got back inside the rear of the plane he was becoming hypoxic from the lack of oxygen. The nervousness that he had to experience caused his body to eat up that life saving oxygen faster than normal. His crew buddies plugged in his normal oxygen line, reviving Johnny rather quickly and this accompanied a series of back slaps, hugs and thank yous from the guys he just saved.

I found out about this incident that evening while at chow and talking to the other waist gunner on Lt. Grammy's crew. The next morning, while walking to the flight line I saw Lt. Grammy and stopped to talk to him about what Johnny did yesterday. I asked Lt. Grammy if he was going to put him in for a medal or at least a citation of bravery. Lt. Grammy said no, he wasn't because that was his job. I just looked at Lt. Grammy and said, "for God's sake he probably saved all of your lives." Lt. Grammy answered sarcastically, "so what." I was shocked and couldn't believe such an attitude would or could come from an American officer and a pilot. I knew that rank had it privileges and nothing I could add would sway his thinking. I could do or say nothing but to stare at him for a time, then saluted him and walked away. I could not help but to thank our lucky stars he was the exception and not the rule of officer conduct.

I couldn't get Lt. Grammy's attitude out of my mind and decided to do something about it. I talked to as many crew members as I could in all four squadrons and they all agreed Johnny Oaks should be given a special citation. We even took it to group headquarters but were told they could do nothing and the request for a citation had to be initiated by the planes commander. I then took the problem to T/Sgt. Jim Campbell at the group public relations office and he said he will do what he can. He wrote the story up and sent it to Johnny's home town newspapers.

He stopped me that day outside the orderly room to tell me that the Stars and Stripes European edition will be publishing Johnny's story in next months edition. He did suggest we do not tell Johnny in hopes that he will be surprised when he reads it. As Jim Campbell walked away he said, "Fili, we'll get Johnny his medal yet, only because he deserves one." I had to respond, "Thanks a million Jim."

After stowing our gear on our bunks Charlie and Paul with their laundry bags over their shoulders thumbed a ride to Oria and their war time family. Pop, Randy, Chief and I opted for a walk out to the flight line to see Sam Grybel and our own ugly bitch. We found Sam but not our bomber. Sam began to tell us that a new crew went out on their first mission with our plane the day after we left for "R and R" and they didn't come back. We just looked at each other and finally Pop said, "I sure hope it wasn't that problem with the elevator trim tab that caused them to go down." Sam said, "I made sure they knew about the trim before they left, the report I got was that they were hit in the right wing with flak and it burst into flame." I could not help but notice the agony Sam was feeling as he continued, "I went over to S-2 to find out if any chutes were seen and no one could answer me."

Pop, put his arm on Sam's shoulder as he knew he was worried that his maintenance was at fault, a syndrome suffered by all crew chiefs. Pop said, "Sam, rest easy because we have complete confidence in you and in no way was it your fault that our plane didn't come back." As Pop finished talking I could not help but notice the moisture in Sam's eyes. Yes, without a doubt Sam was, and I hope still is, a most trusted man and mechanic and we would want no other to maintain the bomber we fly in.

Chief, with his ever present smile softened up that situation with some of his humor and asked Sam, " Hey Sam can you find me a ball turret to fly in, I don't want to stay here in sunny-muddy Italy forever. I gotta get home to help my daddy take care of his pigs and help them make little pigs for us pigs to eat." With that Sam smiled and said, "come on with me, I got something to show you." We walked two planes away and Sam stopped and said, "there she is, and she's all yours, all brand spanking new and with a new paint job of the left side of the cockpit." Yes, our new B-24 Liberator had a name, "DESTINY DEB". A beautiful brunette clad in a bikini bathing suit standing straight up, holding the reins and riding a bomb down to the Nazis. They were beauties indeed, both of them, Destiny Deb and our own new ugly bitch. Climbing up into the cockpit, the nose turret section, the tail and the bomb bay, they all smell fresh, new and with an abundance of anxiety at wanting to get busy teaching those Heinie bastards a lesson they won't forget. Randy volunteered, "I'm going to get Varvil and the other officers and maybe together we can christen her with tender loving care." During our remaining days in Italy we never did meet the crew that new Liberator was taken from.

(A reunion of the 450th Bomb Group was convened in the Dayton area in 1988 and was attended by Lenus Bahti. While at the reunion Bahti found a member of the original crew that brought Destiny Deb from the States to Italy. At the conclusion of the reunion this one crew member shouted to Bahti as he was leaving, "don't forget You guys still owe us forty bucks for the painting.")

After chow and taking care of personal hygiene our barracks was filled with laughter, conversation and just nostalgic friendship. All six of Varvil's charges were lined up on the left side of the barracks entrance which gave us full view of the comings and goings. On the far side were various members of different crews. Eddy Clapprood, Charlie Fasolas, Steve Kusmirak, Lloyd Kittleson, Bob Peterson from Lt. Wagner's crew. There was Joe Baz, Mel Openshaw, Mike Dellario from Lt. Edward's crew. There were Al Russo, Ed Herrman (Ed was still in the hospital on this night) and Arlie Griffin of Lt. Ley's crew. And there were so many others that time has erased their names from my memory. All in this barracks was scheduled to fly again tomorrow. All of us knew of the possibility that some of us will not be returning after tomorrow's mission!

Each time I entered the briefing room I couldn't help notice the casual conversation becoming more subdued as the bombing missions became longer and the aerial gun fights more fierce and the clouds of flak becoming thicker each day.

This day was no different, we were going to the very core of Germany once again, Steyr, Austria hopefully to put the finishing touches on those ball bearing and engine assembly plants. And this day was no different on the queazy feelings in our intestines and the lines at the latrines becoming longer and quieter. Even on the flight line our crews conversations became more subdued and resigned that we have to make like a warrior again. As I walked through the plane, while we were taxing out for takeoff, performing my duty of inspecting everyone's battle gear the thought occurred to me that I wouldn't mind being on that sandy beach in Wildwood, New Jersey and let the sea gulls pass their stinky droppings onto my head. Varvil nestled Destiny Deb into formation for the first time in the number six slot of the high right flight of six bombers. Lt. Ley was in the fourth slot. In looking up and over to his bomber I had to chuckle at a happening after briefing. Ed Herrman, his tail turret gunner, being just released from the hospital, was returned for duty. A new tail gunner was assigned in his place. He begged and pleaded with this new gunner to relinquish his assignment and let him, Herrman, fly with his crew. It was a back and forth discussion with Ed being the victor. Before donning my oxygen mask I waved to Ed and he returned the gesture.

It really was exciting to sit in my new nose turret and nestling my butt comfortably in. I couldn't help but notice the weather conditions. We could barely see through the haze and at times we would lose sight of the other two flights below us. No doubt the thought occurred to Varvil and Bahti that they had better take turns in blinking their eyes or they just might collide with another plane. We weren't in the air for more than forty five minutes when the lead echelon of eighteen planes turned left and headed back to Manduria. Our flight leader kept right on going in a Northerly direction. Randy called, "Waist to pilot, looks like the other formations are turning back, what the hell is that guy in the lead plane doing. It looks like the mission is scrubbed." Bahti answered, "Yeah, Paul just got it on the radio, the mission is scrubbed, I guess he just wants to maintain a safe separation in this hazy weather before turning back." We waited for him to turn, five minute — ten minutes — twenty minutes and he still did not turn the formation back and he was still climbing for altitude. We had to go on oxygen and he still was climbing. Boyle came on the intercom, "navigator to pilot, what's that frigen man doing, trying to get another medal, let's turn back ourselves and maybe some of the others will follow us." Then Varvil broke in, "can that kind of talk, you know very well we're too far north to break formation and become a sitting duck for fighters." All this while we were in a soupy haze that allowed us to barely see the other two flights. We were just eighteen bombers and heading nowhere but maybe to oblivion.

Suddenly we broke out of the haze and into an azure sky and I was somewhat relieved to be able to see the ground, the blue Adriatic Sea to my left and looking down I spotted the controversial port of Trieste. Our leader started to turn to the left and out of no where all hell broke loose. There were so many German fighters attacking us it became difficult to even see the sky. And just as quickly our formations tightened up wing tip to wing tip to have better concentration of fire power. They came at us from every conceivable direction and it was obvious they knew where we were and just waited above those hazy clouds for us to break out into the clear sky before commencing the attack.

The shouts from all the gunners and Boyle calling out the attacking fighters from the astro dome, "Fili, he's coming in at ten o'clock high," and screaming, "Fili, get him before he gets us," And at the same time I was shooting at a fighter coming up at us from twelve o'clock and slightly low. He came so close I could almost recognize the features on his face as he passed to the left and descended. I didn't have time to call to Randy, at the left waist gun, that one was coming past his window. In following that fighter I saw one plane going down out of the lead flight and on flames. Then Boyle and Bahti both came on the intercom and in unison shouted, "hey Fili, over there at two o'clock high there's three fighters coming at the formation keep an eye on them. My head was on a swivel watching those fighters darting in and out of all three formations from high and low and from all clock directions. But those three fighters kept coming with their cowl guns sparkling and I knew those sparks were not birthday greetings. They were coming at us so fast I had difficulty in turning my turret to meet them, let alone shoot at them.

Although it took those three fighters only a few seconds to make their pass it seemed like an eternity as my eyes were glued on them. The bombers in number two and four slots were in their line of sight before they could get to us. Then Bahti roared, "there goes number two out of formation, looks like they shot out their three and four engines and he's banked at ninety degrees, fire coming out of the waist windows." Number two was quickly out of my line of sight, on his way down. It happened so fast I didn't get a chance to see if any parachutes came out. Those three fighters continued their attack. They were after Lt. Ley's plane and they were succeeding with an assist of a direct hit from a rocket fired from an ME-110 that was staying just out of gun range in the rear of the formation. Ley's left wing burst into flames and suddenly there was fire coming out of the waist window and I could see Al Russo scrambling around and Ed Herrman trying to get out of his turret. Then the unexpected happened, the whole rear of the plane was enveloped in flames and the pilot, Lt. ley banked to the right to leave the formation. I could have shed more tears than was humanly possible as I screamed into the intercom.

"Oh my God! the ball turret just fell loose from the plane, (God will be the only one to know if the gunner was still in it), and Russo just jumped out of the waist window with his body on fire." I tried to follow him down in the milliseconds it took for Russo to leave my sight. I could almost hear his screams as he fell to earth hoping that some one's guardian angel was around to save him. I never did see if Ed Herrman ever got out of his turret. The agony of seeing him struggling in the flames to save his life was tormenting beyond belief knowing that he choose to be there when he had other options. Those three fighters took two bombers with that one pass and we would have been next if they didn't run out of air space. They went past us so fast I could only guess that the relative speed must have approached five hundred miles an hour. It was quite obvious that Lt. Ley pulled out of formation to protect the other planes in the event that his plane exploded. Varvil pulled Destiny Deb up into the fourth slot and nestled in a absolute tight formation, literally wingtip to wingtip. The fighters left us after shooting down four of our eighteen bombers in less than ten minutes of battle. And that ten minutes of aerial battle seemed like an eternity. Apparently they were running low on fuel and ran out of ammunition.

Two other bombers did not return that day as they collided in midair over the Adriatic Sea and no parachutes were seen coming out of either bomber. One of the bombers and it's crew was piloted by Lt. Hartman, from the 721st squadron and an original crew from Alamagordo, the other bomber and it's crew was a new replacement fresh from the states on their first and last mission and piloted by Lt. Whalen. The lousy weather with poor visibility was a contributing factor in causing that collision.

There was no buzzing of the runway that afternoon nor were there any smiles on our faces indicating a successful mission as we jumped off the personnel carrier to get our coffee, donuts and two ounces of whiskey. Everyone was looking at each other hoping, with blank stares, and looking for some answers of why the formation flight leader did not turn back when we had an opportunity to do so. The answers and consolation we wanted did not come at that moment nor did they come at a later time. Walking back to our barracks we could do nothing but shake our heads in disbelief. The disbelief that Russo, Herrman and the rest of the crew won't be able to snuggle on their cots ever more. Even in the chow line or at the table the silence was deafening and the usual evening chatter in the barracks was noticeably absent. Quietly we could do nothing but to snuggle in our own bunks with a silent prayer thanking someone somewhere for watching over us this day.

I guess it must have been a little after midnight, when we were all asleep, there was an explosion of the likes we have never experienced. The light of that explosion shown brightly through the windows and cracks in the walls and gave the appearance of daylight outside. Everyone jumped out of their bunks and was running into each other trying to get to the front door. Someone was yelling "the Germans are bombing the field, put the lights out." Being the first bunk at the door it could be expected that I would be the first one out. Not so. I was the first at the door but tripped over my blankets and half the barracks walked over me before I could get up. The sky shined as bright as daylight but quickly faded away. I ran back inside to put some clothes on. As it turned out it wasn't the German's but one of the bombers exploded in it's parking area. It seems a mechanics noticed a small fire at the auxiliary power unit and ran to get a fire extinguisher. Upon returning with it the plane exploded in a ball of fire as it consumed seventeen hundred gallons of high octane gasoline in less than two minute. The poor fellow didn't have a chance and he was burnt to a crisp. As bad as that mishap was it did serve to take our minds off yesterdays mission and eased the pain of those memories.

The next ten days we flew on several missions hitting at rail junctions and air fields in various locations in central Italy in support of the ground troops that were trying to break the siege at the Monte Cassino Monastery. The Germans were well entrenched in the tunnels and caves that surrounded that hilltop.

The flying schedule for April 4, 1944 indicated that every available crew will be at briefing, seven am, and no excuse will be accepted, the notice read. At the barracks the question was, "What does the brass have in store for us tomorrow."

Being an experienced crew with thirty missions behind us would make anyone believe that we were calloused to this war and nothing could unnerve Varvil's charges. If anyone thinks that they have to be an idiot. For all those missions we went on, or will go on, briefing still scares the shit out of us and this day is not going to be an exception.

As the map curtain was raised we saw the red string again take us out to the Adriatic Sea. The First thought, we were going back to Germany. But the string abruptly changed course and headed east and once again there was that shocking silence as the string continued for about three hundred miles until it stopped in the area of the Ploiesti Oil Complexes. We knew of that first low level raid on this target on August 1, 1943. That was where the crews found hay stacks open up with anti aircraft guns and began shooting point blank at them, like they were sitting ducks in a shooting gallery. And where those same guns were mounted on railroad cars and gave chase to those bombers.

But the Briefing officer started by saying, "Gentlemen, we are not going to Ploiesti today. Today's target is the massive railroad yards on the outskirts of the City of Bucharest in Roumania. There was a small sigh of relief from all the men in that room, but we still knew we would be in the vicinity of those oil refineries. This renewed the need once again to do something about that queasy feeling in our intestines and again long lines assembled at the latrines and once again without any conversation.

It was a beautiful day as we assembled over the Adriatic and headed east. We skirted the border of Yugoslavia and Albania, Albania supposedly being a neutral nation, and over Lake Scutari. It was a sight that I had never seen before. Those Albanian Alps climbed to the heavens and the lake was so clear we could see those peaks going down in the lake an equal distance. For the want of a camera I lost a picture that will probably never be seen again. Up ahead I could see the Danube River and wondered why Johann Strauss named it the Blue Danube since it was a dirty muddy color.

Past the Danube I saw beautiful patchwork farms lands that as a young inexperienced traveler thought were only to be found in America. Then it occurred to me that that is where I should be. The peace and serenity that I perceived could easily convince me that I was flying over the beautiful and well groomed farmlands of the Dutch country in eastern Pennsylvania. Or flying over the fertile lands of the Napa and San Joaquin Valleys of central California or so many fertile and productive farms lands that is commonly called the bread basket of the world in America. In passing over the Danube River I didn't know I was entering a culture that dated back to the glory days of the Roman Empire and a land that was a way point for the many Crusaders on their way to free the holy land for Christianity and the world. I was unaware that Roumania spawned the first petroleum refinery in 1856 and that the Roumanian Nation was born three years later in 1859. I did not know then, nor did the Roumanian people know, their Roumanian black gold, "OIL", would give birth to so many diabolic attempts to control oil and a world wide economy and cause such worldly destruction of lives, private property and even destroy societies. All these planes now flying over these lands and the Roumanian people, though well intentioned, could not have envisioned or prevented the chaos in the ensuing years.

The sights and sounds of both flights, the real one I am riding in and the imaginary one I envisioned at home, were tranquil for it is spring and mother nature is displaying her many colors as she awakes from her wintertime hibernation. The hiss of the air passing over the plastic shield of my nose turret, passing over the skin of this four engine Liberator bomber and the blossoms below seem to be a part and need for each other. I couldn't help but become enraptured with the grandeur of Planet Earth at the same time I couldn't understand why I am going to do what a soldier must do, fight in a war.

My tranquility was quickly erased when off in the distance I could see the clouds of mushrooms being built up as the lead groups approached the target area. I wasn't aware of it at the time but we were about to begin our participation in the greatest air battles ever conceived in the history of aviation. For high above those blossoms of nature that caught my fancy a new episode of a world at war was about to have the curtain raised. We were approaching the center of the stage to break the backbone of the Hitler war machine, the massive PLOIESTI OIL COMPLEXES. Without transportation Hitler could not distribute the much needed oil supplies. Thus the reason for starting this campaign in destroying the railroad marshalling yards. This curtain will not be lowered for many months and only after hundreds of bombers were blown out of the skies and thousands of airman will have paid the eternal price, their lives.

We were briefed not to expect much opposition from enemy fighters as they will have inexperienced pilots in the cockpits and have no desire to tempt fate. We approached the target from the northwest and started our bomb run from the initial point and observed about a half dozen fighters paralleling our route but staying out of gun range. Then I had to start my ducking and flinching routine, the flak was down right thick from those exploding shells. We made it through with only a few holes in the fuselage. Just when we thought the flak was over a shell burst just to the left of the nose and level with a piece of shrapnel exploding through my plastic window, struck the two inch thick bullet resistant glass plate in front of my face and bounced on the floor. Till this time I really didn't have much faith in that glass plate even when I was told it will with stand a direct hit from a twenty millimeter shell. My faith was restored rather quickly.

We were expecting one hell of a battle over Bucharest but none occurred, all bombers returned to the base with only minor rips and tears from shrapnel, that were repaired overnight. We became somewhat complacent about the defenses of Ploiesti and wondered just what all the stink was about. We'll just have to wait and see if and when there will be another trip east. Our wait lasted only a few hours, we were scheduled to fly again tomorrow.

For some unknown reason all was quiet as we entered the briefing room and sat down. The string was taking us right back to where we were yesterday only about thirty miles north of Bucharest. Yes, the Allies were going back to Ploiesti in force. The briefing officer began by saying, "Gentlemen the 450th is going to lead the Fifteenth Air Force back to Ploiesti." And once again we heard in unison, "Ah Shit" and deep breathing. The briefing continued, "On this mission you can expect to encounter between two and three hundred German fighters flown by experienced pilots to and from the target. At the target you can expect little fighter opposition since the Roumanian Air Force pilots are thoroughly bored with the war. There are more than one hundred and forty anti aircraft guns around the city of Ploiesti and the oil complexes and all are manned by bored Roumanians." I leaned over to Randy and whispered, "is this guy trying to tell us this mission will be a piece of cake. If he is and you believe him then you both better get ready for a ride in a straight jacket to the flaky farm." Randy just nudged me to be quiet. I couldn't help but remember what we read about the low level raid and the preparations that was made for their coming. That guy over there in Roumania, Colonel Gerstenberg, or whatever his name is, must be a mind reader to know what we are planning to do and then place his guns and planes in the right place.

That briefing wasn't exactly over powering but it did exact it's toll on our digestive tracks as we again lined up at the latrine. The 450th was to be first over the target followed by the 376th and the 98th bomb groups. We later learned that when the gunners of those two groups asked the briefing officer about enemy fighters they were told not to worry too much about enemy fighters as the 450th will be in front of you. They remembered the threat Berlin Sally made six weeks ago. The German Luftwaffe kept it's word and really did seek us out first. Maybe that's why they were so aggressive when we got caught coming out of that hazy overcast at Trieste.

It was a somewhat relaxed ride down the runway, the climb out and assembly into formation was routine as ever with Varvil sliding in on the left wing of our CO Colonel Mills. It didn't dawn on me until we approached the coast of Yugoslavia that the only plane in front of us was the formation leader and he was off to the right. And the lead planes are the favorite targets for all German fighters. We will be fired upon equally with the Colonel's plane and his right wing bomber. Not a very pleasant prospect of equalling out the odds of survival.

After passing the Danube river I called to the guys in the waist section, "Hey all you dare devil gunners in the rear look over to the left at about ten o'clock and see those mountain peaks. They're called the Carpathian Mountains. And do you know what else they're called, That's the home of Count Dracula and all his vampires. So keep a sharp lookout for any strange looking birds resembling Vampires and don't let them fly in our windows." Bahti came on the intercom, "all right Fili, knock it off. You had better keep a sharp lookout for those German fighters, you know they can creep up on us in a surprise attack. We're only about a half hour away from the IP."

Paul, from the right waist window, came on the intercom, "I think I see some fighters off in the distance and level." Randy said, "There's about a dozen on this side too, level and traveling in the same direction as we're going." Varvil added, "keep a sharp eye on them and let us know if they change direction."

Randy and Paul reported together, "it looks like they're flying faster than we are and getting ahead of us." From my position in the nose I could see both sides quite easily and reported, "yeah, they are going ahead and on both sides," Both Varvil and Bahti added that they have them in sight. They were barely visible when they started to cross over in front of our formations. My eyes were glued on their every move and then it dawned on me they're preparing to make a head on attack when they appeared to get larger by each blink of the eye. And again it dawned on me that from my nose turret I could very well be facing the whole German Luftwaffe alone. Then I shouted, "Here they come at us and at the same level. Christ, they're going to go right through the formation with their guns blazing. I counted twelve ME-109s all lined in a neat row across our path coming straight at us with all their guns spewing bullets at these three bombers. I looked through my guns sights and had one fighter zeroed in and shooting in short but rapid bursts point blank into his prop spinner at the same time shouting, "go down you frigen bastard, go down," But he kept coming, and he kept firing at us, and I kept firing at him. The relative speed was so great that neither of us had the time to figure the proper trajectory lead and as a result he didn't get us and I didn't get him. They went through the formation so fast, and as they passed our rear dove down and attacked the second echelon. Charlie reported, "looks like they took two bombers down with them." They only made that one head on pass and opted for hitting the outside flights as they did over Regensburg.

 Those pilots were extremely aggressive and tossed caution to the winds and pressed their attacks relentlessly and dove so close we could see the whites of their eyes. So close that one ME-109 tore off his wing when he clipped the top of the left vertical stabilizer of number six in the lower right flight. That Lib made it back to Manduria without much difficulty. Once again our formations tightened up wing tip to wing tip to send a concentration of fifty caliber bullets to those fighters. Just as we were approaching the IP I was shooting at a fighter at ten o'clock low and saw one of the 720th's bombers fall out of formation, on fire and start down in a spin. While in the spin I saw two men come out of the waist window and their parachutes opened. I watched the bomber go down and back out of my sight. Then another bomber in the same lower right flight pulled out of formation and almost completed an outside loop before falling off on the left and went down in a flat spin, no chutes were seen coming out from my vantage point.

By this time we were on the bomb run and we expected the fighters to break off the attack but they did not. They continued to attack the formations right through their own exploding anti aircraft shells. The smoke generators were ineffective this day and that made it quite easy for the bombardiers to hit their assigned targets.

As we rallied to the right and headed back to Manduria. I looked back and could see clouds of black smoke rising from the refineries that were adjacent to the railroad yards. Those German fighters were still pressing the attack on the outside flights looking for wounded planes that fell out of formation. I couldn't keep quiet any longer and on the intercom, "I don't know who's in charge of these rendezvouses but whoever it is had better quit. Where the fuck were those P-38s and P-47s that were supposed to escort us? Why are there so many fuck up's anymore?" Boyle came back, "Fili, I know how you feel and I feel the same way. I saw those two planes go down, they were Lt. Wagner's crew and Lt. Edward's crew, so save your anger until we get on the ground. I had to respond, "yeah, it's easy to say but you didn't see those shells zoom up in front of my turret, if they had of been a millisecond slower or we had of been a millisecond faster that first shell would have gone right up my ass." Twenty minutes after bombs away the escort showed up and chased those fighters away. A lot of good they were after losing those wonderful men.

The escort stayed with us until we reached the center of the Adriatic then broke off to go home. Boyle once again opened my turret doors, shoved a cigarette between my lips and his and lit them both. He just stared at me and before he could say anything I said, "don't say it, cause you know we'll go up again. And don't ask why we will; because I don't have the answer." Boyle went to his desk and began folding up his charts and I sat there trying to hold back the tears. I could only think about going back to an almost empty barracks. Just on those two bombers we lost twelve of our buddies. Whether they got out safely or went down with the bomber we probably will never know. I couldn't help but to think of each one of them. Joe Baz, Bill Signs, Mike Dellario, Mel Openshaw, Jack Schoonover, all on Lt. Edward's crew. And the others Eddy Clapprood, Charlie Fasolas, Steve Kusmirak, Larry Miller, Bob Peterson on Lt. Wagner's crew. I know the names here are of enlisted men who lived in our barracks but our sadness was equally traumatic for the pilots, navigators and bombardiers on those bombers and all our prayers are for all of them.

It was only to obvious our barracks is going to be a quiet and lonely place tonight. I just sat alone on my bunk that night sipping my whiskey and trying not to think about what lies ahead for the rest of us. Five more of our bombers and crews went down on that first high level bombing mission on Ploiesti. How many more will go down and how many more men will have to pay the eternal price before this asinine stupid war is over? Again no one wanted to ask how many of our original crews were still flying simply because we were afraid to ask. Was I angry? You could bet your lifes earnings I was. It wasn't until many years later did I realize life expectancy of a bomber crew there was not very good with the survival rate at less than three in ten.

The Fifteenth Air Force statistics for April 5, 1944 over Ploiesti were an indication of things to come. Two hundred and thirty four engine bombers made it to the target. Thirteen bombers were shot down, ten B-24s (five of these B-24s were from the leading 450th group) and three B-17s, eleven downed by enemy fighters and only two were brought down by flak. One hundred and thirty healthy able bodied American Airmen, human beings, either killed or captured. The briefing officer reported that we should expect little or no fighter opposition in the target area but we had to fight our way onto the target and fight to get off the target.

The enemy put up one hundred and eighty two fighters and forty one of these were destroyed mostly by the gunners on the bombers. The Fifteenth Air Force sent up one hundred and seventy five escorting fighters to protect the bombers, only two Allied fighters, two men, were lost to enemy action. If those Allied fighters were in the air where were they when they were needed? If they arrived before the target as they were supposed to do instead of a half hour after the target it is conceivable that the numbers of lost lives and bombers would have been much less. On a more positive note the bombing accuracy was nearly eighty percent. For leading the Fifteenth Air Force over Ploiesti the 450th received an Oak Leaf Cluster to it's Presidential Unit Citation.

After parking Destiny Deb we discovered that we had so many flak holes in various parts of the wings and fuselage and my turret needed a new plexiglas dome we had to sit out the next week until the repairs were made. I did manage to retrieve that piece of flak from the floor of my turret and I carried it with me for more than twenty years before losing it.

We were on our way east once again on April 16, 1944 and headed for the railroad distribution point north of Ploiesti at the city of Brasov. We were briefed that there will be no screw ups in the escort today as a new group of P-51s will be escorting us to and from the target. This will be their first mission. With that statement everyone just snickered, laughed and said "we'll see." The briefing officer continued, "The Luftwaffe with their ME-109s and FW-190s will be no match for those Mustangs that can fly faster and farther than any fighter plane in existence today. Gentlemen, this is the end of the line for the German Luftwaffe. You will have P-38s take you to the Danube River and the Mustang's will take you to and from the target. On the way back you will be escorted by P-38s and P-47s from the Danube to the center of the Adriatic. The escorts did make their rendezvous

About twenty minutes past the Danube River I called to the waist, "you guys back there look over to the left to that mountain range. On the other side is Transylvania and we just might fly over the home of Count Dracula so again I'm warning you to keep a sharp lookout for any of his vampire bats." Charlie came back, "hey, Fili, why don't you can that horse shit and talk some sense." "Why, Charlie, don't you believe in vampires," was my answer. Boyle interrupted our attempts to ease the tensions, "the IP is that break in the mountains."

That mountain pass invited my attention. We were high enough that I could see the other side. The railroad yards were clearly visible. The visibility was clear enough for me to see the air field on the other side of the city and that fighters were taking off to meet us. I was on the intercom with this news and added, "I bet if those fighter pilots knew these mustangs were here they wouldn't be so anxious to come up to fight. Their radar only shows a lot of planes approaching, we'll know in the few minutes it takes for them to get this high."

Those Luftwaffe pilots started to attack just after we dropped our bombs. The flak in the area was ineffective due to the metal strands (called window) we dropped out the bomb bay that disrupted their radar. They had enough time to make one pass at the formations and succeeded in taking out two bombers before the mustangs arrived from the rear of the bomber formations. The only two bombers lost this day were from the 450th. Two mustangs were shot down and a total of sixteen German fighters will never fly again. The trip home was uneventful with escorts all over the place.

As usual the coffee, donuts and whiskey was enjoyed to the fullest. After Chow we were treated to an air show of sorts by one of those brand new P-51 Mustangs that buzzed the field several times before landing and taxing up to the hanger. All six of Varvil charges were there as the pilot climbed out of the cockpit. He was a bird colonel and as he stepped out onto the wing he shouted, "I'm here to show you gunners what a P-51 looks like so you won't shot at us anymore." Someone in back of us shouted, "Yeah, Colonel you better take a good look at a Liberator so you won't point your nose at us cause if you do we'll shoot at you." That P-51 pilot started to get hot under the collar when an unknown major shouted to him, "maybe you haven't been told Colonel, but I gave my gunners instructions to shoot at any plane that points it's nose at us and so did every other bomber commander. Besides that's standard combat procedure." That P-51 Colonel quickly cooled his temper.

We didn't know at the time but one of those two Mustangs that was shot down today was credited to a waist gunner. It seems that the mustang pilot's guns jammed and he was only attempting to nestle under that bombers wings for security. But his approach was definitely wrong in being nose first instead of sliding under sideways. In certain positions it was extremely difficult to determine if the fighter was an ME-109 or a P-51. Their profiles were almost identical with the exception of the air scopes. The ME-109 had an air scoop under each wing and the P-51 had only one air scoop under the fuselage. Before that Colonel left there was a cohesive understanding with the bomber crews and the fighter pilots. We gunners let him know how glad we were to see him and his mustangs here in sunny Italy and welcomed him or any of his pilots to seek cover under our wings, but please don't point your nose at us.

The following day we flew to bomb the marshalling yards in Sophia, Bulgaria. We encountered a feeble attempt by German fighters to penetrate the formations but were driven off by the heavy fire power of the bombers. It was not determined if the pilots were Bulgarian or German and only assumed that they were Bulgarian because of their lack of aggressiveness. The Flak was light, not very accurate and only one bomber returned with a small hole that was repaired rather easily. Not having our nerves shattered on this mission we were able to enjoy a leisurely cup of coffee and donuts. The two ounces of whiskey was saved for an after dinner drink while sitting on the steps of the barracks, just talking about anything that came into our minds.

On April 20, 1944 the group took off on a mission without Varvil's charges and they all made it back despite our absence. The mission took them to northern Italy and the marshalling yards at Treviso, a small rail head near the city of Venice. Although this target was within the range of several German airfields no fighter attacks were made probably due to the presence of the escorting fighters. The group experienced light and inaccurate flak to and from the target.

It was hard to accept other men taking the beds of our buddies who were shot down in the past couple of weeks but we had no choice. As much as we could we gave advise when asked by these newcomers. But realistically we had to hold back our real feelings that life expectancy of a bomber crew wasn't anything to write home about. Just about everyone in the barracks was scheduled to fly tomorrow April 23, 1944.

There was a lot of non descriptive chatter in the briefing room that morning but only from the replacement crews most of which were going out on their first mission. The red string went up and up and once again into the heart of the German industrial areas. We were going to Vienna and the Schwechat aircraft factory.

Some of the newcomers almost cheered that they were going to Germany. I couldn't help but to wonder how loud they are going to cheer when and if they come off that flak infested target? How talkative will they be when they get back to their barracks? How fast will they drink their first two ounces of whiskey. Our learning was slow with easy targets gradually working up to the fierce aerial battles. Their learning will be quick and traumatic. Fortunately for them they will not have to contend with going on bombing missions without any escort or to experience the unrelenting fighter attacks. Those newly arrived P-51s will see to the unchallenged bombing runs.

We were in the number two slot of the lead flight behind an awesome number of bombers ahead of us. I spotted that big black cloud ahead of us and called to Varvil, "looks like we'll have to turn back, that thunderhead may be too strong for us to go through." Varvil said, "Fili that's not a thunderhead that's the flak from Vienna." I got real nervous at seeing that cloud, so I raised my voice and added, "I know that's a flak cloud but can't you make believe it's a rain cloud so we don't have to go through it," Deep down in my heart I knew Varvil or any of us would not turn and run but the more I see these flak clouds the more I seem to be running out of knowing how to flinch and dodge those shells passing by and sometimes exploding within earshot. Flying into that cloud I could no longer flinch and since there were no fighters to content with I just put my hands over my face and hoped for the best. I held them there until I could no longer here the hissing of passing shells or the nearby flak explosions. Flying in that nose turret presented an unbelievable panoramic view of Planet Earth but only when no one was shooting at you. We were In the heart of Germany and it was almost a thrill to have no opposition from those ME-109s and FW-190s. Apparently the P-51 Mustangs were just what the doctor ordered. An hour south of Vienna Boyle performed his ritual with two cigarettes and this time we just looked at each other, saying nothing but taking deep drags on the cigarettes. The ride down the Adriatic was down right comfortable after what we just flew through. At the base once again I made a bee line for the medic and his whiskey bottle then the donuts and coffee.

We old timers, Varvil's charges, of the original forty two men, just the six of us are left in this barracks and we were noticeably quiet that night. Not taking part in any of the mundane conversations of the replacement crews. Maybe we were bored with their kind of talk or maybe we were conditioned by our combat experiences. But we had to get our rest or maybe we just wanted to go into oblivion. Yes, we are flying again tomorrow.

VARVIL'S (CHARGES) CREW
MANDURIA, ITALY APRIL 23, 1944

Standing L to R - Randy Haney, Waist Gunner; John Foster, Ball Turret; Edward Bell, Bombardier; Glenn Boyle, Navigator; Bob,(Pop) Culver, Engineer & top turret;
Kneeling L to R - Paul Swearingen, Radio Operator and Waist Gunner; Lenus Bahti, Co-Pilot; Dana V. Varvil, Pilot and Aircraft Commander; Author Bill Fili, Assistant Engineer and Nose Turret; Charlie Kourvelas, Tail Turret.

AUTHOR'S REVISIONS FOR THE SECOND PRINTING

During "BIG WEEK" of February 22, 1944 the 450th Bomb Group suffered severe losses in manpower and aircraft. The outcome of these bombing raids was that one crew of the 450th committed a cardinal sin. It was reported that one aircraft commander dropped his landing gear in the sign of surrender. Immediately three ME-109 fighters came along side to escort the bomber to a German airfield. One fighter was on each wing and one on the tail.

The report, concocted by some unknown person, stated that the pilot ordered his two waist gunners and the tail turret gunner to shot at the cockpit. They, supposedly, had killed the two wing fighter pilots but the tail turret could not move as fast and the tail fighter pilot escaped and reported the incident to his superiors. The bomber, supposedly, made it back to Manduria safely.

Subsequently, the bomber crews of other bomb groups were advised not to worry about encountering enemy fighters since the 450th "COTTONTAILS" are nearby and would be their escort since the German Luftwaffe would rather attack them.

In the past forty nine years since that eventful day many German fighter pilots were questioned about the incident and their response was "They had no knowledge that it really did happen." Several American airmen took it upon themselves to search for proof and could find none in the American or German Archives. The reason the German Luftwaffe did attack the 450th more aggressively was simply that they had to pick on one particular group and we from the 450th "COTTONTAILS" were selected and so advised by Berlin Sally.

To add to this legend were the Hollywood movie moguls who produced a movie in the 1960's about a B-17 Crew flying from England that did drop their landing gear in a sign of surrender. Again there is no proof that such an action took place. It just did not happen, not by a B-24 or a B-17.

A final disclaimer must be written to the credit and heroism of those opposing combatants of the skies. There existed, in that European War of the early nineteen forties, overwhelming respect between the German Luftwaffe and the American and Allied Air Crews. A humanistic trait unparalleled in the history of Mankind.

THE SIEGE AT PLOIESTI

Strike photo taken 5 April showing heavy concentration in railyards & through Astra oil storage tanks seen burning...

When the air war over Europe commenced in late 1942 the Allies formed the Eighth Air Force to be based in England. It was the Eighth Air Force that bore the brunt of unescorted bombing missions knowing that overwhelming fighter opposition would be encountered. In the true tradition of American heritage and determination they were never turned back by the ferocity of battle. The Eighth had to put an end to the inhumane and barbaric terror caused by the relentless and indiscriminate bombing of the British Isles. They had to protect the oceans and the shipping lanes from the submarine wolf packs so that war goods and men could be assembled for the all out assault on the European Mainland. The Eighth had the awesome responsibility to gain air superiority over Europe and they partially succeeded before the Fifteenth Air Force began to operate from southern Italy in January 1944.

After "BIG WEEK" (February 22, 1944) and the massive attacks to destroy German fighter production the direction was made clear for an all out effort to deny the German Wehrmacht it's most vital commodity, "OIL". Under orders from General Eisenhower the air battles of Ploiesti began. Finally the stage was set at noon on April 4, 1944 as the huge fleets of bombers turned east and headed to the backbone of Hitler's war machine at Ploiesti. The curtain would not be lowered until August 23, 1944. In this period the most decisive and bitterly contested battles of any war would be waged.

Without a doubt other European Cities, such as Berlin, were defended with more anti aircraft guns than at Ploiesti. What made the Ploiesti area so bitterly fought was that those flak gunners had more practice with the constant, almost daily, bombardment from the bombers. In addition the gunners at Berlin had to defend a fifty square mile area as compared to only a five square mile area at Ploiesti. It cannot be denied that the air battles over those oil plants could not have been fought and won successfully without the help of the bomber crews and fighter pilots of the Eighth Air Force based in England. Indeed it was a team effort to win total superiority of the air over those European sky's that brought defeat to the German war machine.

As in any battle, there are two sides and Ploiesti had one of the most capable and brilliant strategists of all the leaders in the Third Reich to defend it. Colonel Alfred Gerstenberg was reportedly to be one of a very few men that ever stood up to Adolph Hitler and lived to tell about it. To contain Gerstenberg's arrogance toward him, Hitler banished him to the Ploiesti oil complexes as he considered them to be the least vulnerable of all his industrial centers. But not to this professional soldier for Gerstenberg knew that the Allies would have to destroy Ploiesti if they were to succeed in their efforts to put an end to the war. Upon arrival in Ploiesti Gerstenberg began the careful deployment of anti-aircraft guns, vigorous training of his fighter pilots and spending some time alone trying to guess when and from what direction the attack would come. Before the end of the battles for Ploiesti more men and bombers would be downed at this target than any other in history. His flak gunners were so accurate that their shells would not just damage a bomber but would invariably be a direct hit, lessening the chances of survival for the airmen. During this campaign the United States Fifteenth Air Force sent more than 5,500 bombers against Ploiesti, dropped more that 13,000 tons of bombs, (that's equal to 52,000 five hundred pound bombs), and succeeded, long before the Russian occupation of Roumania late in August 1944, in denying the German Wehrmacht a major portion of needed fuel without which air forces cannot fly, mechanized armies cannot advance or retreat and the industrial might becomes bogged down.

Not only American bombers were sent to Ploiesti and to keep the pressure on the German defenders the British were constantly sending bombers on night missions. Those missions were successfully executed by 230 Wellington, Halifax and Liberator bombers that made up the 205th Royal Air Force Group. The 205th together with the U.S. Fifteenth Air Force comprised the Mediterranean Allied Strategic Air Force commanded by General Nathan Twining.

Before this all out campaign Ploiesti had been attacked on two separate occasions. Once in June of 1942 by 13 Liberators flying from Egypt known as the Halverson Project No. 63 and again by 162 Liberators flying from the libyan desert and known a Tidal Wave. The Halverson Project was a homefolk moral builder as they were destined to bomb Tokyo. But Colonel Jimmy Doolittle accomplished the feat first, the Halverson Project being a back up in the event the Doolittle mission was unsuccessful. The Halverson fleet then headed for Ploiesti and enroute all the bombers lost their way due to obsolete navigation charts. Hence, the mission was ineffective except that the Nazi Cartel was warned that it could and would happen. Twelve of the thirteen Halverson bombers did reach the target area without dropping a single bomb on any of the refinery complexes. Post mission briefings were not made public.

The next attack, Tidal Wave, was the famous tree top attack by 162 Liberators that had to fly a 2400 mile round trip mission. Except for a disastrous wrong turn by the mission leader the raid was partially successful from both the offensive and defensive view. The defenders of Ploiesti were shocked at the courage of the flyers in those bombers flying so low and so close to achieve their goals. Some of the bombers had to fly between smoke stacks only to find that they then

General Joseph Clark, Author William J. Fili and Colonel Jacob Smart at the Air Force Academy in August of 1973.

had to fly through towering plumes of dense smoke hoping that there was nothing to stop them on the other side. The Liberator crews witnessed the results of Gerstenbergs efforts to defend those refineries. They saw haystacks and rail cars open up, all with anti-aircraft guns shooting point blank at them. When the mission was over the Ploiesti refineries were a sea of flames and destruction but at a costly price to the bomber crews. Of the 162 Liberators, 53 were destroyed, a few made it to Turkey where they were interned. Of the approximately 1620 attacking airmen 310 were killed and 130 were taken prisoner.

Partially successful as it was this type of attack could never be repeated. Not until heavy bombers could be based within a reasonable operational radius where it would be possible to attack again and again until it's destruction is achieved. But Tidal Wave did prove something to Hitler. He knew he made an excellent choice in selecting Gerstenberg, who was now given the pseudonym, "THE PROTECTOR".

It is interesting to note here that Tidal Wave was the brain child of a brilliant pilot and strategist in Colonel Jacob Smart and he was to lead all the bombers. Around Midnight on the Eve of the Tidal Wave Attack a message was sent to Colonel Smart from the White House advising that he was not to go on this mission. It was a personal blow to Colonel Smart for this would have been his mark in aviation history. His place in the lead plane was filled by General Ent who was not as familiar with the details of the mission. No one knew why Colonel Smart was relieved of duty other than being told that he was too knowledgeable and a valued leader to have his life placed in jeopardy

This photo shows Colonel Jacob Smart at the far right and in the rear and was taken at the historical meeting between Winston Churchill and Franklin Roosevelt in Casablanca in Early December 1943.

Less than a year later Colonel Smart did go on a bombing mission with the Eighth Air Force over Germany and, as if ordained by fate, he was shot down and placed in a POW camp. This devastated Allied Headquarters. This Author had the privilege of meeting with Colonel Smart in August of 1973 at the Air Force Academy together with General Clark, the Academy Superintendent. It was then he found out the details of why Colonel Smart was relieved of his duty on Tidal Wave.

Very few persons, regardless of rank, had any knowledge of the Manhattan Project, (the atom bomb project). However Colonel Smart was one of the leaders of the project. High Command was afraid the Germans would use some form of truth serum to get him to talk if he should get captured. When Colonel Smart was captured he was relentlessly interrogated by the German's. The German high command found out who Colonel Smart was since they had a photograph of him standing behind President Roosevelt at that historic meeting in Casablanca. But the German concern had nothing to do with the atom bomb project. They wanted to know how Germany was going to be partitioned when the war was over. Upon hearing this a ton of concern was lifted from the shoulders of Colonel Jacob Smart.

Earlier and more successful bombardment of Ploiesti could have been possible if Joseph Stalin had allowed the Allied bombers to make shuttle runs. Meaning the bombers could take off in Africa or England, bomb the oil complexes and land in Russia. Another bombing attack could be made on the return trip. Forty six years later this question still remains unanswered. Undoubtedly, the war could have been shortened and millions of lives spared but Joseph Stalin and Russia proved to be an uncooperative Ally.

After the first two attacks on April 4th and 5th, 1944 it became apparent that the task was by no means going to be easy. No commander or crewman realized the significance of the bombardments more than the enemy. The Germans found that their aerial defenses would not stop the never ending stream of bombers with their cargoes of destruction. The bombers carries formidable armaments with well trained gunners who knew the value of self preservation, "Get the enemy before he gets you." Added to the destruction of the enemy's fighter force by the bombers and their escorting fighters was the inability of the Germans to provide replacement aircraft at a rate equivalent to their losses.

What developed from the lack of adequate fighter protection and flak that was good, but not good enough, was the Protector's most successful defensive technique. A series of smoke generators were strategically placed around the refineries to hide the targets from the sharp eyes of the bombardiers and their precious bomb sights. These smoke screens offered only a temporary respite for the protector as the eyes of a new bombing system called "Pathfinder" radar was now installed in some of the bombers.

Particular appreciation must be given to Colonel Kraiger of the OSS and his Intelligence team for some of the data and photographs contained herein and to the 28th Statistical Group for it's compilation.

The tree top attack on Ploiesti was the only battle in the air or on the ground where five Congressional Medals of Honor was awarded. A sixth Congressional Medal of Honor was awarded to Lt. David R. Kinsley, a bombardier, for his actions on June 23, 1944. Lt. Kinsley removed his parachute and put it on a wounded crew member, helped him out of the crippled plane and was last seen standing in the bomb bay and going down with the bomber. No greater love hath no man.

Above - An artist's view of the city of Ploiesti that was surrounded by many oil refining complexes. Below - A view from a P-38's camera from 30,000 feet. The white dots are bomb craters misdirected through the smoke screens.

P-38 photo planes recorded the visual defeat of Gerstenberg's smoke pots that led to the expulsion of the German Army from Roumania only four days after these pictures were taken.

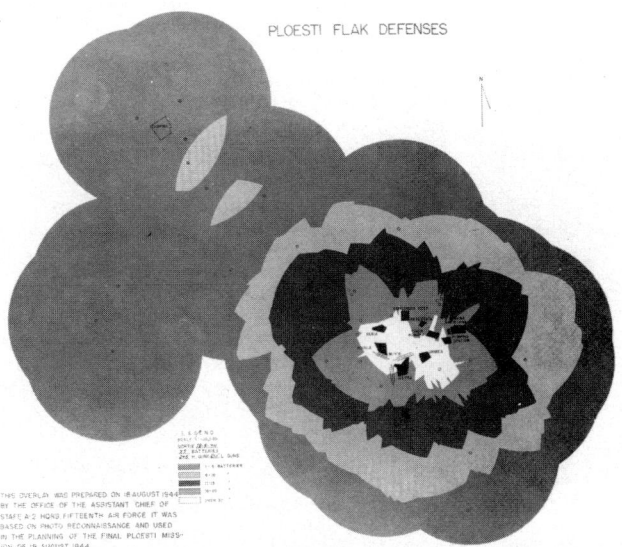

Above - This overlay was prepared on August 18, 1944 by the 15th Air Force Hdqt's based on aerial photos and was used in planning the final assault on August 19, 1944. Below - This overlay was captured from German Hdqt's in Bucharest by Colonel Kraiger's intelligence team and illustrates accuracy of high altitude photo recons.

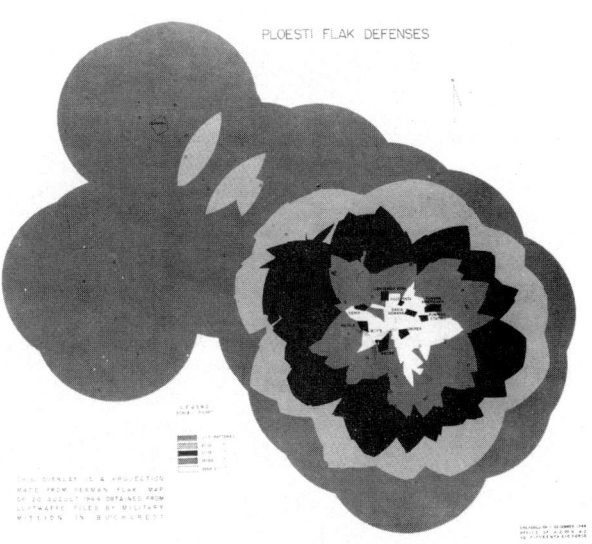

P-10

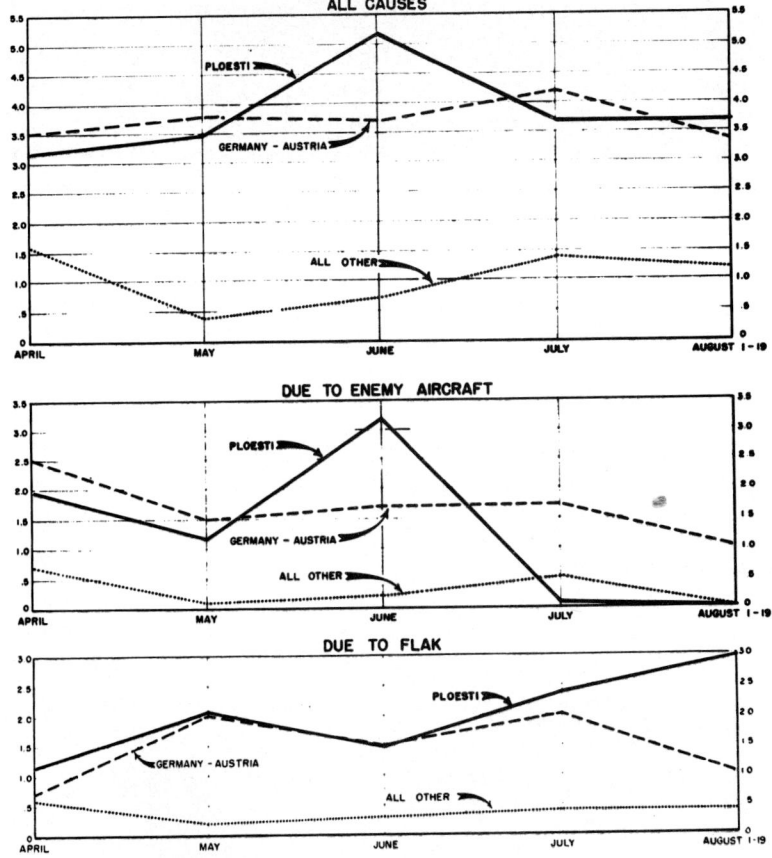

Combat loss chart that compares the number of downed bombers at Ploiesti with other targets in Europe.

DAMAGED 128MM RAILROAD GUN AT PLOESTI

Above - Photo of a 128 MM anti aircraft gun mounted on a railroad car that chased the bombers in the thirty mile run between Bucharest and Ploiesti.

Right - Photo illustrates the physical size of the anti aircraft projectile that was shot at the attacking bombers as they passed overhead.

When the smoke had cleared on the morning of August 20, 1944 the petroleum refining capacity at Ploiesti was at a stand still amid a sea of destruction. The German high command admitted that the attacks on the Ploiesti complexes was the single blow that sped the defeat of the Wehrmacht.

Above - R.O. White & a buddy after being freed.
Below - Ex-POWs heading for the rescuing B-17s.

Above - General Twining greeting freed POWs.
Below - 63 Ex-POW gunners from the 450th Bomb Group.

P-15

Above - POWs standing in the bomb crater that landed in the camp yard and made Bill Fili hit the dirt only seconds before it landed. Below - R.O. White & John Briggs examine the camp bomb shelter. Building in rear is the camp infirmary, bombed out only an hour after the wounded were removed.

Above - Maternity building where Joe Baz found the lifeless body of the sixteen year old girl who shielded his body with hers from the bombs. Below - Author Bill Fili in center waiting for his rescue plane. To his left is Harry Harris and Duke Brioli.

Above - POWs being deloused before being admitted to society. Below - Varvil's crew, the beaus of Destiny Deb *3 days after being freed and deloused.*

Above - the 450th Bomb Group leaving Ploiesti after the April 5, 1944 bombing mission. Below - the sea of destruction that was left behind.

Above - P-38s on their way to dive bomb Ploiesti.
Below - The punishment taken by men and machine.

Above - Liberators over snow covered Alps on their way to Regensburg.
Below - Flying Fortresses on their way to the aircraft factories at Schweinfurt.

When the smoke had cleared.

P-22

EIGHT

5:30 AM comes all to quickly when enjoying a sound and peaceful sleep and the wee hours in the morning of April 24, 1944 was no exception. The almost rude awakening was compounded by the harsh and commanding voice of our first sergeant, who for the first time, stomped into our barracks, turned on the lights and shouted, "Alright all of you daredevil pussy cats, drop your cocks and grab your socks you're scheduled to go hunting some more Heinies today before they get you." Yes. our first sergeant, a master sergeant and a twenty four year veteran of army service was gruff on the outside. But his insides were being torn to shreds by the thoughts of so many men he came from the States with who are now only a memory or are trying to survive somewhere in a prison camp. Quietly I could hear the torment and anguish in his heart as he stomped out of the door and in a choked up voice that he tried to disguise be bellowed, "good luck kids, God bless you all."

Jumping out of our sacks, taking care of our bodily functions, chatting at breakfast and corraled in the briefing room was routine. Once all inside the S2 officer climbed on the make shift stage and started to raise the curtain. We could see the red string heading out to the Adriatic Sea, by now it was the standard operating procedure, hoping that it was going to turn north. That was not to be our luck this day for then it turned north north east for about fifty miles and then turned due east for another heart pounding trip to eastern Roumania and those oil complexes at Ploiesti. At seeing this the non descriptive chatter ended just as quickly as it started being replaced with blank stares on all our faces. Suddenly you could a pin drop above the heavy breathing. Somehow this day was going to be different from the last time we were there just three weeks ago, and I didn't know why. The fact that Varvil was finally being recognized for his leadership ability and promoted to flight leader couldn't be the cause. Maybe what was brought to our attention last night by some wise cracking replacement gunner caused my ominous concern or maybe I was just thinking too much. Our crew, the Beaus of Destiny Deb, a new name for Varvil's charges, was one of only two remaining crews of the original eighteen in the 720th squadron that came from the States together and survived thirty four death defying aerial battles over Europe. Secretly we all knew this fact but refused to openly discuss it. It did nothing for our peace of mind to have been reminded of it by a callous and thoughtless replacement gunner. Will this day be our turn or will it be Lt. French and his crew the ones not to return.

Briefing over, everyone quietly and slowly leaving the room I could not help but to notice the line at the open air latrines getting longer by the second. An inherited human phenomenon associated with being told that you once again have to fight a battle four miles up in the air. There has to be a limit on just what could be endured by the human digestive tracks, a limit that always eluded us, or maybe that's what fate had in store for us.

On leaving that briefing room I literally ran into Doc Wagner. Captain Alfred W. Wagner wasn't just the run of the mill squadron flight surgeon. He was more like the caring country doctor who felt the same pain his patients felt. And so too did he feel the anxiety of being scared of war as we felt. Being face to face, Doc Wagner took my hand in a real warm sincere handshake (after forty six years I still feel the warmth and sincerity of that handshake) and said, "Bill, (this was the first time he called me by my first name instead of Sarge) how do you feel, are you ok to fly?" I said, "Sure, I feel great Captain." He asked, "Is everyone else on the crew ok." Everyone is just fine Sir," was my reply. He ended by wishing us all good luck and added "I'll see you all when you get back." I got the strangest funny feeling that Doc Wagner was desperately searching for a reason not to let me or anyone on our crew fly. I saw and felt that same anguish and torment in his eyes and voice as did our first sergeant this morning. Doc. Wagner had the heart throbbing responsibility to keep all the flying crews healthy, physically and mentally, to fight those aerial battles, to shed their blood and even to die. The results of this days mission would be all that Captain Wagner could take and was his last day as a squadron flight surgeon. By midnight he had written his request for a transfer to the general hospital where his work would be less personal.

On the flight line and after checking out all the flight systems on our bomber, guns and ammunition in good working order, we were advised that there will be a delay in take-off as headquarters had not yet heard from the photo recon plane. Randy pulled out a pack of cigarettes, offered one to Boyle and me. I instinctively, pulled out a pack of matches, lit Randy's, then Boyle's and started to light mine. Boyle tried his best to stop me and, in resisting his attempt, I started a slow trot around the plane with Boyle hot on my heels and managed to light mine. I became aware right then that Glen was extremely superstitious when he shouted at me "Woe on you," and other vituperations for lighting three cigarettes on one match. I laughed it off then and would still laugh at it today, forty six years after the incident. Finally green flares were shot from the control tower and we all scrambled into the plane.

Starting the engines, taxing out in a long line and waiting the prescribed thirty second interval for take off was just another routine we learned to follow. Pop was sitting on the top of the fuselage at the ceiling hatch and I was standing between Varvil and Bahti. I don't know why a previous take off incident popped into my mind. A few weeks ago one Liberator was taking off in the direction of Manduria and as the main landing gear was being retracted and only about thirty feet high the entire bomber exploded and instantly was enveloped in a ball of flames. The next succeeding bomber had already reached take off speed and, due to insufficient runway, could not stop and continued through the flames and miraculously made it through. One gunner was blown clear of the exploding bomber and survived but with severe burns. I guess I was hoping we don't have an encore today.

Climb out and the gathering of eagles was once again a simple routine with no problems occurring to cause us to abort the mission. Without a doubt we wish we had at least one reason to use. Above us was an azure cloud less sky with nothing but clear crisp air ahead and the blue waters of the Adriatic Sea below. As we crossed into Yugoslavia all guns were test fired and made ready for action on a split second. Then there was the anxiety of approaching the most formidably defended target of this or any war in history.

Sitting in my nose turret I enjoyed the panorama of natures beautiful scenery ahead and to both sides. We were the lead bomber of the high right six plane flight. With nothing in front of us but open air space I suddenly felt alone in that giant of a bomber. In looking through my bullet proof glass window to two hundred miles away my thoughts strayed to that day three weeks ago. The tension we all felt was not conducive to accepting any of my stupid humor about Count Dracula and his vampire bats. I wondered about those men who were shot out of the sky, some without a chance of surviving the four mile fall to the ground. For some reason providence brought Barney into my mind. While still in Alamogordo Barney and I were in fierce competition for the favors of a cute little Spanish girl that worked in the PX. Barney took offense that I won out. But that was quickly sedated when we reached Italy. I could swear that I did hear Barney's voice. I jerked my head around in both directions to see the person talking to me or if the door to my turret was open, but it wasn't. How could this be? I asked myself, he was shot down over this target three weeks ago? The voice seemed so real and simply said several times:

"Bill, You'll make it." "Bill, you'll make it." Then just as quickly as providence sent Barney's voice to me the urgency of this fateful mission faded those words as we approached the target area as I called "nose to the pilot, Target area with smoke screen in full bloom dead ahead." Boyle responded, "Bill, choose your words more carefully, the target is straight ahead, not D— ahead." I retorted, "yes sir, super." Suddenly, Varvil turned the plane to the right. Nose gunner to pilot, "Why are you turning toward Bucharest, Ploiesti is dead, eh, I mean straight ahead?" "Because some desk jockey at HQ said we have to use the rail yards in Bucharest as our IP," was Varvil's retort. From his tail turret Charlie chimed in, "I'll bet he was a politician that got his commission by kissing ass somewhere in the pentagon." "Nose to Pilot, That's going to give us an asinine stupid thirty minute flak run! And I suppose he wants us to count the flak bursts so he can put more pins in his map on the wall, I'd like to shove those fucken pins up his frigen ass." Randy, added his quip, "Didn't you know, he gets an oak leaf cluster for his good conduct medal for every seventy two pins he puts in the map." Varvil added, "all right you guys, knock off the chatter and keep a sharp eye for some Nazi fighters. They might help to keep you from thinking too much."

Sitting in his tail turret Charlie was helping Varvil as to the position of the other planes in our formation. Four and six position were vacated just before the Danube River, heading back to Manduria with apparent malfunctions. And now as we are starting our bomb run number two dropped out of formation and is heading for the formations just coming off the target after dropping their bombs. We have just three bombers left in out flight as Bell is setting his up his bomb sight. Being flight leader may have it's advantages but being required to stay on the bomb run and not being able to evade some of the flak is not one of them. Fortunately for us, if fortunate is the proper word, we didn't have to contend with any enemy fighters, those mustangs saw to that.

My vantage position in the lead plane provided a panorama view of what lies ahead, and what I saw, I didn't like one bit. In this position one is absolutely alone and watching that black cloud of bursting anti-aircraft shells getting blacker by the second I again had to wonder what a nice young kid from Fishtown like me is doing here? No answers came back. Nose to pilot, "can't you go around that stuff, I don't think its very healthy in there?" Again, no answers. As we entered we could feel the plane starting to bounce around and as the milliseconds ticked away the bounces became more violent. It seemed like another eternity on that bomb run, Varvil had switched the control of the bomber to Bell's bomb sight and we had to fly straight and level through that flak. It must have been at least ten minutes from Bucharest to Ploiesti with those flak shells bursting all around us. I went into my usual ducking and flinching routine and in the course of turning my head from side to side I noticed we were alone, a single bomber and a sitting duck for those anti aircraft gunners and couldn't help but to wonder where the other two wing bombers were just as Bell called out "bombs away". I couldn't help but ask myself, did they go over the target? As best he could, Bahti tried to count the flak bursts and to tell Varvil which way to turn away from the next bursts as we could easily see those guns were set up in batteries of four or five guns. Except the ones that were mounted on railroad flat cars and traveling between Bucharest and Ploiesti. Bombs were away less than a minute when suddenly the plane lurched upward, Randy came on the intercom, "Waist to pilot, A shell just went right through the bomb bay and gas is coming out of the tanks like a cascading waterfall, looks like a hole about three feet round." Nose to waist, "Randy don't light a cigarette." It was stupid, I didn't realize the seriousness of that hole. Just then the plane was thrown to the right as Pop called, " we just took another shell inboard of number two engine and gas is pouring out of the lines, I'm going to try to hold the hose together with my hand, if I can reach it - I got it." With his hand outside the fuselage in air that had to be twenty degrees below zero plus the cold of high octane gasoline had to be taking it's toll on Pop's hand as he said, "I don't know how long I can hold this line, there's no feeling in my hand." Bahti, called out, "number four engine just took a hit, I'm going to feather it." Alone in my turret and not knowing what really is taking place, I could only surmise that those gunners on the ground were using Destiny Deb as a clay pigeon in choosing just what part they want to hit next. Suddenly, a shell burst to the left of my turret and a piece of steel shrapnel again came crashing through the plexiglas and hit me in the left temple. Charlie, later told me that, I let out a scream, "I'm hit, I'm hit in the head." Blood was profusely dripping down my cheek, but I was conscious and apparently not injured in a way that I would be incapacitated. Boyle and Bell opened the doors to my turret and helped me out and clipped on my parachute. The rush of air coming through the many holes in the fuselage was deafening, Boyle had to holler into my ears, "we're going to have to bailout, are you all right?" I nodded my head in the affirmative. Boyle then took a squatting position in front of the nose wheel well, our exit door. I had to laugh at seeing him there, squatting with his hands alternating between holding them on his headset, listening for the bailout signal and holding them in front of him as if praying. It was humorous only because I was still dazed from that piece of shrapnel and not being able to fully comprehend our perilous situation.

   Varvil's voice was serious as he said, Pilot to crew, "prepare to bail out, I don't think this plane is going to make it back to

Italy." By this time Charlie left his tail turret, Chief, left his ball turret and together with Randy and Paul were waiting for the bailout bell. Pop had to let go of the fuel line and needed help from Bahti to clip on his chest parachute, his right hand rendered useless from burns due to the cold air and high octane gasoline. This left us with one good engine and one that coughs in spurts, not conducive to keeping anything in the air let alone a lame defective bomber and we were losing altitude rapidly.

Varvil came on the intercom, his voice was noticeably choked, he wanted so much, with all his being, to be able to get his crew back safely to our home base. He was compelled by the awesome situation to tell us, "time to go you guys, God bless you all," — and hit the bailout bell. Varvil wanted to help, or to say more, but urgency prevailed.

We always wondered about that bailout bell and how loud it would be, if we could hear it. For obvious reasons we were reluctant to test it while in the air. Maybe we all, unknowingly, were superstitious about it. It was loud!

Back in the waist all four were saying "after you sir", and, after realizing their fate decided they had better get the hell out of that bomber. Charlie was last out the camera hatch following Chief and Paul as Randy dove out the waist window. On the flight deck, Varvil stayed in his seat to hold the plane level while Bahti went down to the bomb bay to help Pop who had a white knuckle death grip on the bomb racks. Above the noise of the rushing air coming up through the bomb bay Pop yelled to Bahti, "I can't go." Bahti said, "get the hell out of here, you idiot, this plane can blow up any second with all that gas coming out of the tanks." Pop continued, "I can't do it." At this point, Bahti pried Pop's only good hand off the racks, placed his foot on Pop's hips and kicked him out of the bomb bay and then jumped out himself.

Up in the nose with Boyle squatting in front of the open nose wheel doors, when the first clang of the bailout bell was heard Boyle was gone in a flash, not waiting for that bell's hammer to hit the second time, his head set was still on his ears as he dove out, praying hands and all. Bell said, " your next Fili." I retorted, "after you sir" and he left without saying another word. I wasn't that brave to just dive out of an airplane two and a half miles up. I sat down, facing the rear, and let my feet dangle in the fierce slipstream and didn't like that position. So I shimmied around to the side of the door with my feet still dangling and didn't like that stupid position either. I Put my back to the nose wheel and thought if I just put my head down the slip stream would pull me out. So I did a rehearsal just as the bomber lurched up then down and found myself falling away from the plane, some rehearsal.

I was falling on my back and looking up at Destiny Deb as she sped away with her wings rocking violently from side to side and not knowing that Varvil was still inside. I looked up at her for the last time and waved goodbye to a not so old but dear friend. Varvil had to climb back into the cockpit three times to level the wings so he could get out. When his parachute did open Destiny Deb started a left turn and headed straight toward him and would have recaptured him if it were not for that sputtering engine. It sputtered once more, as if ordered to do so by providence, to alter its course away from him. That traumatic sight would be sufficient to cause any heart to skip more than just a few beats in the strongest of men.

Meanwhile I was still falling toward terra firma at, as I was told, terminal velocity, even though it was not the least noticeable at the time. Sky divers in the years to come would know the thrill of falling free in open space and become quite exhilarated at it. But that late April day in 1944 over Roumania it was indeed quite frightening to a first time novice parachutist. I was upside down headed to a farm area head first. I gazed at my right hand still on the red ripcord and remembered my instructions to count ten then pull it. Instantly, I decided that ten had passed and pulled the handle. The opening of that life saving canopy was one hell of a jerk, pulling me upright, as I felt an uncomfortable feeling in my lower back. Even though my crotch was well padded with my high altitude flying gear that harness still pinched the hell out my jewels so I tried to move the straps around, a useless waste of effort. Besides the ground was coming up rather quickly.

Approaching the ground, I began to see the farmers, men, women and children, all scrambling for cover in fear of a one man invasion. I recalled some instructions on parachuting before leaving the states. After leaving your plane and coming close to the ground one should try to relax, relax I did. Letting my body go limp, landing on the side of a hill and tumbling ass over head down that hill until my parachute snagged in a bush. By then, I felt like jamming that "relax bit" down that somebody's throat.

After several attempts to stand, I was pretty rocky from the ordeal, I managed to stand erect and became steadier by the second. I started to remove my parachute harness and found that rip cord still in a death grip in my hand. To this day I cannot figure how I tried to manipulate the shroud lines with that rip cord still in my hand.

Shedding the harness, I surveyed the terrain and saw figures darting between the trees and working their way down and up that hill to determine who or what dropped down from their peaceful sky. I Reached inside my flying suit for a cigarette, lighting it, and waited for my reception party. Those farmers stayed a short distance from me until I yelled to them, "Alo! Alo!" and pointing to my chest yelled, "Me American!" Not knowing what else I could say. One man, timidly, came to me and asked, "Ruskie" (Russian), I answered "No," and again pointing to my chest, "American," Finally he understood and called to the others, "American" and the others, men, women and children gathered around me. The first man shook my hand, and, not knowing what else to do, I offered him a cigarette, which he took. I quickly became at ease, surmising that I was safe and in the hands of the underground partisans. An older man came up to me and wanted to shake both my hands and directed a man behind me to tie my hands behind my back with the straps of my mae west. Now I was assured of being the most naive kid that ever lived as it was apparent I was not in the company of friendly's.

Then I noticed an elderly woman standing a few feet in front of me, she had tears in her eyes, and suddenly she made a lunge for me. I could not help but to hold my breath with my eyes as wide open as the Holland Tunnel and instinctively became resigned that this is the end for me in this life. Her lunge took her past me as she was screaming to someone doing something behind me. I was reluctant to turn around, but I did, and saw another bearded man standing directly behind me with an axe held high over his head, and revenge in his eyes, about to plant the sharp edge in my skull. She stopped this man and saved my life. Directly a young girl brought a wet rag to the elderly woman who started to wipe the blood from my face. The compassion shown to me by that woman and the others who were there came from the heart and was totally unexpected after what we did to their country. A few minutes later the man who tried to part my skull with his axe came up to me, shook my hand, and as I looked into his eyes I saw the appearance of tears. He was telling me he was sorry. I later found out through an interpreter that on April 16, nine days ago, the bombers went over his house and stray bullets or shrapnel killed two of his children as they sought safe confines inside their home. I didn't have the heart to tell him that those stray bullets might have come from my guns because I flew that day to bomb the air fields and railroad yards in Brasov. How could anyone want to hurt, intentionally, these peace loving people who did no harm to anyone, did not start this war, did not want to participate in the war and did not deserve the hardships and agony's that were being forced upon them? I had to put all those thoughts aside before I went stark raving mad at the World in general.

The first elderly man motioned me to start walking up the hill and all the others followed. At the crest I could see we had to go down to reach the little village to the left about a half mile away. At the bottom a small cart trail would take us to the village. During the trek down that hill I felt my tied hands fall free from the bonds and let them dangle normally by my side. My captors, by then, didn't seem to care whether or not they were tied.

The strain of those emotions I felt crystallized when I found the inside of my mouth as dry as death valley and began to swell, making it somewhat difficult to breathe. Not knowing what was taking place I convinced myself that my nerves were getting the best of me, distracting my mind from sustenance and focusing on survival. I persuaded my captors that I needed a drink of water. Agreeably, they directed me to a spring by the roadside and bade me drink from it. I hesitated, however. That hesitation was somehow humanly appreciated, for one of the men walked over and drank from it first to demonstrate that its water was palatable. I seemed to drink several gallons, my custodians and the children meanwhile gathered around me, and laughing hysterically, were wondering when I would stop. Having drunk enough I just stood there briefly, gazing at the little lake across the road trying to paint a picture in my memory bank, that I should never forget this day, this place, and the people who were so kind to me.

With everyone calmed and a little laughter showing on all our faces we resumed the trek to their village. During this, I reflected how, within seconds, I had gone from mortal fear to bewilderment to near death to being almost feted and of course lucky and finally enjoyment just to be alive. If someone had told me of this experience, I, no doubt, would have called the flaky wagon for a trip to the looney farm. It was traumatic to run that gambit of human emotions in the short circumference of a watch's second hand. I motioned to the elder man I would like to sit down a few minutes and this rest was denied as he motioned we have only a short distance to go.

Still walking on this same cart path we came to a fork coming from the right and wonders will never cease. For walking in the same direction from that fork were Charlie and Paul also escorted by farmers and children. They allowed us a few minutes to speak to each other and then pushed us forward. Charlie, being from sturdy stock, was not harmed. But Paul had turned his ankle on landing and needed some assistance to walk. Charlie and I helped him as best as we could as far as their proud little village. A typical immaculate country community similar to those usually found in rural American townships. We were marched into the village square and directed to sit on the porch of the main building, evidently their meeting house. We no sooner had put our butts on a bench when Chief was being escorted into the village square from the opposite direction. Then and there we knew that at least four of us had survived the demise of "Destiny Deb". After greeting each other we sat on that porch pondering our fate. I asked Chief if he saw any of the other guys. He replied in his slow droll manner and silly smile:

"While I was coming down I saw Randy, I guess it was Randy, landing in the middle of some houses and two soldiers captured him even before he stood up. The poor guy didn't have a chance, he became a prisoner right away."

The three of us looked at each other and began to laugh as I asked chief: "what the hell do you think you are, a tourist." A camera "bug" would have a collectors item in a shot of the expression on Chief's face. Wide eyed, he asked the inevitable question:

"You mean we're prisoners, too?" We assured him that this is one bet he would win. Then Chief glowered at me from the slits in his narrowed eyes as he said:

"So, you wanted to be the third on a match! Why the hell did you have to take us with you?"

As the four of us sat on that porch, we became aware a general town meeting was convening to inspect us and, we suppose, to decide what to do with us. After about an hour a strikingly beautiful well dressed lady approached us. She seemed to be about thirtyish and without a doubt could easily pass for the American movie siren, Lana Turner. As she approached us she started speaking, very courteously in British English. In our predicament, it could easily be misconstrued as a sexy "hello." Perking our ears for want of a compassionate word we heard nothing, for this beauty had nothing but scorn for us Americans. She inquired: "Why do you come all the way from America to bomb our very small country. We did you no harm, we cannot even fight back?" She hesitated a second and again asked, before we could respond; "Why?"

Charlie, Paul and Chief looked at me to respond to her questions. Her very appearance demanded I be polite as I said; "Mam, no plane can fly that far. We came from Italy and hoped to return." It was evident that the average citizens of Roumania were being told by their government leaders these American bombers were flying from the States. At hearing this she kept silent as she pondered my answer. With initial contact made with these Roumanian people without the language barrier I had to inquire about our obvious status. "Mam, are we prisoners?" She very indignantly replied, "Of course you are prisoners, and I'm amazed that you would take the trouble to ask." The next appropriate question; "Are we prisoners of the Germans or the Roumanians?" Her response was like a ton of troubles being lifted from our shoulders as she said; "We Roumanians would not permit the Germans to take prisoners in our country and yes, you are prisoners of the Roumanian people.

As the conversation was subsiding, two Roumanian soldiers appeared and ushered us inside to the room to left of the entrance and locked the door. There was just a plain table and two chairs, one of which we insisted that Paul sit on. A few moments later the same two soldiers came back in and while one stood at the door with his rifle pointed at us the other began to search us and took away all our pocket possessions and our escape kits. Much more gracious, however, the village women brought us some tea and bread on the assumption that we would be hungry. As we ate the man who was going to axe my head came in with the lady who stopped him. The man once again came over to shake my hand and smile, his hands folded as in prayer, he bowed, a gesture that I returned in kind for I took it as another apology. My three buddies looked at me with a startled stare and they almost spoke in unison; "what the hell was that all about?" I told them I would let them know later.

About an hour later, those same guards returned and upon opening the door motioned us to go outside. There they had an open body truck and, again with motions, told us to climb onto it. Obviously they're going to take us somewhere else was my response to Chief's question; "where do we go from here?" We were riding on that same cart path, being bounced around by the ruts for about (we could only guess since they took our watches) an hour. Around the next bend came a town much bigger than the one we left. The truck pulled up to what looked like the local lockup as six gendarmes came outside to escort us in. Going up the front steps I noticed the name above the door "Pitesti" I assumed the name of the town. Once inside we were ushered upstairs to a dormitory like cell that had some cots. It was good to see Randy again as he was there waiting for us. In his hillbilly tone and humor he asked, "what the hell kept you, been here waiting for company and all they could find were you guys. looks like we know where we will be for the next dozen or so hours, if that's any consolation." A soldier brought us some tea and brown bread with marmalade. As we ate we inquired about the rest of our crew. The soldier held up his right hand and counted five, indicating that five more were captured. He also held up his left hand with his index finger as he said, "La Mort". It didn't take much thinking to know that "La Mort" meant death. We all looked at each other and instinctively knew if it was anyone it had to be Varvil. Because Varvil was that kind of a man. He was the captain of his ship and his men was his accepted responsibility. We could only hope and pray that tomorrow will tell us another story.

If it wasn't for the ordeal and trauma we four were subjected to that day I don't think we would have slept a single wink thinking about Varvil. But, when night did fall and as the lights were dimmed we all passed out from shear exhaustion. During the night I had a need for a bowel movement, why it took so long I'll never know. But, the guard took me to their type of latrine and what I saw was so shockingly primitive. The urinal was a trough in the floor on one side of the room and the other side had several pads about three feet square. In the center and toward the rear was a funnel shaped hole. Just in front of the funnel were two raised pads. Apparently when one is about to defecate one should place their feet on the pads and squat, hoping that both holes are aligned properly. It took some getting used to. This time our American ingenuity didn't prevail and so we did it their way.

As providence would have it we all awoke at the same time. I started to move off the cot but found difficulty in straightening my legs due to some pain and tightening of the muscles in my lower back. I asked Randy to come over to lend a hand so I could stand up. As I strained to stand I remembered I was upside down when I pulled the rip cord on my parachute and felt something happen or snap in the same area of my back. When erect I had to walk very slow and in somewhat of a stiff position. Randy tried to massage the area and it did help some. I resigned myself that somehow or someway I will have to cope with it and try to work it out.

The guards knew we had to take our morning turn in the latrine and escorted us there one at a time. After which they brought us some more tea, bread and marmalade. Chief asked, "Don't these people eat anything else but bread and marmalade?" Chief, I said, "don't complain, after all consider what we did to them yesterday, I would guess that we are lucky to get anything!" "Maybe you're right, Bill" was Chief's end of complaining.

While we were sitting at the one table in that lockup eating our so called breakfast a commotion from downstairs startled us then a guard started up followed by other foot steps. With wide eyes and gaping mouths we watched in anticipation and suddenly exploded with a shout of sincere joy as we saw Varvil, Bahti, Bell and Pop coming up the stairs following the guard. I invited them into our little room for our tea party. Hand shakes galore and unbelievable smiles were indicative of the weight removed from our minds. Varvil was the first to speak to tell us Boyle was all right but he broke his leg on landing and they took him to the nearest hospital. With all greetings ending we seemed to begin a ritual of asking each other silently, "where the hell do we go from here?" Varvil, was still his quiet reserved self observing our situation and how he could extricate us from where ever we were. Bahti, with his red and ruddy Finnish smile could only keep saying, "son-of-a- buck what are we doing here?" Bell was just walking around the room periodically not saying much to anyone as was just about everyone else.

Bahti noticed the way I was walking and inquired about it just as Varvil called the guard to get a doctor to look at my face and eye. I told Bahti about the parachute opening and he started to massage my back. Bahti was a powerfully built man without an ounce of fat on his body, he seemed to know the human male anatomy and knew what he was doing. He had me lay across a chair that he turned down and had me exercise my back and with his masterful massaging my aches seemed to vanish. He told me the aches will come back but will gradually subside as long as we keep up with these mini treatments. Shortly a doctor came into the lockup and examined my left eye and found no apparent damage that would require immediate treatment. He then looked at Pop's hand that was treated and bandaged before he arrived here. Pop will just have to wait for the healing process and hopefully with no long lasting effects from those burns caused by the cold and high octane gasoline. We would later learn that to have all ten men survive those exploding bombers over Ploiesti was nothing short of a miracle. Three survivors out of ten was the norm. Providence had to be with us that day.

For the rest of that afternoon I compulsively intruded into everyone's private discourse and making myself a general nuisance. When silent, I visualized Boyle lying in that hospital trying to make a pass at some cute perky nurse. To lighten the situation I interjected, "Look at this way, you guys, three on a match is not such bad luck, we're all here aren't we. maybe I brought us all good luck!" No one bought my analogy and all cast ominous glares my way.

It must have been about four o'clock when a Roumanian lieutenant entered our room and beckoned the guard to unlock the door for him to enter. He was a personable young man, I would guess reaching for thirty years, and could speak a little English. He informed us that we would leave very soon for an internment camp in Bucharest. We tried to pump more information out of him without success. We wanted to know if other Americans were there at which point he changed the subject by telling us we would travel by train. A guard came running up the stairs and, after shouting something to the lieutenant, they both left. We could only guess that our transportation to the railroad station had arrived.

Once on the train with a multitude of guards at both ends of the car we were ushered to one end, away from other Roumanians. It was a pleasant enough ride if it wasn't our thoughts of how fighters usually seek targets of opportunity and moving trains were their favorite foes. We passed through countryside not unlike our own in the United States. We would soon learn that, in those days, Roumania might well be called "Little America" and as the lieutenant informed us their capital city, Bucharest, was known in European circles as the "Paris of the Balkans." In the years past, many details have escaped my memory, such as the time it took to travel to Bucharest. (It couldn't have taken more than a few hours). It was obvious that we were approaching the City as more and more homes and buildings were noticeable.

The sun was setting in the west as daylight began its ritual of turning into night as the train inched into the station. We could not help but notice the destruction brought on these people by our bombers from the first time we were there on April 4, 1944 until yesterday April 24, 1944. Silence was only too prevalent at seeing first hand just how much damage we had done to the city and to the people themselves. Alighting from that train, amidst an army of guards, all we could hear were the yells from the people shouting to us, "Murders! Gangsters!" shaking fists at us, spitting in our direction and some of the children were throwing stones at us. The stone throwing youngsters were quickly dispersed by the guards but the adults would not budge. However, those guards did manage to keep them at a distance from us. We did not understand why we would be called "Murders! and Gangsters!" No doubt they had their reasons.

Those guards, we found out later, were older men who were conscripted to military service for such a purpose as this. They may have been older but they maintained their dignity and would not take any nonsense from us smart assed Americans. We also found out they were our protectors as well as our guards and keeping us from being lynched.

Breathing became a little easier as we were ushered into the bus and on our way to the internment camp. Leaving the railroad station we had to pass an area where a grave about a block long and twenty feet wide and twenty feet deep was being prepared for the nearby bodies. The lieutenant explained that grave will be for about three thousand bodies that were killed during yesterdays air raid. It seemed one bomb group, assigned to bomb the railroad yards in Bucharest were late in arriving at the target. After most of the bombers flew over the city heading for Ploiesti, the air raid wardens assumed todays bombings had ended and sounded the all clear signal. People came out of the shelters to go about their business when that last bomb group arrived and dropped their bombs in the middle of the masses of people causing such a high casualty rate.

Was it strange, therefore, that the train station mob wanted to lynch us? It was hard for me to take my eyes off that scene and only did so as the bus turned onto another street. How grateful I was knowing that the bombs in our bomber did not rain such death and destruction. Once again silence and deep thoughts completely enveloped all nine of us in that bus. Our airmen-warrior facade was gone, replaced by compassion for the people of Bucharest amidst a multitude of questions, questions that seemed to ask the same thing "why?" "why?"

When we arrived at our destination there was still enough daylight to know our new home away from home would be a military garrison converted to a prisoner of war camp. And as such we were quartered in a military target. Not knowing whether or not any other prisoners were inside we expressed our objections to our escorting lieutenant who indicated that he would make a note of it. Those notes are no doubt still collecting dust on some shelf somewhere in or near Bucharest. That garrison covered nearly a full city block and from outside appearance would be equally as hard to get in as it would be to get out. Our lieutenant did tell us that this place, just one month ago, was the quarters for the royal regiment of King Michael. Apparently the young king was more desirous in saving grace in the eyes of the Americans than he was prone to please the Germans.

The bus pulled ahead thru the two gigantic steel doors after they were opened. The bus stopped at two more closed huge steel doors. After the first two were closed and locked we were ushered out of the bus and into a room to the left of the entrance. There were no chairs in that room so we sat on the floor for about a half hour when a guard opened the door and left it open. We could see clear through to the courtyard since they opened the inside doors. It is hard to describe the relief we felt when we saw other Americans walking around inside that courtyard. That courtyard was huge with sufficient area to hold a dress parade. There were also some smaller service buildings in its center and suddenly a switch was triggered in my memory bank. Watching movies, states side, we had been shown predicaments similar to our present one. Then, however, nothing could have been more remote from our minds that the prospect of an actual experience. Looking around that garrison, we could only assume that our captors would try to use some form of torture on us to obtain their desired information before letting us join the rest of the prisoners.

Our examination of the interior of our new home came to an abrupt halt when entering was a short stocky Roumanian captain. Speaking fluent American English, slang words and all, he greeted us, "Hello, I'm captain Christescu, how is everyone? Does anyone need medical attention?" We answered in kind that we were all well as could be expected under these circumstances. Not saying another word he left and entered a room to the right of the entrance vestibule but first making sure that sufficient guards were posted to keep us in our place. He send one guard to escort one crew member to his room (the exact sequence of who went first and so on escapes my memory). However, I do recall, on entering that second room, I observed that it was rather small, that a desk was in the center and captain Christescu was seated in one chair on the tables other side and I was beckoned to sit in the other chair facing him. He took out his revolver and placed it on the table nearer to him than me and handed me a paper. Christescu said, "Fill out this paper as it is required by the International Red Cross in accordance with the Geneva Convention." I looked at the paper and found questions that as a soldier I did not have to answer and simply wrote down my name, rank, and serial number and handed it back to him. His composure seemingly lost he picked up his pistol, slammed it back down on the table, and pushed the paper back to me ordering me in an arrogant tone to fill out the rest of it. I don't know how many scenes like this one I've seen in the past in the movies but this was real. Did he scare this nice young kid from Fishtown, you bet your ass he did! I started to push the paper back to him when I heard a scuffle behind me at the door. Faster than a machine gun could fire a hundred rounds my mind was rummaging through its memory bank trying to find a scene in a movie where the good guy really did extricate himself from his would be torturer or his executioner about to enter that door behind him.

The door flew open with an unexpected suddenness and a small frail body reached past me and grabbed that paper at the same time yelling, "don't tell this frigen son-of-a-bitch anything". The frail body somehow seemed familiar and it was difficult to try to think with such rapid fire unexpected occurrences and captain Christescu picked up his revolver and put it back into its holster.

Stupefied, dumbfounded and amazed, I looked harder at the little fellow again and then took my turn at bellowing!

"Fasolas, you aren't dead, are you?"

"You stupid ass," he retorted, "Do I look dead?"

Just then, two guards dashed into the room and, each seizing one of Fasolas's arms, they swept him off his feet and whisked him outside with his feet dangling and kicking and hollering "let me down, you fucken dumb bastards."

The outside guard then closed the door and left the captain and I alone again. I looked at Him, he was sitting there with a silly grin on his face which soon faded but remained soft. Taking the paper which I was supposed to fill out, he did exactly that for me. Having completed his writing, he handed it to me and asked that

I check its accuracy. I looked at that form on which he had written every minute detail of our mission; our bomber group and squadron, our home base, and the role of each crew member. Everything! I pushed it back to him the third time.

And asked, "what the hell did you ask me for?"

Smiling once more, he simply replied, "We all have a job to do don't we?"

Anyone can pass through life thinking and talking about the unexpected and the ridiculous happening, yet never see them. For me, they did happen, and in a prison camp of all places. I sat there, expecting to defecate in my pants, wondering what kind of torture they might inflict on me and unwillingly entertaining all the wild ideas which bombard the human mind in such situations. Then, into that cramped interrogation room stormed one of our guys to upstage the enemy interrogator who was supposed to scare the shit out of me, In fact he did everything but. What matters is that, true to script, Captain Christescu was unnerved (so I later learned) and immediately concluded the interrogation of our crew.

At the captains call, those guards conducted us through a long narrow corridor and into the dormitory like room. There we were greeted by fellow American airmen and just glancing around we could see some of the men whom we thought were killed in the last few air raids over Bucharest and Ploiesti. Ironically, we found them eating Roumanian pastry as if on a picnic, yes, munching on cakes and cookies purchased when they sold their watches or other personal belongings to the guards or the canteen operator. You can be assured that Americans are not the only enterprising people in the world for someone required only a few days to contact a local politician, most likely cut him in on the profits, to be permitted to establish a canteen in that camp. However, it only lasted a few days that is, until we ran out of things to sell then we went back to their bland tea, brown bread and sour watery bean soup.

Randy spotted Mel Openshaw, and brought him over to where I was standing. It sure was good to see him and to know that he was alive and well. Mel took Randy and I to the rear of the room and showed us the last two upper cots where we were to sleep that night and from now on till that certain someday. I climbed up on that bunk and decided to stay there as it was almost completely dark outside. Besides I was too weary to do anything else and I was in no mood to converse with anyone that is, not just yet. I guess I just wanted to feel sorry for myself. In looking around "our" room it seems that I was not the only one with that frame of mind. Bewildered faces were in abundance that night. I wasn't on my bunk more than a few minutes when I heard the one door at the opposite end of the room closed and a lock snap closed. The ultimate indication that I was in a prison camp.

AUTHOR'S REVISIONS FOR THE SECOND PRINTING.

During my first day in that prison camp I noticed the absence of some men who I knew were shot down but they were not in this camp. I assumed they had been killed in the air battles and I did not want to question anyone and add to their personal trauma.

Forty eight years later I received a letter from Jack Schoonover whom I thought went down with Lt. Edwards crew and was killed. Jack wrote to me to tell the story of why he was not on that mission with his crew.

Jack was experiencing an unusual physical impairment during fighter attacks and at the target. The flight surgeon was giving him medication that enabled him to perform his duties as the Flight Engineer on his Liberator. On April 5, 1944, the first high level mission over Ploiesti, Jack went to the medical office for his pill. Instead the doc took his temperature and grounded him. That evening, after Jack found out about his crew, had to be the most heart ripping trauma anyone would have to experience. It took a few weeks for Jack to compose himself before flying once again, but with a made up crew as he did not want to get to close to anyone again. He then finished his fifty missions. His last mission was to Munich and was the Engineer for Major General Nathan Twining, Commanding General of the 15th Air Force.

While completing his missions Jack had became a loner and spent most of his idle time with a bottle of vino under an olive tree just waiting for his turn at whatever fate had in store for him. Without a doubt the happenings on April 5, 1944 would affect Jack for the rest of his life. Perhaps that medication was the cause of his present day condition.

Today, Jack lives in Fair Oaks, California and is confined to a wheel chair with severe COPD. In Jack's words, "I stay home, write letters to friends, give the politicians hell, play with my roses and generally get in the way. I see a lot of TV, read books and magazines. All in all it's been a wonderful life and I still enjoy it." If anyone deserves God's Blessings Jack should be first in line. Surely there is a special place in Valhalla for men like Jack Schoonover.

AMERICAN LOSSES AT PLOIESTI

LOW LEVEL RAID AUGUST 1, 1943
53 BOMBERS SHOT DOWN WITH 530 MEN — 130 TAKEN PRISONER

HIGH LEVEL RAIDS APRIL 4, 1944 TO AUGUST 19, 1944

```
    314  BOMBERS SHOT DOWN     3140 MEN    1027 TAKEN PRISONER
    111  FIGHTERS SHOT DOWN     111 MEN      28 TAKEN PRISONER
    425                        3251         1055
```

WHERE DID THE FIGHTERS AND BOMBERS COME FROM

8TH AIR FORCE ON LOW LEVEL RAID BASED IN ENGLAND
(flying from the Libyan desert)

B-24	44th BOMB GROUP	51 POWs
B-24	93rd BOMB GROUP	18 POWs
B-24	389th BOMB GROUP	17 POWs
B-24	98th BOMB GROUP ALSO ON THE LOW LEVEL RAID	
B-24	376th BOMB GROUP ALSO ON THE LOW LEVEL RAID	

15th AIR FORCE ON HIGH LEVEL RAIDS BASED IN ITALY

930 B-24 BOMBERS			310 B-17 BOMBERS		
98th	BOMB GROUP	59 POWs	2nd	BOMB GROUP	11 POWs
376th	BOMB GROUP	84 POWs	97th	BOMB GROUP	76 POWs
449th	BOMB GROUP	97 POWs	99th	BOMB GROUP	62 POWs
450th	BOMB GROUP	133 POWs	301st	BOMB GROUP	20 POWs
451st	BOMB GROUP	62 POWs	463rd	BOMB GROUP	85 POWs
454th	BOMB GROUP	26 POWs			254 POWs
455th	BOMB GROUP	68 POWs			
456th	BOMB GROUP	26 POWs	166 P-38 FIGHTERS		
459th	BOMB GROUP	67 POWs	1st	FIGHTER GROUP	6 POWs
460th	BOMB GROUP	25 POWs	14tH	FIGHTER GROUP	3 POWs
461st	BOMB GROUP	31 POWs	82nD	FIGHTER GROUP	8 POWs
464th	BOMB GROUP	44 POWs			17 POWs
465th	BOMB GROUP	26 POWs			
484th	BOMB GROUP	17 POWs	P-47 FIGHTERS NOT KNOWN		
485th	BOMB GROUP	8 POWs			
		773 POWs	166 P-51 FIGHTERS		
			31st	FIGHTER GROUP	2 POWs
			52nd	FIGHTER GROUP	5 POWs
			325th	FIGHTER GROUP	4 POWs
					11 POWs

FINAL ANALYSIS OF LOSSES AT PLOIESTI

367 BOMBERS SHOT DOWN WITH 3670 MEN
111 FIGHTERS SHOT DOWN WITH 111 MEN
3781 MEN SHOT DOWN – ONLY 1185 SURVIVED AND RETURNED HOME

NINE

After locking the door the guard turned on the only dim ceiling light. It was barely sufficient for me to examine my new home. The room was about fifty feet long, twelve foot high ceilings, with double tiered bunks on both sides and a three foot aisle in between the rows of bunks. The bunks were butted against each other and to get into the lower bunk one had to crawl in through the ends and to get above, climb up over the end. The room was so small and crowded that I didn't have to strain my eyes to notice the small groups of men, in three's, in four's, and some five's. Some groups were huddled on the top bunks, some on the lower bunks and still others were in the aisle. And yet it was easy to see the loneliness of the men just looking out into space through the steel bars. Their voices were low; they were talking about anything that came into their minds. Mostly it was talk about home and what will be the first thing they will do; the first word to be said to an American girl; the first food eaten from an American table; these firsts were talked about, if and when they do get home. The low voices were for no reason other than an acceptance of the perilous situation we found ourselves in. There seemed to be no resignation that these firsts would not be realized. And there was no sign of surrender, only a sincere desire to see this thing through whatever it takes.

They talked of their families, swapped stories of home life, described their moms and dads, brothers and sisters. I overheard one fellow talk about his marine older brother and his harrowing experiences on Guadalcanal and his night mares about fighting the sneaking little Japs. And of his trip home from combat after he had half his guts blown out by a grenade. Another fellow told of his father who tried vainly to work and support a family for years even though he was miserably sick from being gassed in the Argonne Forest in World War 1 - it caught up to him in 1936. Finally, as I listened, I realized these men were allowing their very private thoughts to be heard, thinking out loud so to speak, hoping for a compassionate ear. And there were many in that room that night. I was too bewildered and afraid to share my thoughts and anxieties with anyone.

The beds were only about thirty inches wide and the room accommodated sixty two beds and I now occupy what was the last empty one with Randy at my right side. There was a steel bar extending up at the head of the bed where I hung the tin cup they gave me. The mattress was burlap covered straw that smelled like the horse or cow left it's excrement on it, which hardened, and kept the straw in a rigid state to poke at me through the burlap. It was like laying on dull needles sticking into various parts of my anatomy every time I moved slightly. It was something that a nice clean cut young American kid like me was just not used to. I could not help but think about those clean sheeted beds my mom always provided me with.

The course burlap and straw were endurable after a fashion, but those filthy, crawling, biting and itching lice were not. Laying there in what was supposed to be a bed, I realized how scared a young man I was. My first night in a prisoner of war camp, was I supposed to be anything else? What was my life expectancy and would I see tomorrow and how many other tomorrows would I be able to look forward to?

In between thoughts, thoughts that were continually being disturbed by those crawling lice being attracted to this virgin clean American. In a matter of minutes after laying down they were on my feet, in my hair, ears, nose and as expected in my crotch. I don't know if I could have endured the worry and the not knowing of that first night if I wasn't kept busy chasing my new found tenants. They did have a purpose, at least at that very moment.

My concern about myself was overshadowed by the thoughts of my family back in Fishtown and their not knowing what was happening to me. Reaching out to them mentally was impractical as well as impossible and this effort exhausted me into a deep sleep. It was a sleep of peace and tranquility that would be welcomed by anyone, especially a person in my, and all the other men's predicament. We were to be denied even this short respite though. As if fate had preordained our situation, we were to be antagonized in a way that even we could not understand. In fact, we still think it unbelievable to this day forty six years later, that we are alive to talk about it.

Being in a prisoner of war camp one would think the war would be over for them. One would think that our only concern would be survival and getting enough food to sustain life. As one of our inmates, an Englishman from Leicester put it, "one can be wrong, Yank, and usually is when he applies stupid logic to our situation".

I was suddenly aroused out of that deep sleep by one of those nasty lice crawling up my nose and by the fellow in the left top bunk. His hand was gently but firmly against my shoulder to wake me up. After removing the pest in my nose, I sleepily asked what was the matter? I slowly began to comprehend what he was saying.

"Hey, buddy, you had better wake up, there's an air raid going on". "Oh", I said, "what do you want me to do, Stop it"? "No, buddy, but I think it would be a good idea to get up anyway, just in case". "Hell, just in case of what?" I said. I sort of guessed that I had better listen to this voice of experience since he is a veteran of this POW camp, a veteran of at least three weeks. I slowly got to a sitting position at the end of my bunk and let my feet dangle over the end. It didn't take long for me to become fully awake watching the men standing in front of the eight foot high steel barred windows. They were able to open the top window and then I became aware of the outside noise. I heard the roar of airplane engines, the anti-aircraft guns shooting in volleys of four rounds each. The outside looked almost as bright as daylight but with an eerie yellowish glare that somehow did not look normal.

The men at the windows were like the quarterback calling the signals. There goes a Whimpy behind a cloud over there and did you see that Halifax caught in those searchlights and those ackack shells exploding all around it.

Another one said, "How the hell do they get through this mess of lights to find the target"? "How the do they keep their sanity"?

Yet another would say, "You couldn't get me to do that for all the money in China or chowder in Boston". Then the laughter would start when he was reminded that that was the reason he was under those lights that night. He did just what he just said he wouldn't do.

All hell broke loose when the Englishman from Leicester cried out, "Why the bloody bastards are dropping the green flares on top of us". He raised his fist at the Whimpy that ducked behind that cloud and shouted, "You bloody idiot don't you know I'm down here"? As he left that window he shouted to us, "we're in for it now!

Some Yanks shouted back, "What the hell are we in for; and what do you know that we don't know"?

The Limey answered, "you stupid bloody Yanks, don't you know how night bombing is done"? "No wonder the war is lasting so bloody long"! At this some of the Yanks were getting irritated at his remarks and a few of them took his words as a personal insult and headed for him with the fire of confrontation or physical violence in their eyes.

I looked over at the window, being mesmerized by those powerful yellow flares that lit up the whole city of Bucharest. I saw small trucks with machine guns on them and soldiers firing into the air. I asked stupidly, "what the hell do they think they can do with such a small machine gun, their bullets will never reach those bombers". I found out they were shooting out the flares that seemed to be suspended for an eternity from their small parachutes. Sounds almost impossible but some fellows told me they were pretty good at it. Their efforts were comforting to them in putting some of the flares out but didn't dim the night sky one bit because of the thousands that were dropped. And each airplane would drop more flares with their bombs.

Still sitting on the end of my upper bunk, I noticed my and knees were shaking violently, the kind of shaking one gets when they are soaking wet from a cold rain or suddenly come down with a chill and fever. But I had no fever or cold and the temperature was a balmy seventy degrees with a light breeze coming in the window. I asked myself, "Why am I shaking, what the hell is the matter with me"? I answered myself. "I must be scared, but scared of what"?

I reached into the pocket of my flying suit for a cigarette and put the end into my mouth, then took out a match. When I lit the match, you would have thought I had killed someone the way everyone was shouting at me to put out the match. I yelled, "what for"? In unison I was told the bombardiers would be able to see it even through those flares. I shouted back, "Oh bullshit, they couldn't see a match inside a building". Then someone reached up and put it out and offered the end of his lit cigarette to light mine. After lighting my cigarette, I noticed I still had the shakes, and taking a couple of deep drags of the cigarette and a few deep breaths the shaking seemed to subside a little bit. It also took some of the tension away from the Limey, when I lit the match just about everyone got off his back and onto mine.

Then Limy started to explain what he meant and in an almost resigned to his fate low tone of voice. "You all saw that Halifax come over, the one that was caught in the searchlights and then ducked behind the clouds. Well, he was the pathfinder, the locator of the target area. It was his job to find and to light up the whole area, and sometimes he has to make several passes to cover the entire area with flares. And then you saw that Whimpy come over and just miss the search lights and duck behind another cloud. Well Yanks, that bloody Whimpy had to locate the target and drop the green flares over the actual target".

"So what", called one Yank from the other end of the room.

"So what, you stupid bloody Yanks", roared the man from Leiscester. "I'll tell you what, the next planes, and I don't know how many there will be tonight. The next planes are going to drop their bombs into the center of the green flares, that's what, and guess who's in the center of the green flares"!!! In that room that night of April 25, 1944 and at that very moment a very, very, deep silence overtook everyone. It was an eerie silence except for the outside distraction of airplane engines, ackack guns and small machine gun fire. I was still sitting on the end of my bunk finishing that cigarette down to where it burnt my fingers and I was still shaking. But now I knew why and I didn't like it and didn't like what I was thinking. Neither did the men at the windows who looked and listened to the sky and then alternately at the Englishman. Those few seconds seemed like an eternity, an eternity that we may all be traveling to this night.

We were locked into this room by our captors, the soldiers of the Roumanian Army. They had no intentions of letting us out and if they did let us out, where would we go? We started to hear the roar of more airplane engines getting louder by the second and time was getting short. Short for what? For making decisions? What the hell kind of a decision could we make in this locked up room? We began to hear whistling bombs with explosions nearby and each explosion seemed to come closer and closer to our room and then the whole building started to shake and the floor heaved as it would shake in an earthquake. All sorts of advice and incoherent vocal meanderings came from just about everyone and none of it made any sense at all. Was this what we were waiting for, the beginning of the end for us? Was this what we were born for?

Some of the more gallant men stayed by the windows, others stayed in the aisle between the rows of bunks, and me still sitting on the end of my bunk and still shaking and shivering violently without any control. It was like a very sharp needle being placed in delicate and sensitive spots on the human anatomy or being hit on the head with a baseball bat when one of the fellows at the windows yelled, "I saw it! I saw it come out of that plane, his raised hand pointing to the sky, and it's a blockbuster headed right for us"!!! He continued shouting, "It's a blockbuster, It's a blockbuster"!!! as he half jumped and half dove for the confines of under a bed. Instinctively, everyone dove also for the protective cover under a bed. I know it sounds stupid and ridiculous and it is stupid and ridiculous. How can a bed protect anyone from a two thousand pound bomb? To answer that, simply, in our predicament, we will take all the help we can get.

No longer was I sitting on the end of my upper bunk, for, I too was in a head long dive for a bed across that small aisle and somehow seemed to have a head-on collision with a fellow who aimed his body for the same bed. We never made it because we landed on the floor just as that blockbuster exploded outside our building. The floor heaved so violently that I thought I was being lifted to the pearly gates for a visit with St. Peter. Besides some other fellow was faster than us two. The two of us just laid there, huddled against each other looking for some sort of paternal protection as other bombs were exploding in rapid succession and almost equal force and vibrations in the ground. That first bomb was so close it blew out all the windows in that room.

The time on that floor was forever for us, an eternity for the hour it took for all those British bombers to drop their bombs. We were later to find out that they hit their target a devastating blow as the primary target was another military garrison like the one we were imprisoned. It was fortunate for us that they flew low enough to identify the real garrison and the stray bombs strayed a little bit farther or shorter to spare us that heavenly vacation from which there would have been no return.

After the bombs stopped falling and exploding, the anti-aircraft guns were silenced and all the flares were shot out or burnt themselves out, we very slowly managed to get ourselves off the floor or leave the protective confines of under a bed. There wasn't much talking after that scenario only an air of thankfulness. We did not have to listen too intently to hear the deep sighs of relief as we went about the clean-up and straightening-up task. As our Limey buddy walked past his fellow P.O.W.'s each one would put his hand on his shoulder and smile, a sort of unspoken apology, and said, "Thanks, you bloody Limey". Never again, in this camp anyway, would the Limey and the Yank have any doubts about each other. The bonding of this friendship was as solid as the rock of Gibraltar.

Man can find humor in just about any situation he becomes involved in, and being on the receiving end of a load of blockbusting bombs is no exception. In the middle of all the frightening scare, there came a time for laughter. When the guy at the window yelled that he saw a blockbuster come out of the Whimpy he joined all the others in diving for the safety of being under a bed. While half-diving and half-flying somehow his belt got caught on the metal post on the end of the bunk. This snare caused him to swing around like a yoyo and left him dangling from the post. He was yelling for help to get him down. His feet were only inches from the floor but it had to scare him half to death as if he were dangling from a high cliff. Someone did help him down finally but only after that first bomb exploded and scattered the glass all over. He wasn't hit with glass as the snare caught him at a bed that was in between windows.

After the laughs, the sighs, and I have no doubt some tears, unnoticed in the darkened room, that brought the much needed calm to our bodies, we all started heading to our bunks. I did not realize before, but my bed was directly opposite a window. When that bomb went off outside the building, that shattered window sprayed it's glass all over my bed and some with such force that it imbedded itself into the plaster wall behind and into the straw mattress. I may have been shaking before, but now thinking of what would have happened to me and to my face had I been sitting on the end of my bunk when that bomb exploded. The thought makes me want to start shaking all over again. Now that I know what the unknown is I will respect it more in the future, if that makes any sense? Then again does war make any sense or the need for a Prisoner of War Camp? It took me most of the night to pick the glass out of my mattress. My bunkmate Randy offered to help but I told him to get some sleep and rest it may be needed sooner than we think. Anyway, I wouldn't be able to sleep the rest of the night. After finishing that chore I just sat on the end of the bunk with my feet dangling but not shaking as before thinking of this situation and the sheer lunacy of man's inhumanity to man. I didn't get any answers or reassurances of survival.

As I sat there and probably thinking the same silent thoughts as everyone else was doing earlier. I remembered reading about the boy scouts that caused this whole messy war to start in the first place. A New York Times editor was quoted in November 1923, one month before I was born, that Adolph Hitler's followers numbered less than one thousand. He further described Hitler and his gang as a bunch of boy scouts playing games of war. And now, as I sit on this filthy bed, an empty belly and lice crawling all over me I wonder what kind of a merit badge they will earn for this scenario. Rationalization was all but impossible.

Without thinking I pulled out my pack of cigarettes and withdrew the last one and put it to my lips. Then I pulled out a book of matches and it too had but one match. I tore off the match and started to strike it against the abrasive end of the cover. I faintly remember seeing a spark of some sort and heard the beginning of an explosion and found myself in an apparition of floating in the air space of that room. Then everything went blank, for how long I didn't know and never found out. I do remember opening my eyes looking straight up to the ceiling. My eyes began to burn as if irritated by sand and as I wet my lips with my tongue I tasted plaster. By this time one of the guards outside in the corridor had turned on the single light in the center of the room. I could see a mist of dust like fog had enveloped the room. Then I realized I was on my back on the floor in the aisle between the rows of bunks. I began moving my body slowly to determine if all my parts were still fastened together. I first sat up then stood up, looked around and thought, "Good God, did my match do this"? Just as slowly all the others were arousing themselves and going through the same ritual, trying to find out just what the hell happened?

As the dust settled we could see that much of the ceiling plaster had fallen on just about everyone and everything. We guessed right as we found out the next morning it was a delayed fused bomb or that the fuse just malfunctioned. But landed just outside the outer wall to the corridor and partially demolished it. How lucky we were to have that extra wall for protection because the inside wall wasn't much more than a block and plaster partition compared to the outside masonry wall. Protection for prisoners of war from their own bombs. What irony.

Another episode of knee shaking, heart pounding and just plain asinine stupidity! How much more are we going to experience this night? After cleaning up as best we could I was mentally assured that I was not going to sleep the rest of this night. I managed to bum a cigarette from Randy. I asked him to light it for me as I didn't want another show like the one we just rung down the curtain on. Randy went to his bunk and once again I'm sitting on the end of my bunk with my legs dangling. I think I finally fell asleep in that sitting position. My first night in a POW camp sure was a show stopper! A show that I hope and pray will never have a curtain call.

Oil storage tanks of Columbia Aquila refinery on fire as B-24s approach on their bomb run. (National Archives Still Pictures)

Lil Jughaid, piloted by Robert Nicholson, and other B-24s from the 98th leaving the target low to the ground. Fire and smoke are from crashed B-24. (National Archives Still Pictures)

TEN

The rustle of my flying buddies awoke me from the sound sleep I fell into after that earth shattering experience last night. I found myself flat on my back with my legs still dangling over the bottom of my bed. As I started to move I could feel nothing but pins and needles from above my knees to the tips of my toes. That awkward position had limited the blood circulation in those extremities. A little hand massaging and they were as good as new. But that awful taste of plaster dust was still in my mouth. Randy and I jumped off the cots and asked a fellow inmate if there was a place to wash or rinse out our mouths, "Not yet," was the response. He added, "besides it's breakfast time so you had better get your tin cup for the surprise of your life." We looked at each other and Randy said, "well at least we're going to be feed." Everyone started to line up in the hallway so we just followed the crowd. In front of Randy I reached the Roumanian soldier who ladled a tinted liquid in my cup and handed me a small piece of bread. I followed the guy in front of me and asked, "What is this in the cup?" He said it was tea. "Is this breakfast, a cup of colored water and a small piece of bread?" I asked. "What you see is what you got," was his answer. Randy and I just looked at our tin cup and at each other several times and accepted what was given to us, simply because we had no choice, except to starve or die from dehydration. By this time everyone was out of the room and into the court yard and looking over the crater last nights bomb had caused.

Suddenly someone grabbed me from behind by the back of my collar and the seat of my pants and started to march me around the yard. My feet were half dangling and half scraping the ground as a pair of powerful hands were holding me in that position. I shouted, "for Christ's sake, who ever you are let go, your pinching the hell of my nuts." He marched me over to a wall and shouted "now I got you, you son of a bitch and I'm going to beat the shit out of you." I still didn't know who this guy was or what I did to deserve such treatment. Finally, after what seemed like forever he let go of my collar and pants while my face was still pushed against the wall. With my both feet flat on the ground, I pulled the crotch of my pants down to relieve the pressure on my testicles and slowly turned around. In turning, my face was then up against someone's chest. Off to the side was Randy laughing hysterically. I slowly tilted my head back to look up to a familiar face. It took a few seconds for me to compose myself and suddenly realized it was an old acquaintance from gunnery school in Fort Myers, Florida, the biggest guy in the class named Bill Lamphear. He too was laughing his head off. I couldn't help but to ask, "just what the fuck do you think you're doing Cisco." He said, "I told you when you left gunnery school hiding behind that first sergeant I would get you some day for that caper you pulled on me." I said, "aw, come on Cisco, you can't hold that against me, we were just having a little fun, not here in a prison camp anyway." "Cisco softened his voice and smiling he said, "no, I guess not, but just remember you owe me one." Then he put his giant arm around my neck in a bear hug and said, "Fili, it sure is good to see you and Randy made it alive and how the hell did you manage to get on the same crew." Again after composing myself and my voice I Said, "That's a long story Cisco I'll tell you about it sometime when we have nothing else to do."

Back in gunnery school in order to maintain our bodies in good physical condition to accept the rigors of combat flying we were required to participate in sports and do strenuous exercises. Bill Lamphear was the biggest man in the class and like all of us was either twenty or twenty one years old. That was when Caesar Romero played the part of "The Cisco Kid" in the movies. Bill was the splitting image of Caesar Romero so I knicknamed him Cisco. A name that has stuck with him to this day more than forty six years later. Cisco was extremely athletic and his favorite sport was boxing. In fact he had a secret desire to some day be a professional boxer in the light heavy weight division.

In the rear of our barracks at gunnery school was a boxing ring and one evening a series of entertaining boxing matches were scheduled. After several preliminary fights the main event was with a light heavy weight boxer from another squadron. His opponent didn't show up and the match was about to be cancelled. But I talked Cisco into going into the ring because, as I told him, I knew that boxer was a push over and that he, Cisco, could take him on easily. Well, Cisco agreed to put on the gloves and continue with the match. The first round was simple with Cisco and the other boxer just feeling each other out with a few light jabs in various parts of the anatomy. But the second round was different. The other boxer started to show his boxing dexterity and peppered Cisco's face with such rapid fire one two punches Cisco's head was bobbing around like a punching bag so much he didn't know what the hell he was doing. After about one minute into the second round Cisco turned his back on his opponent, threw off his gloves and climbed out of the ring. He looked in my direction and saw me laughing like I never laughed before. Somehow he knew that I knew the other boxer was a professional and was just toying with him. Cisco, started to make a bee line for where I was sitting and knowing discretion is the better part of valor, I high-tailed it out of there and stayed out of Cisco's way for the remainder of gunnery school. But Cisco sent me a message, "Fili, you can't duck me forever, someday I'll get you." Who would have thought our next meeting would be in a prisoner of war camp, of all places. After renewing my friendship with Cisco I began looking around hoping for more familiar faces and sure enough I found them. It was like a college home coming party to once again see those faces that vacated our barracks back in Manduria three weeks ago. Yesterday I was surprised to see Charlie Fascolas and Mel Openshaw. But today brought the biggest surprises. Mike Dellario, Joe Baz, Bill Signs and Harry Lamb from Lt. Edwards crew. Joe Baz told me that when Lt. Edwards finally leveled off their bomber from that spin they were in they all bailed out. But when Edwards pulled his ripcord his parachute didn't inflate and he fell to his death with a streamer following him. Then there were Eddy Clapprood, Steve Kusmirak, Lloyd Kittleson, Bob Peterson, Charlie Fascolas from Lt. Wagner's crew. It was such a warm feeling to know some of the men got out of those bombers before they hit the ground and exploded.

   Everyone was asking about the other crews in the squadron and how they were doing. We had to tell them that as far as we know Lt. French and his crew would be the only original crew to make it back home after fifty missions. It didn't take long to fit ourselves into the routine of prison life.

Within the next two weeks we were to endure two more night raids by the British, each of which succeeded in scaring the shit out of us. By then , however, we were "conditioned troops" with no more Apollo acts from upper berths to beneath beds on the opposite side of that room, or so we thought. Although we still sought, wanted and needed all the help we could get, "bed bottom or no bed bottom."

About the first of May, the air raid siren sounded while we were still locked in our room, why? We didn't know for sure other than they were expecting the return of the bombers that morning. Daylight raids were not as frightening as night raids. If we could see the bombers we might be able to determine their target, hoping that it was not in our general direction. In following a certain prescribed method the 15th Air Force used a constant pattern of bombing. This technique would maximize the destruction of a given target. The formations consisted of six or seven airplanes each with a given target to drop their bombs from high in the sky. The bombardier in the lead plane would identify the target, drop his bombs and the other planes would then toggle their bombs out of the bomb bay. That day, though, we were shocked at seeing them approaching at a lower altitude of possibly twelve to fifteen thousand feet in lieu of the twenty one to twenty three thousand feet. At the higher altitude their direction was revealed by the vapor trails caused by the heat from the engines. While at this lower altitude their direction was revealed by visually seeing them.

Their intentions became quite clear to us, that day, when they turned directly toward our prison compound, a clearly defined military target. Silence was awesome in those few moments, as we watched the bombers approach, with the stark reality of being on the receiving end of our own bombs. Is this going to be judgment day for us? Is this going to our grand exit from the human race? Is this going to be our reward or punishment for deeds, good or bad, in our past lives? Our silence, with wide open eyes and gaping mouths, continued as we watched those bombers come ever closer by the second. Our stares were shocked into reality when we saw the unnatural ripples of air moving in waves, similar to the movement of the ocean's waves, as mother nature's protective covering of planet earth was being disturbed by bombs falling at terminal velocity. We knew it would be only be a few seconds before bomb impact as we felt the sudden gust of air, whose velocity was mechanically being increased, coming into the windows. The first explosions shook the very concrete floor we were standing on and rippled up through the walls we were leaning against. Only a few of the inmates darted to the seemingly protective confines under a bed, the rest of us being awestruck and waiting for "our" bomb knowing that we could do nothing to change it's trajectory. The bombs were continuing to fall, for what seemed like hours, in their ever endless search for something to destroy and their explosive force continued to violently shake our prison floors and walls. We not only could hear and feel those bombs exploding but the smoke and debris hurled into the air seemed to be too close to calm our well shaken nervous systems. We were helpless to do anything but watch — and wait.

Our minds were suddenly distracted from our own perils when we saw one bomber burst into a huge fireball after being hit with an anti aircraft shell. That big red fire ball disintegrated as quickly as it started as we watched the bomber begin it's uncontrollable descent to Earth, we were hoping to see ten parachutes. Our eyes were glued in the direction of that bomber when we saw three parachutes, maybe from that same bomber, slowly descending. One of the parachutists was descending over what looked like a huge oil fire caused by the exploding bombs. He suddenly started to rise in his parachute, a striking example of the rising heat that keeps those hot air balloons above the ground. I could not help him, but instinctively, said a silent prayer that the heat would not erode his silk parachute. Those prayers, mine and everyone's, were answered when after rising a short distance a breeze moved him away from the fire and he then descended to safety on mother Earth. As for the bombers they were attacking a munitions depot a mere half mile from our garrison and succeeded in hitting it a devastating blow with very few bombs missing the target area.

Who knows whether those day and night bombing raids were destined to save us from total boredom, even complacency? Our immediate objective, like that of the Bounty Captain Bleigh and his loyal crewman, was to survive if at all possible. A prerequisite of that was not to succumb to despair. Our long range belief was that this war could not go on forever, that we would someday return home in peace.

During those approximately two weeks of imprisonment in the garrison we learned two phrases which the guards would direct toward us at air raid times. With the 15th Air Force approaching Bucharest in the daylight and the sirens wailing the guards would shout "Adapost", meaning Air Raid Shelter. So we were ushered inside and locked in our room, supposedly as a shelter from the bombs. Again, with the British taking their turn at dropping bombs at night the guards would bellow, "Lumina" meaning lights out. (Ridiculous as it sounds, they would yell "Lumina" when we lit our cigarettes inside our room.) Aside from requiring bowel movements in their stupid toilets every time we heard the air raid siren wail we had very little that we could do except chit chat with our fellow inmates or to play bridge with the few decks of cards our captors gave us to help us pass the time. Still, the total scenario was far removed from what the general public was conditioned to believe about prisoner of war camps through post war movies and television shows. Being on the receiving end of your own bombs made true believers out of us that "War is Hell".

A few days later, the third or fourth of May, I suffered some sort of intestinal attack, to judge by the severe pains in my abdomen. Sometime in the wee hours of the morning I called a guard to the door and requested a visit to the commode hoping that I needed a bowel movement. Nevertheless I could pass nothing but gas and returned to bed, pains and all. It was a long night, the crawling lice being upstaged by the severe pain. When morning finally came, I found that I wasn't the only sick prisoner. Nunzio Tripaldi with his body doubled up in fetal position was enduring pains more severe than mine. This caused us to demand that our captors return the morphine taken from our escape kits and they complied without hesitating. We administered two vials of morphine to Nunzio at one hour intervals. Unknown to us then, his suffering was so severe that, subconsciously, his body remained doubled up and his agonizing groans of pain continued, although he had passed out. We then demanded that he be admitted to the military hospital.

Our Roumanian captors once again didn't waste any time in dispatching an ambulance. Randy and Pop, knew of my pains and discomfort, suggested that I go with Nunzio, but I declined preferring to stay in that garrison compound. My refusal to go on that ambulance trip was to be the smartest move I probably will ever make in my life. I suppose that, like everyone else there, I felt safety in numbers. Around noon, that same day, the sirens wailed again and the long lines to those Roumanian style commodes formed, this time I declined. I didn't know why in 1944, but there seemed no better real laxative for us in that garrison, than the sound of an air raid siren. It was quite similar to our need to visit the latrine immediately after we were briefed on the days bombing missions. In the intervening years, I have learned enough about the subconscious and the psychosomatic to recognize that I was still a sensitive and idealistic young man whose strained nerves over activated my digestive glands to reject that frigen diet of "bland sour bean soup."

When the ambulance arrived we had discovered another inmate, Joe Rendlemen, shot down on April 5, 1944 with our barracks buddies, had severe pains both in his back and stomach. But Joe refused any morphine and opted to stay awake. Both Joe and Nunzio were taken to the military Hospital only a few blocks from the railroad freight yards and passenger station, the apparent target for that day's bombing raid by the 15th Air Force. They were not the only American patients in that ward. There were nineteen American, British and Australian airmen being nursed back to health and the healing of their wounds from the fierce aerial battles. That hospital wing was two stories high. Half of each floor on the inside end was for the Allied wounded prisoners and the other half, on both floors was for wounded Roumanian soldiers. During the blitz on the railroad yards this day a few stray bombs fell in the hospital area and that particular hospital wing. As fate would have it one bomb came crashing through the roof of the section that had only Roumanian patients and exploded as it passed through to the first floor, completely demolishing the first and second floors. All of those Roumanian convalescents were killed.

Who could blame any Roumanian from becoming outraged at such an occurrence. They particularly noted that nothing befell the Allied airmen except for the plaster dust and associated debris. Even our guards changed their attitudes toward us, becoming convinced that we truly were gangsters. We were then hard pressed to find the words to convince our guards that this was an accident. Had I accompanied Nunzio and Joe to the hospital I would have been awake, as was Joe, throughout that entire ordeal. The mere thought of it terrified me and succeeded only in increasing those awful tormenting intestinal pains. In discussing that bomb with Nunzio a few days later he told me that he was either asleep or sedated throughout the bombing and remembered nothing. But Joe couldn't stop shaking every time someone mentioned how close he came to going through those pearly gates. Such an oblivion for Nunzio could only have been a blessing in disguise.

Unfortunately, the Roumanian citizenry had other thoughts on the matter. They were convinced that our much publicized bomb sights were so powerful and accurate that that bomb was purposely aimed at their Roumanian soldiers and away from the Allied airmen in the hospital for the purpose of demoralizing the people of Bucharest. It took some time but eventually we did persuade our guards that it was an accident. We then asked them to please tell the people of Bucharest "that bomb was an accident" and that no apparatus exists that could do such a dastardly thing.

In any event, constant bombardments by the 15th Air Force in daylight and the British at night inevitably increased the number of guests quartered by the Roumanians in that small garrison. When our numbers reached an overflow condition we were informed that larger quarters were being prepared and we will be transferred shortly. Although housed there a scant two weeks, I felt that I had been imprisoned for life. Every minute seems so precious in such confinement. And, the longer the stay, the more precious life and time becomes. The desire to survive intensifies, self awareness increased and the ripple effect of determination emerges as the adult human spirit's supreme ideal. To paraphrase a remark of a South Pacific Marine about strained spirit's dependence on Providence, "There are no atheist's in a prison camp."

Those several weeks in that internment camp allowed us sufficient time to evaluate our position. Our minds wandered to those incredible predictions made before we left the States. Indeed, our very presence in that compound had been so accurately portrayed that we almost believed we were acting out some play or were stand in characters for a novel in the writing.

Recaptured was the completion of our phase training in Alamogordo, New Mexico and our last training flight to the Herrington, Kansas staging area. There we had been issued complete new wardrobes and indispensable gear for the fully dressed and armed airmen. Our planes were being double checked by aviation experts and our minds were checked for any mechanical malfunction, like saying at the last minute, "I don't want to go". Then we had to listen to lectures. We were given warnings of the fantastic casualty rate of the Strategic Air Corps. Only forty percent would finish their missions, thirty percent would end up in prison camps and thirty would be killed. This was grossly under stated as only one crew in eighteen in our original squadron did in fact finish their fifty missions and were returned home.

Our lecturer was a special agent of the Office of Strategic Services, OSS, and a professional spy. His very mannerism convinced us to believe what he was going to tell us. Namely everything that did happen to us, including the gun Captain Christescu laid on the table to scare the shit out of me as he began his interrogation. He told us of the prison camp committees we would be forming; escape committee, nuisance committee, food committee and any other committee we could think of forming. Of course, when hearing this in lecture form we could do nothing but laugh hysterically at such nonsense. Now, as we sit here in this prison camp in Bucharest we are convinced that he who laughs last will laugh best. We were definitely not the last ones laughing. That professional spy really told it like it was going to be. In hindsight, if we had believed him, I doubt if anyone of us would have gotten on that bomber the next morning.

That lecture returned quite easily to my mind because, after only two weeks as a prisoner, I found myself serving on one of the more important committees, in fact I was hood winked into heading the escape committee. Inasmuch as our captors had separated commissioned officers and the non- commissioned officers we required a non-com to take charge. As we all belonged to the first three grades, it was expedient to determine who would be our elder. He proved to be Pop Culver. Pop, thirty eight years old, ruddy complexion, with a happy go lucky smiling disposition, from Joplin Missouri and was forever talking about how many Indian Squaws he had for wives. He never divulged the number. Appropriately he recruited a short order cook and a food committee, the later proved to be a waste of time as our jailers had other ideas on how to feed us.

A few days later while I was talking to Cisco, another fellow joined the conversation. Cisco introduced him as R.O. White one of his crew buddies. During the talk I asked them if anyone had tried to escape? This brought a little laughter from both of them. R.O. called another buddy, Joe Rendleman and told Joe what I had asked. Joe and I seemed to hit it off when we both found that we were from Philadelphia. Joe from West Philly and I being from Fishtown. Joe said, "so you want to know about escaping do you." "I'm no daredevil, just curious." was my reply. Joe invited me over to the curb to sit down while he tells me a story, and added, "a true story." Joe began. About three days ago a few of us decided to try to escape. Besides myself there was R.O. White, Donald Eschback and John Chunka, who could speak fluently in Roumanian. We decided that in the far end of this building here on the right side of this courtyard was a food storage room. If we could slip into it on our afternoon walk we might be able to stay there until dark, which we did. We hid behind some shelving, waiting for darkness when a soldier came in, sat down and started to peel some potatoes. We thought he would never stop and it was hard to keep still since we were only about eight to ten feet away from him. We couldn't even breathe hard and I had awful pains in my stomach from holding in my pee. Finally I had to let it go very easy against the wall and half of it went down Chunka's pants. We thought he was going to smell the pee but he got up and left.

We waited until it was close to midnight and jumped out of the rear window on to the street, but still inside the garrison walls. We crawled on our bellies past a stable, where three German soldiers were grooming some horses and conversing in their language. We made it past the stable to a fence that we could climb over. Joe said, "since I was the smallest they boosted me over first. We landed in someone's yard just as the lady of the house was coming out the back door with the trash." Chunka spoke a few words to her and she pointed in a direction that Chunka motioned us to go. So the four of us started to walk down a deserted street. We ran into two teenage boys who just looked at us with puzzled expressions on their faces. We walked for about two blocks and turning the next corner ran smack into two cars, each with two men in long black leather overcoats. Then two more cars pulled up from the street we just left. They questioned us and Chunka told them that they are out on a weekend pass. That went over like a lead balloon and we were jammed into the cars and taken back to the garrison and to a room on the opposite side from where we are sitting. That's when things started to get real nasty. They started asking more questions that we just could not answer. When we got out of the cars they took their rifles with them, and pointed them at us until we got in that room.

Well, we couldn't answer them so they started to use their rifle buts on our ribs, legs and, when we were on the floor, on the back of our heads. Joe added that at one point while on the ground he felt a boot on top of his head holding him down and could only think, "aw, shit, they're going to shoot us now after beating the shit out of us." But for some unknown reason they let us up and jammed all four of us in a booth that wasn't much bigger than a phone booth and fastened the hasp closed. We were jammed in so tight our lips almost touched. We took one deep breath and the hasp broke. They heard this and came running over to us and the fighting started all over again, but this time we fought back. Suddenly, before they killed us someone came in and put a stop to the fighting and we were rushed back here to our cots. Joe ended with, "I forgot to tell you that we didn't know there was a midnight curfew and no one was allowed on the streets. Those two kids probably got caught and then told those Gestapo men that they saw us.

Joe got up from that curb and said, "that's it Fili, if you want to take the chance of getting the shit beat out of you or worse yet get killed with a bullet in your head, go right ahead and escape." I just looked at him as he walked over to the commode building.

After hearing this tale of escaping and the associated perils, Pop became fascinated with the idea of forming an escape committee and began trying to enlist a suitable leader for it. Although several of our men seemed to have pasts that could be questioned, they were reluctant to assume this daring responsibility. On one of those early May nights, Pop casually mentioned the problem to me and the brick wall he was running into. What he said, should have told me that Pop was a loving administrator but no Errol Flynn type of a leader. Only when he followed it with a lightning -like request that I head it, did I gain my first full insight on that which had become his hallmark. Looking at Pop, right in the eyes with my dumbfounded expression I asked.

"Who-Me". "Yeah! you," Pop replied. "You're kidding I hope." I retorted. "Come on Bill I know you can do it". Pop continued, "I'll give you all the help you need and you can have a free hand." The thought went through my mind with lightning speed and the duties I would be expected to fulfill. I was far from a daredevil, not a brave man in any sense, not even aggressive in life and death situations. In attempting escape, it occurred to me, one could get instantly shot and instantly dead, a fact that told me that such a situation does nothing for ones health and extended life. It also occurred to me that as a planner of possible escapes I could never place myself in jeopardy. It would be incumbent on me to provide directions and sustenance to would be escapees. Another five minutes of dialogue with Pop I said, "Ok, Pop, you're on, but don't say I didn't warn you. I'm going to have some fun with this caper." We shook hands and went our own ways.

I accepted the post because I had no desire to expose myself to risks but did hope to be useful in steering others in the right directions. The assignment proved to be more precarious than I thought. In this compound we had some emotionally immature young airmen who, although brave airmen, could not appreciate the dangers of an attempt to escape.

Anyhow, having accepted Pop's invitation I proceeded to form my committee, that included only one other, Chief Foster, our master lock picker who will be getting lotsa practice. Chief was a natural lock mechanic, ideally suited for this elite committee. However, our aspirations at a cloak and dagger life were destined to be put on hold. We were advised that we would be transferred to our new prison compound the next morning.

It's more than fourteen days since we arrived at this garrison and I began to smell so bad that I wanted to get away from myself. You can imagine how we all felt when advised that this afternoon we will be able to take a shower. We were marched, in groups of twenty, to a building in the center of this garrison, a shower room. Had we known about those shower rooms in those infamous repositories of human suffering in places like Buchenwald and Auschwitz I have no doubt we would have opted for living with our stinky bodies as long as we could. When we arrived at the shower room we were told to leave our clothes in the outer room for delousing and then shower. After showering we put on our clothes went back to "our room" and climbed onto the same bed that was lice infested. Well, I'll say no more except that it did feel good to have some of the dirt, grime and stink off our bodies. I have no doubt those lice enjoyed these clean Americans.

That morning of May 8, 1944 was extremely bright and cheerful and helped to ease the insecurities about our relocation. The air was noticeably still at 9:00 AM when we were ushered into the cobblestone street circling the garrison interior. The usual pleasantness of the guards had evaporated and was replaced with stern and foreboding facial expressions telling us they would not tolerate any nonsense from us wise cracking Yankees. We could not help but notice the flat body truck to our rear that had a mounted machine gun and two soldiers standing ready for action. To be sure, one could almost hear a pin drop. Our quietude was mutually noticeable, our eyes acting as our voices and mildly puzzled expressions covered everyone's face.

Slowly, we began departing through the two banks of huge steel doors where we had entered seemingly only a few days earlier. While most of us took the clothes on our backs as sole possessions, some still had kept their heated flight suits, while others carried the one army blanket provided by the Roumanians. Outside the garrison we were turned to the left and began our march through the streets of Bucharest. In the lead was another flat body truck with another machine gun and two soldiers also ready for action. Once outside we could not help but notice the fresh cadre of guards also with stern looks on their faces. These new guards were young warriors apparently battle field tested who would accept none of our impish ways, and none was offered. Were we scared? You could bet your Aunt Minnie's high button shoes we were. Indeed, the difference between these new guards and the garrison guards was like the difference between strong American coffee and the weak tea they were serving us. Those gentle, farmer type guards, to whom we had become accustomed to talking to, had been replaced by serious, no nonsense professionals. Contemplating these new guards only intensified our concern about this relocation and our new prison camp. Their very presence seemed to almost freeze us into silence and did command our respect. In all honesty, I must admit that they showed neither arrogance nor hostility toward us, nor did they unduly command or rush us. Their facial expressions was conventional for anyone with such a stern task to perform. And, hardened veterans or not, those new guards did perform with calm alertness and compassion.

The non stop march took a little more than two hours. We would have to be blind not to notice the people, the buildings and the life style of Bucharest's citizenry. For one thing, we were shocked to see the billboards advertising American products like Lux Soap and Coca Cola. For another, we gradually realized that the Roumanian people could not be distinguished in dress and mannerisms from our families back in the States. We saw their buildings and stores as near identical counterparts of any in our home towns, their corner food markets and candy stores almost made us feel at home. And we could not help but notice the large number of German soldiers observing our march as they roamed the streets of Bucharest. In discussing our march later many of us seemed to agree on noticing the absence of a hostile look on those German's faces.

As our march proceeded, however, we noticed the crowds becoming larger and some of the people began following our formation. I guess it was about fifteen minutes into the march when some of the younger adults started jeering at us and holding up a clenched fist and calling us murders and gangsters and started moving off the sidewalk's toward our line of march. They then began a chant of words we could not understand. The older adults seemed to understand our plight and remained silent. Our pulses began pounding noticeably at not knowing what will happen next or what may have been planned by those jeering people on the side walk. Like a long awaited gift at Christmas time our anxieties were somewhat relieved on hearing our new guards order those trouble makers back on the sidewalk and as forcefully as pointing their rifles at them. They wasted no time in retreating as ordered. We were convinced that our guards had every intention of protecting us prisoners-in-transit from citizenry wrath as well as preventing any attempts at escaping. Believe me, there is blessed irony in being a captive when you are a well protected captive!

Yet, I could not blame the Roumanian people for their feelings toward us. How would I have felt if they had flown over the City of Brotherly love, Philadelphia, to bomb my home community, possibly killing and crippling many of my neighbors, even members of my family? Had not the west coast of America been on air raid alert the day after pearl harbor? Had not Japanese submarines tried shelling the beaches of southern California? I had to admit to myself, all us Americans were intruders - invaders. And Bucharest, with its beautiful and peaceful way of life, was being systematically destroyed by bombs dropped by airmen like me. Bucharest's people were being forced to accept the atrocities of a war in their country, a war they did not start, did not want and did not deserve. As human beings with fundamental rights to life and private property, they seemed entitled to try retaliation for the encroachment on their human and property rights. The people of Bucharest had a right to feel that their very way of life, of existence, of identity, is being jeopardized. If only we could do something to prevent its extinction. But, we were helpless to do anything for them except maybe say some prayers.

Suddenly, my mind recaptured newsreel clips of war prisoners taken by the Allies in the North African campaign. Those vivid pictures had shown thousands upon thousands of men on forced marches through desert sand and heat, an ocean and a continent distant from their homes, their loved ones and being subjected to the hardships of war prisoner life. Over the many years I tried to analyze or to find a reason for this P.O.W. thing and could never find an answer to the "why" of it. Was it, then, asking to much now that the compassion I felt for those unnamed and disarmed soldiers of foreign nations be shown to me by the average citizen of Bucharest? I can only hope that someday the average citizens of all countries would put the pagan politicians who start these wars out in front of their respective soldiers, to be the first to do battle.

Anyhow, the march to our new compound continued with a more relaxed attitude and no more incidents from the people. As we drew nearer to our destination, that melancholy gradually dispersed like gray clouds being chased by fresh winds. Still no words were exchanged between us inmates only softened looks on our faces. The expressions of our guards never changed, they remained keenly alert of our movements as well as those of the sidewalk spectators following us.

At long last, and with beaming smiles, our new prison compound was sighted. It is hard to describe the relief we all felt seeing that building with its apparent assurance of sorts that those Roumanians were sincere in trying to supply humane conditions to our limbo like status of war prisoners.

ELEVEN

Our new "HOME" was a former girls high school that was taken over by the Roumanian government specifically to house the ever escalating numbers of P.O.W.'s they shot out of the skies. It stood two stories tall almost a full city block long and about ninety feet in depth. It was situated on a neat and very clean street that allowed the citizenry to walk on the opposite side of that street. Its first floor rose about ten steps from the sidewalk. Completely surrounding it, except for the entrance doors, was a high wooden fence topped by spirals of flat sharp and barbed wire. In fact, that fence reached high enough to block visibility from the school's first floor. (The second floor windows, however, provided a clear view.) At those entrance doors stood rotating, round the clock guards, inside and outside. The main door itself opened to a central hallway separating the quarters for the officers from those of the non-coms and an entrance to the huge staircase leading to the second floor. Indeed, no sooner had we entered that entrance doorway when the officers were ushered to the left and the non-coms were sent to the right on both the first and second floors.

At the top of the second floor staircase was an auditorium, elevated about three more steps from the hallway. A Guard was posted before its door, no access to it being permitted just then. Directly below the auditorium and accessible from the first floor hallway was a cafeteria style room where we would be served our meals. Fortunately for our crew, all five of us non coms found beds in the same room and Pop Culver was able to enjoy a single private room since he was the senior non-com in the compound. The battle tested guards who had been assigned as our protectors and jailers during the march through the city streets then assumed their stations throughout the building - inside, outside and in the corner towers. Another two guards were assigned to the halls directly in front of the cafeteria and the auditorium on the first and second floors respectfully. And additional guards were placed at each end of the hallways on the first and second floors. These experienced guards, unlike the overly friendly guards we were accustomed too, gave us the impression that they did not want to become too close or friendly and kept their distance and declined any and all attempts at conversation.

Our entire first day in that new prison compound was spent getting acquainted with the building. It's rear included several courtyards, each enclosed by that high fence and the barbed wire topping. From their towers on each end on the building, the guards could completely oversee those yards. With sour bean soup and brown bread again being our mealtime menu, we had ample incentive to locate their stupid toilets, though we never really resigned ourselves to them!

The morning of the second day brought us all a form of relief, if that is the proper word. Those professional transfer guards were relieved by the older guards from the previous lockup in the garrison. It must have been as amusing as a scene from "Hogan's Hero's" to watch us P.O.W.'s going around shaking hands with these older guards to welcome them to "our" new home. It was just as pleasing for them to be in that schoolhouse than being sent to the Russian front where it has become a real battle for the survival of the fittest. How could we blame them for dreading those snowy steeps, as contemporary news reports confirmed the Fuehrer's forces were faring there worse that Napoleon Bonaparte's Grand Army had fared six generations ago! At breakfast, Captain Christescu had announced that we would meet our new commandant later in the morning. Knowing how calloused some of us smart assed Americans can be at times he asked us to show some respect for his rank. It seemed, at first, a puzzle that he should make such a request. Then, aware of our earlier impish hostilities, each of us decided privately on no further disrespect.

Before noon, a general meeting was called in the center hallway of the second floor, when our new commandant appeared. He was an older man, about 55, over six feet tall and weighed close to four hundred pounds. He had the jolly face of a huge Santa Claus and enjoyed the rank of Colonel. He spoke from the top entrance step to the auditorium. Still, his first address, translated by captain Christescu, appeared to be very gruff and intolerant of us Americans. He simply cautioned us to abide by the rules and to make no trouble for the guards. He further cautioned that one principal rule forbade showing our heads at any window after 6:00 PM and that the guards had orders to shoot at any head seen in a window after that hour.

After that address, the Colonel proceeded to count and check every man in his charge. A table and chair being set before him in the center of the hallway he motioned all the officers to line up to his right and all the non-coms to line up to his left. On the table was a roster of us inmates. The Colonel began calling names and surprised us by being able to pronounce them quite correctly, each man approaching him, saluting him and repeating his name. The Colonel then checked that inmates serial number on his dog tag against the number on "his" roster by asking each to call off his number slowly. His desire was to hear the number spoke as one, three five nine etc. (We later learned that he was rather proud of learning English numbers before arriving here.) For a while, everyone complied, slowly, as requested. As this process continued, each man counted was directed to enter the auditorium, on the stage, guards were stationed.

But in every American group, there has to be a wise guy who refuses to go along with the rules and this group was no exception. Directly ahead of me was Eddy Clapprood, a wise-cracking New Englander, decided he was going to be totally different. At his turn he recited his number as thirteen million, one hundred fifty thousand, nine hundred and seventy seven! With an astonished wide eyed look on his face at never hearing such a large number, the big Colonel stood up and with a flustered look on his face, glanced at Captain Christescu and Lieutenant Hawkeye, picked up his roster and promptly walked down the stairs and out the front door. Christescu ordered everyone out of the auditorium, locked the doors, stationed the guards and then announced the end of this session until further notice. For a period of time we, too, were astonished at what had transpired. Then, needless to say, we all laughed loudly on realizing what had happened. By the same token, that unexpected incident persuaded us that the Roumanian Colonel's gruff tone was pretty much play acting, that he was an inwardly gentle and compassionate man with an unpleasant job. It also persuaded us to believe that the Colonel was determined to do the best he could to try to understand these obstinate wise cracking young American airmen. I was standing in front of the auditorium when Len Bahti came out. He had the usual big Finnish smile on his face and as he passed me he said, "son of a buck, the guys a pussy cat"!

Without my knowledge, too, a scene was being staged for the Colonel's benefit in one of the second floor dormitories. Seven men coaxed Mike Dellario, a professional barber, to cut letters out of their hair so that, when lined up side by side, the tops of their skulls would spell out "VICTORY" to anyone who viewed them from a slight elevation. Accordingly the next morning at breakfast, these seven imps stationed themselves about four rows of seats from the cafeteria's entrance. That doorway being about two steps higher than the floor, the Colonel could oversee the entire hall when he entered. In line with their expectations, he appeared for breakfast and, on entering the large room, hesitated long enough for those seven to stand, to bow in his direction and to recite in unison, "Good Morning Colonel." At seeing this, the Colonel again became flustered, called the guards to escort those men to their dorms and notified us all that we would not be admitted to the courtyards for exercise until those heads were completely shaved! So, in our rooms and in the hallways did we stay for the rest of the day.

With the monotony of confinement "getting" to us, someone proposed the brilliant idea of testing whether those guards outside really had orders to shoot any head seen in a window after 6:00 PM. That someone was the escape artist R.O. White. R.O. was rather young for his experiences, having enlisted in the infantry at only fifteen years of age, then moving to the Royal Canadian Air Force. He transferred to the United States Army Air Corps just after Pearl Harbor and finally at only twenty three years old found himself here in "our" prison camp. R.O. was extremely well built with broad square shoulders, narrow waist and full of perversity. He was forever entertaining an insane desire to tantalize anyone as a means of getting a laugh. (Call it an impish sowing of wild oats.)

R.O. enlisted the aid of one of his crew mates in the person of Cisco, yes, it was my buddy Bill Lamphear. Cisco was just the opposite of R.O. Tall, well built, athletic and with a physique of a light heavy weight boxer that he aspired to be. Cisco was a lumberjack from the northern woods of the Michigan Upper Peninsula. R.O. talked Cisco into a little fun play with the guards, just for that night after 6:00 PM. Yet, Cisco did not fully understand what R.O. had in mind and R.O. had no intentions of telling him. The right end of the second floor was selected for this caper. R.O. stationed Cisco at the far left hand window with him at the far right hand window, the guard tower being in the center of the two windows and about thirty feet distant.

At 6:30 PM the caper went as follows: R.O. at the right hand window would raise his head to look out the window and holler to the guard "hello" and Cisco would raise his head to look out at the guard to determine if he actually raised his gun to shoot at R.O. R.O. gave Cisco the signal and started to raise his head as Cisco prepared to look out the window. But, R.O. retrenched quickly, before exposing his head but still hollered "hello" just as Cisco raised his head. The guard seeing only Cisco's head did just what he was ordered to do and shot at Cisco. The bullet hit and imbedded itself in the window sash. It took several seconds for that caper to sink into Cisco's mind and what he allowed himself to be talked into. Cisco, looked over in R.O.'s direction and saw him rolling on the floor in a fit of laughter.

With a single lunge over several beds, Cisco screamed,

"You son of a bitch, I'll kill you."

Hastily jumping from the floor, R.O. darted out of that room and down the hall as fast as he could possible travel and with Cisco in hot pursuit. When Cisco caught him he just grabbed him by the throat and said, "you bastard, don't you ever forget, I owe you one."

Needless to say after R.O.'s traumatic test we were all convinced that those gentle guards would indeed obey their commandant's orders to shoot at any head. It also served to convince us that R.O. White was the man to watch and warned us not to let him talk us into any of his debacles. To this day, I have never forgotten R.O. or his antics. Somehow, though, he proved to be the most amiable participant in those memorable but least enviable days of our service.

Morning of the third day found us in the dining hall and those same seven men, this time with cleanly shaven heads, again at the same table. As expected, too, when the Colonel arrived, the seven arose, bowed and once more said in unison, "Good Morning Colonel." Determined not to let anybody put anything over on him, the Colonel counted the bald heads numbering seven, shouted "Opt" and began scanning the cafeteria for that "opt" man. (He was looking for the eighth bald headed man.) By then, we were the bewildered parties! One of the shaven seven stood,, holding his hands high, started to spell "VICTORY" with his seven fingers in a move to convince the Colonel that all seven in question were accounted for. He would hear none of this, however, starting to spell out on his fingers "VICTORIA"! As we could not convince him of our non Latin spelling of that word he expelled us from the dining hall and before ever having breakfast. He further threatened no more food until we produce the eighth bald headed man. Fortunately as we started to file out Captain Christescu arrived and a short conversation took place with the Colonel. The big man shrugged his shoulders in disbelief. Turning to us in leaving the hall, this would be gruff man, simply smiled and brandished his right index finger at us naughty boys. And, of course, he rescinded his no food order.

Let me share an observation here. We could hardly have been captured and incarcerated by more affable and compassionate people than those Roumanians. We were to become rather close to the Colonel during our days there. Though playing many tricks on him, which he took in stride, we grew to respect and to even like him. I cannot imagine mutual respect more evident in any theater of war.

Nevertheless, hardships abound in wartime, in any place affected, as a prisoner or as a combatant. We could not expect better treatment than given Roumanian civilians. Simply stated, we were cared for by the Roumanian people with their best facilities available. The food we received was the same provided for their own soldiers in the field. It was just not as nourishing as we Americans were accustomed to receiving. As for work, we were required to do none since officers and non-coms could not be forced to do manual labor under the Geneva Convention International Agreement.

In any detention facility, it could be expected and predicted that medical problems would arise. Accordingly a few of our men at the schoolhouse began suffering sore throats. I believe that Len Bahti, our stocky Finnish co-pilot from Minneapolis was the first to contact this condition, which soon affected about fifteen of us very seriously. Upset by this turn of events and ignorant of what was happening, we demanded immediate medical aid. So, a doctor was sent to diagnose and prescribe treatment. Meantime, the fifteen were segregated in a first floor room to the right of the main entrance. (It seems that this was done fatalistically, in obedience to some indefinite instinct or divine order.) When the doctor arrived, he began his examinations and quickly determined our illnesses to be diphtheria. Pallidly, he advised Pop Culver on procedure, isolation. As Americans we knew nothing about diphtheria. I later was advised it ranks high among the most dreaded of the communicable diseases, that it effects different persons differently and it's after effects can sometimes be worse than the sickness itself. After about a week in the isolation ward in the military hospital all the men were returned to the schoolhouse. Ruddy Len was fortunate, having kept his wrestler type physique in good repair, he could fight off such a dreaded disease. Recovery would come easy for him. With medication, he would be up and around in ten days, although practice would be required to strengthen his vocal cords. Charlie Fasolas, that mini Italian from Beaver Falls, Pennsylvania would have to once again learn walking and talking, a genuine ordeal for an aspiring vaudevillian. Indeed little Fasolas could easily be mistaken for that famous comedian Mickey Rooney, in size, looks and actions. Godfrey, the amiable Australian, would need nearly two months to master walking without buddies at both sides trying to steady him.

Anyhow, as soon as the doctor determined the extent of the epidemic, he immediately set the wheels in motion, less this illness spread to the citizenry of Bucharest, and had the serious cases transferred to the hospital. Early next morning, a staff of doctors, nurses and Orthodox nuns appeared at our doors. Being a beautiful sunny day, the weather permitted their setting up medicine tables in the large center court yard. Everyone had to take the schick test. The medical team proceeded to insert a serum just under the skin on our forearms, telling us they would return in three days to re-examine us all. Before they returned, in fact that very night, my right forearm wore a red spot that almost circumvented my entire arm indicating a positive reaction. I knew then I would have to take a series of three inoculations as did about thirty four other inmates.

After receiving the first shot in our upper left arms we were told that we would receive two more shots at two week intervals and that there might be a reaction from the shot in the form of slight swelling of the arm and nausea. That "slight-sickness" reaction proved slightly euphemistic, in fact, the understatement of the year, of the century. My arm swelled to almost twice its size and I had no choice but to endure an accompanying high fever. I felt extremely nauseous for about two days and could not eat what little food we were served. I can only surmise this is when I lost most of my weight during those days. I weighed about one hundred and eighty pounds the day I got shot down and when I returned to Italy I weighted only one hundred and forty pounds. It goes without saying no person ever gained weight during those days in Bucharest. So severe was the reaction, indeed, I entertained second thoughts about allowing them a second injection. My only real consolation was that I did not suffer alone, for all who had positive reactions to the schick test likewise had positive reactions to that first needle. In the long run, we managed to survive that ordeal, thanking God for the will to do so. Again in retrospect, I must insist that our heritage of American birth helped us overcome a diphtheria outbreak in circumstances where only limited medical facilities were available.

After a week or so, we were informed we could use the auditorium a few hours a day in both the mornings and afternoons. A piano being there, this privilege was pursued with delight. Several of our men were rather good, in fact they were accomplished "ticklers of the ivory's" and encouraged us to pass time a-plenty in songfests.

Aside from the jolly, over weight commandant and Captain Christescu, we had another officer-jailer whom we already had nicknamed "Hawkeye". (Not to be confused with the amiable "Hawkeye" of the long running TV series of the 1970s "MASH". Indeed, we had our "Hawkeye many years before that show "MASH" was ever a gleam in some producers wallet.) We gave that handle to him as he seemed to be squinting in one eye all the time. (We later found out that he had one glass eye.) Hawkeye had clearly become extremely envious of our affection for the Colonel, for Captain Christescu to a lessor degree and for the remaining guards. For some reason, at first indeterminate, we could not accept him. Only in time did this reason crystallize. It seems that an officer in the Roumanian Army could punish a private soldier by beating him manually or in any manner he chose.

A guard arrived late one evening for the changing of the guard only to have punishment administered to him by Hawkeye, but not in our presence. When, the next morning, we saw that sorrowful looking guard with a black eye, bruises on his face and a long gash on his left cheek, he very reluctantly charged them to Hawkeye's belt buckle. It was an unspoken agreement among all of us who first saw these injuries, "we will have to find a way to put a stop to that insane way of administering punishment". That way, surprisingly, came to us later that afternoon.

About mid afternoon, a few of us were relaxing in a song fest and enjoyed the concert hall playing of Donald Eshbock, a likeable fellow of French ancestry from Detroit. Donald seemed to lean toward playing all those classic tunes about Paris and her people, he received no objections from anyone. Entering, Hawkeye approached the piano and asked Donald whether he might play for us. Politely, Donald arose from the stool and, as Hawkeye began playing, we all departed the auditorium and closed the door behind us. That infuriated Hawkeye, to no end, as he ran out of the hall and tried to order our return. We continued walking away from him, however, and only with extra effort did he restrain his fury in the presence of the hallway guards. After that piano lesson, Hawkeye got the message of our backs and our silence every time he tried to address anyone, the word was out. About four days later, Hawkeye collared John Chunka, our Roumanian speaking buddy from Ohio, and asked why he was being treated this way. John told him we Americans don't beat up on anyone who cannot fight back. At hearing this, Hawkeye went into deep thought and apparently got the message and said, he is sorry and that he will mend his ways. No subsequent beatings of any guards were meted out by Hawkeye or any other officer, at least not to our knowledge. In looking back once more, I doubt whether an ethical lesson in humanity had been so forcefully taught.

Yet, we were always puzzled about the "why" of those guards posted in the hallway ends of each floor and away from the staircases. For, even with their rifles and ammunition supply, they could have been easily overpowered by any of us, had someone chosen to jump them. But, then we would have to consider those guards outside whom we could not overpower. Those thoughts were quickly erased from our minds in favor of other American style pursuits, impish or otherwise.

Enter, once again, that diabolic imp R.O. White. One guard, who usually dutied the afternoon shift on the second floor right wing end, always seemed to be aloof and have to much scorn for us Americans. We continually noticed this and, subsequently, drew the particular attention of reformed (?) prankster R.O. One morning R.O. was in my dormitory sitting and talking to a fellow crew member, Ike. Suddenly expressing a desire to determine what makes that one guard so different, he left the room. Sensing that he has something in mind, Randy, Chief and I followed R.O. toward that guard down the hall. Enroute, R.O. met John Chunka and asked him to go with him. At the hall end, where the guard stood, R.O. pretended to converse with Chunka and then began addressing the guard through Chunka, saying that he was a lousy soldier. The distinctive guard replied that he was a better soldier than any of you Americans whom he described as slovenly. R.O. continued with his chiding, telling him that he didn't even know how to salute with a rifle. Quite indignant, that guard began performing the full manual complement of arms, and he was quite good at it, ending with brisk salutes and at attention. Putting two fingers to his nose to indicate that the exhibition stank, R.O. started to walk away slowly. This different guard stopped all of us, acting out the manual of arms again. We told him, through Chunka, that R.O. could do it better than he. Still unknown to anyone was R.O.'s plan.

R.O. started to reach for that guards rifle, who retrenched, insisting that he would be beaten if caught unarmed. By this time there was a crowd of inmates at this hall end to catch a glimpse of whatever caper is going to take place. Chunka assured him that no one will see him through such a crowd and that he would keep a watchful eye for an officer. Reluctantly, handing his rifle to R.O., the guard began removing the bullet clip, but Chunka persuaded him to leave it in.

R.O. took that rifle and started doing the Queen's salute, a masterful demonstration and surprised even us that he could do it. But, as ever, R.O. was full of surprises. After a few practice swings to feel the weight and balance of the weapon, R.O. began showing his ability as an infantryman. From standing at attention, position the rifle at his side, he began a systematic routine of the Queen's salute. Unlike the other observers, I noticed R.O. starting to dismantle the gun. It was fantastic to watch that young man manipulate the Roumanian's rifle. Removing the bolt and the ammunition clip and slip them into his pocket without ever stopping the movements and undetected by anyone including that guard. Even the guard showed nothing but amazement at such dexterity and he even smiled. Having finished his performance, R.O. returned the rifle to the guard, brushed his hands together to indicate his superiority. R.O. then signalled all of us to leave, he bowed to the guard and withdrew himself. I glanced back at that guard who could do nothing but stare at us leaving. Arriving at my room, we all entered. R.O. started to roll with laughter on Ike's bed as he pulled the bolt and the bullet clip from his pocket. No sooner, however, had R.O. returned the bolt and clip to his pocket than that guard charged in, marched directly to R.O., held up his rifle and indicated by pointing that he wanted the rest of his gun. Shrugging his shoulder, R.O. feigned that he did not know what the hell he was talking about. Still, after a few minutes of pleading by the guard, R.O. relented and gave him back his parts, patted him on the head and departed the room. That once smug guard could only look at the departing R.O. with eyes of admiration.

TWELVE

To revert to a repeated refrain, our heritage of American citizenship was not adequately appreciated by us airmen until we found ourselves Prisoners of War in far off Roumania. As proletarians, rather then patricians, we had learned during depression days to treasure the meagerest blessings, a clean bed without lice and bugs, a choice cut of meat, a glass of milk, aspirin for a headache, or even toilet paper! In that schoolhouse-guardhouse, such blessings were as desperately desired as they were mournfully missed.

One day, for example, a guard passed the word that our main meal, which always comprised brown bread, sour bean soup and bland tea, would include "carni". Cursory questioning disclosed that "carni" was meat. They were going to put meat in our soup that day. Such news not only stimulated us but also persuaded us that life there would truly improve in the days ahead.

Anyhow, the long awaited dinner hour finally arrived. Chief Foster preceded me in the chow line and Randy Haney was just behind me. Our soup bowls half full, (a standard portion) we all received that one piece of bread and then filed onto a bench along one side of a table. Then and there, Chief, the rugged, can stomach anything, farm boy from Pueblo, betrayed his weakness seconds after he had sat down, put his spoon in his soup and lifted the contents to the light. Randy and I were, of course being next to him, first to savor that scene! Chief's sigh of sorrow could not but ignite our chuckles. Inside his raised spoon we saw an eye ball rolling ruefully around and seemed to be looking back at Chief, his face turning green, then white. His secret fear no secret any more, Chief dropped that not-so-loving spoonful, rose with right hand over his mouth and made tracks - we only guessed - to the privy! But, did that bother us? Well, I proceeded eating, only to have my first spoonful of my soup prove to have a piece of jaw bone with a few decayed teeth still attached to it. Hesitating slightly, I placed that jaw bone and those rotten teeth in Chief's bowl, knowing that he would not return to it. I doggedly finished my soup and somehow was satisfied, despite its not containing any of that promised meat. Then conversely, a fellow across the table claimed he had just tasted a piece of meat in his soup. Like Chief, however, he soon vacated his seat and traveled in Chief's tracks when he was told that he just ate a piece of that goat's brains. That little "lesson of life" impressed on us the wisdom of the 1940s adage: "Believe half of what you see and nothing of what you hear. and don't accept promises until they are fulfilled."

Boredom could easily have become epidemic in that camp without the ingenuity of fast talking, enterprising and impy Americans. For instance, on the far side of the right end courtyard , outside our dormitory and just beyond the barbed wire covered fence, were apartment buildings apparently occupied by average working people of Bucharest. In one of those apartments resided a lovely young lady who liked to look out her window at us Americans. We wondered what she was thinking. Donald Eschback, being as familiar with the French language as he was with the eighty eight ivories, began to hold daily conversations with her in decibels just short of shouting. Such far flung socializing not being permitted by the commandant, we had to prevent the guard's hearing this daily dialogue about the war's progress.

After about two weeks, a new inmate, who also spoke fluent French, was walking through the conversation area and stopped to listen to them. Having listened for a few minutes, he began laughing hysterically and, after composing himself, told us they were discussing love, not war news. It seemed that Donald was making up the war news to throw us off guard. Needless to say, we started chiding Donald about his amour only to see him become quite indignant. The more indignant be became, however, the more absurd the incident became. For Donald was obsessed with the notion of escaping merely to get married. That little "affaire de coeur" abruptly ended a few days later, when the lovely lass appeared no more. We conjectured that she had been compelled to move by our jailers.

A walk through various dormitories of that compound revealed our many modes of passing time. Having only five decks of cards, we could play that many bridge games at one time. Paul Swearingen, our dedicated and totally professional ham radio operator, would usually be sitting or laying on his bunk drawing radio diagrams, talking to himself in Morse code (we never did find out if he ever got any answers) or by talking to another radio operator in their unintelligible diddy-dum-diddy sounds. Others might be sitting on their bunks naked as bowling balls, their legs spread apart, playing hide and seek with lice in their pubic hair.

In fact, one late-may day, while passing through the hall, I noticed several buddies, at the window in the dormitory across from ours, who seemed to be talking to some people down on the street. I entered to see at close range what was transpiring. Indeed, the makings of a huge crowd was gathering below and across the street. But, all were gazing and pointing some distance down our building, evidently enthralled by a scenario two or three rooms away. With my youthful curiosity in crescendo, I went to that room only to behold the unbelievable. It seems that their side of the school building, facing north, gets very little sunshine. There sat Donald Moffett in a window, his legs stretched and hanging between the bars! Bare as a cue ball, he simply sat there, his two legs dangling and his pecker between them! Believe it or not, Mr. Ripley, Donald was trying to kill as many lice as he could find in his pubic hair. Unlike our parochial school bred girls back in the Fishtown section of the City of Brotherly Love, Philadelphia, those Bucharest babes at street level were loitering and laughing at the sight. There peep show was to be short lived, however. Two guards arrived, dispersing the crowd and chasing Moffett from that window at gun point. Believe me again, Mr. R. they threatened to shoot Donald if he didn't move. Move he did.

Those spring nights, one had to do nothing more than lie still to hear a building full of prisoners scratching in search of those frigen lice, which bothered us most at night because we were trying to sleep. It seemed they were placed there as punishment or designed torment. They would swarm across every hairy part of the body, the armpits, the nose, even up the ass! After starting to grow a beard, I decided against it for three reasons. First, it turned out bright red. Secondly, my crew buddies, Randy, Chief, Paul and Charlie would sit on me, trying to pull it out, one hair at a time. (Plucking my beard may have been there way of idling time, but it cast me in the role of anyone's servant.) And, you can guess the third factor, the lice.

Two weeks or more in that second compound persuaded me to play my undistinguished duty as Escape Committee Chairman. By then, I realized that time had come to devise a getaway plan for future use. That project, too, would serve as added therapy for us idle - but not lazy - Yankee and Limey P.O.W.'s.

Within the next few days, I persuaded Chief to join me in pulling off a few capers. Accordingly he examined the lock on the door immediately to the left of the auditorium entrance to determine if it was pickable. Chief's report was, "piece a cake". So, as a dry run, that door lock was picked, for we were quite curious why the prison commandant had stationed one guard at that door and one a few feet away on the top step to the auditorium.

On experiment day, our prime problem was to distract the first of those two guards, allowing Chief sufficient time to pick the lock. According to plan, Chunka and a few others would begin a conversation with the guard. They found him to be very talkative, the subject being the Roumanian way of life, particularly his home life. Although that trial run dialogue proved interesting to us, as well as the guard, My eyes remained riveted to Chief. Speaking to the guard, we gradually edged him away from the door and, with slight nudging, maneuvered him to a spot approximately three feet in front of the door. That allowed Chief to place his back to the door, though I, for one, wondered what the hell he was trying to do. Picking a lock without looking at it has to be an amazing feat. Refocusing the picture in my mind, I see Chief with his back to the door, the guard directly in front of Chief, (with his back to Chief), Chunka standing in front of and facing the guard, Myself standing to Chunk's left and facing Chief and three other fellows to Chunka's right feeding questions to Chunka to ask the guard. I was concerned about Chief's progress. He stood there, with that ever present silly smile on his face, his hands behind his back, for a period no longer than one minute when, all of a sudden he opened and closed that door. The surprise came so quickly that he made a slight creaking noise in closing it provoking the guard to start turning toward it curiously. But, within his visual range, Chunka also saw the door opening and closing. Sensing the guard's slight swerving, Chunka interjected a quick joke. The guard laughed at it and, in laughing, forgot the creak he heard. To avoid our jailer's learning that we had opened the door, I inched my way closer to Chief, to stop him from leaving, and told him to relock it. Looking at me with his kind of puzzled expression, he quickly covered his face with his special smile on realizing that the door undergoing testing was always checked at change-of-guard time to make sure it was locked.

That door secured once more, we all politely took leave of its guard, went to our dormitory, laughed in a discussion of those happenings and began planning our next move. While sitting on our bunks, I compulsively asked Chief, whether he was a professional burglar and how the hell did he learn to pick locks and still spent so much time on your Daddy's farm. The answer from the Colorado Kid came in the form of another silly smile. Anyway, it was unanimously agreed that, the next morning, with another guard covering that door, we would initiate a similar conversation and conduct an incursion behind that door to determine what is so precious to our jailers.

According to the arrangements for that early June morning conversation was started with the guard while Chief once again picked that door lock. He opened it, slipped inside and this time closed it silently. I inched toward the door stationing myself just two feet from its right side in full view of the bottom of the door. It was prearranged that Chief would put a piece of wire under the door as a signal that he was ready to come out. On seeing that wire I motioned to Chunka to step up the pace of conversation, thus drowning out any possible noise from the door when it opened and closed again. Emerging from behind that door, Chief locked it. And, once again as we rehearsed, we politely took leave of that guard, who resumed his duty of protecting the door. It has to be understood that we did not over look the guard at the top step to the auditorium for he was not in eyesight of that door, however we prepared for any eventuality and had a few buddies prepared to distract him if need be. Back at our dorm, Chief's description of what that door hid was brief but vivid. Directly behind it was an upper landing of what once had been a fire escape tower. From that landing, he descended a half flight of steps to another landing with a fair sized, steel barred window, egress being impossible. He then descended another half flight to a landing with a solid masonry wall, then still one more half flight only to come face to face with another masonry wall. This whole area had once been used as an exit to the courtyard in the event of a fire. But, had been sealed up recently, probably in anticipation for our arrival.

Our concern, more curiosity than anything else, over the placement of that guard became progressively puzzling. A few weeks later, Chunka would question different guards on different occasions, He gleaned from them that the door whose lock we picked was nothing other than a means of separating the guards for their sakes, making it harder for us prisoners to confuse them. Needless to say, we would have to explore new avenues of egress. Finding such a new challenge nothing more than intriguing it was the needed therapy to keep my mind more occupied by day. In hindsight, it was therapeutic for I slept more soundly at nights, in spite of those insidious lice, not waking up restlessly as during those first few weeks of confinement.

The day following our discovery, Chief and I were conversing in the courtyard when, suddenly, (and this sudden sound was not unusual), the air raid siren stirred up our digestive systems once again. Without haste we were ushered to our dorms, our guards reviving their systematic wail of "Adapost" and rushing us inside the ex-schoolhouse and to its attack shelter. The 15th Allied Air Command was about to return and, not hearing the consistent drone of engines at high altitude, we guessed they might be striking the Ploiesti complexes once again. Sadistic though it sounds, we were excited at the prospect of news from our side, for we knew that some unfortunate crew or crews would endure what "should only happen to others." We knew that some flyers would be shot down and that, more than likely, more than a few would be killed. Actually, we were not calloused to wartime predicaments but only realistic to the facts of our condition. Appropriately, escape routes and discussions were held in abeyance for the remainder of that day. The crews in all the bombers that sunny day were more fortunate than on most bombing days as only two bombers were shot down. Less fortunate were the sixteen out of twenty airmen that did not survive that final plunge to earth.

With all the unintentional killings during the battles of Ploiesti for that black gold "OIL" there surfaced a cliche that is probably as old as intelligent mankind and no doubt was first heard when man began his inhumanity to his fellow man. "There are no atheist in the fox hole, or in the unseen bomber and more appropriately definitely not in any prison camp anywhere on planet Earth. Whenever those air raid sirens sounded every man's heart was, besides beating heavily, silently saying, Please Lord, not this time? The eventual easing of our captors' animosity towards us permitted them to grant more hours in the auditorium, where we not only relaxed with more music but grew downright nostalgic, each of us for his home, our prewar values and our life style, like going to church on Sundays.

For example, the Catholics of our group requested that a priest come on Sundays to celebrate Mass. I volunteered to be his altar boy. First, though, chairs were set up in the auditorium for all who wished to attend these services. Then, a table was placed in front of those chairs as an altar substitute. Thirdly, a small table was set to the left of the altar from which the priest might vest. (some sacristy)! When the good Father, short, pudgy and with a fully grown beard, entered, he carried a suitcase containing an altar stone, linens, altar cards, missal, a crucifix, candles and all the items to present the Mass as it should be. His coat removed, he promptly opened the case. Going over, I picked up the altar cloths to lay on the table. However, he looked at me as though I was some kind of lunatic. He snatched the cloths from my hands and placed them on the altar himself while still leering at me. When I removed the altar stone and the candles from his case to try to be helpful he slapped my hands, gave me another blank stare and seemed to be some what resentful of my presence. Those gestures finally sunk in, he didn't want me or anyone else to help him. There was little doubt at the moment that this kindly old priest was either brainwashed about us or, at least, had made a hasty judgment about me as a person. For the time being, he was neither arrogant nor discourteous. But, he did rush through the Mass and through his packing up. Then, the option appeared, certain, he had learned to hate the Allies. For, as he left, I overheard the Good Father mumbling that odious and too-familiar word, "Gangsters!" Anyhow "our" consciences were clear. I had tried to help in the small way I knew, and the large Catholic contingent really did appreciate having that priest celebrate Mass for them, "man of God" or "no man of God". That Mass still helped to calm the savage beast that may have been inside us.

After a full month in that former schoolhouse, our numbers swelled noticeably. For one thing, I distinctly remember a June 1st head count of almost five hundred and eighty six men in the shrunken dormitories. And, for another, we had already begun eating in two shifts.

Soon after June 1st, a group of inmates received permission to organize and rehearse a vaudeville show for everyone in the compound and this included the Colonel and his staff. However, that permission to use the stage area entailed acceptance of a guard posted there to supervise our activities. Past "performances" had taught those trusting Roumanians not to trust us Yankees. That guard was then instructed to keep us clear of the one door to the right of the stage, close to the rear wall. Indeed we were alerted, and decided that we must discover what lay behind that door. Enter Chief and I. Chief gave a quick cursory examination and declared just another piece of cake. Literally the stage was set for another incursion into the unknown, the maneuvering of a guard and going inside that door to find out if this was yet another game they were playing with us.

Again with his back to the door, Chief managed quite easily to pick its lock and, as prearranged, Pete Beyerle slipped through its opening to investigate. Returning in a few minutes, Pete signaled under the door with "his" piece of wire. Whereupon, we readmitted him to the stage. On leaving that stage, the four of us, Chief, Chunka, Pete and myself, gathered at mid-auditorium, where Pete briefed us on another door leading out to the center courtyard. Then, standing by an auditorium window, we determined that, if one could reach that courtyard by night, he could vault over the fence, hopefully clearing the barbed wire topping, without much difficulty and thus escape.

The next day and during the chorus line rehearsal (all male, of course, for the want of female airmen), Chief again picked the stage door lock and went with Pete to try to open that lower level door. He could and he did, but he locked it again for use at a later time. Later that day, Pete decided on trying to escape. Pete was a very special kind of airman, intelligent, learned the Roumanian language in but a few weeks, possessed a rugged complexion, quite athletic and sufficiently daring to try to escape but not sufficiently reckless to take unnecessary risks. In short, we felt that, if anyone could succeed, Pete would. But, Pete did not want to venture it alone, believing two escapees could provide mutual protection, whereas a third escapee would tend to over burden the entire effort. In one of his crew mates, Joe Fontaine, Pete found a willing partner.

The plan called for the variety show to have its final rehearsal on the following afternoon upon our midday return from the courtyard. During that rehearsal, Chief was to unlock both the upper and lower doors so that we could all leave the stage simultaneously. Chunka would be once again assigned to chat with the stage guard and to assure that he and the guard would leave the stage last. In this way Chunka would sway the guard from checking the lock on the stage door. Pete and Joe would slip through the door as the show was ending hopefully during the applause. we would expect the Colonel and his staff would then turn their backs to the stage after rising to leave the auditorium. To further decrease any detection by our jailers, Pete was to enjoy the last act in the show, a squirrel hunting act. Fortunately, when we all left after that final rehearsal, the guards also left and Hawkeye locked the auditorium door and stationed the guard outside until curtain time.

Show time finally rolled around. Most inmates appeared for the entertainment, though some always declined group activities and still others were continually "uptight" from the general prison camp routine. Last to enter the auditorium were the Colonel, Captain Christescu and Hawkeye. Following them were the senior Allied co-commanders Majors Bean and Haas.

Extreme amateurs though they were, the guys performed surprisingly well throughout. Joe Baz sang "Granada" and his favorite "Gianina Mia" magnificently while Chuck Isherwood played on a borrowed guitar, sang a few hillbilly songs and then did "Cocktails for two" almost as masterfully as Spike Jones. We were treated to a superb chorus line of hairy legs and hairy busts. They tried to follow the routine of the Radio City Music

Hall Rockettes and their high stepping and even some tap dancing before the entire line tripped over each other and collapsed on the stage floor! Before those female impersonators rose, we could not help but notice that some had three were there should be two, others had only one and still others had their home made brassieres wrapped around their necks! Everything considered, even those "faux pas" brought solid laughter and, watching the Colonel, we could see him enjoying himself.

It was now Pete Beyerle's turn to do his squirrel hunt. To hunt squirrel, one must remain extremely quiet to avoid scaring it off. This was to be a pantomime act, therefore, it was perfect for Pete. He moved ever so slowly and noiselessly onto the stage with a stick for a rifle and walking on the tips of his toes. Most of the audience, not having seen the rehearsal, was equally quiet as if in anticipation of something happening. On center stage, on his toes, Pete started a slow circular movement with his eyes looking up to the imaginary trees, suggesting that he was searching for squirrels. On completion of his first circle he started shaking his abdomen. When he crossed his legs in a squatting posture, we perceived that he required an immediate bowel movement! Twitching ever more, Pete finally decided that he could contain it no longer. He then went into a semi squat, placed his make belief rifle across his lap and began unbuckling his pants. While Still looking patiently up at those trees, he dropped his pants, spread his legs, as if over one of those stupid toilets, and squatted. With his "gun" on his lap, Pete then fingered his breast pocket, took out a piece of paper and reached around to wipe his anus, as normally done after defecation! While wiping, however, Pete spotted a squirrel in the trees. Without even thinking about it transferred that paper from his anus to his mouth, he lifted the rifle from his lap and shot that sole imaginary squirrel. Laughs from the audience were tempered by chuckles as various men analyzed the absurdity of such an absented minded act. Looking toward the Colonel again, I found him not laughing but rising with his aides and leaving the auditorium quite hurriedly.

"Those Americans have an awful sense of humor," he reportedly snarled in Roumanian as he was leaving.

Pete Beyerle surprised everyone in attendance including myself for I had not witnessed his rehearsal. Who would have dreamed of so extreme a climax to his pantomime. But it did serve the purpose to throw everyone off guard as to what we were up to. With the attention of all diverted from the stage, Pete and Joe easily passed through that door taking with them their little sacks of food to help them on their way to freedom. Both stayed in that stair case until after eleven in the evening when everyone including the guards would normally be relaxed. Everyone else filed out of the auditorium. Hawkeye scowled very disgustedly at us Americans, locked the doors and posted the guards outside in the usual manner.

By prearrangement, we were to cause some dormitory commotion at the right end of the building so as to direct the guards' attention there and away for the center court yard. To accomplish this, lights were switched on at various intervals and different places provoking the guards to repeat their favorite refrain, "Lumina"! (Lights out). In retaliation for that earlier fiasco, Cisco collared R.O. to hold his head before a window for a guard to shoot at. Having been collared twice R.O. exploded. Hollering at Cisco, "You're nothing but a frigen sore head that can't take a joke go do it yourself, I like my head the way it is, even if it's screwed on different."

Just as Cisco let R.O. alone in entered Majors Haas and Beane who tried to order us to stop harassing the guards. As officers they should have known better than to issue such an order or to have involved themselves with the antics of Non Coms. It is a soldier's duty, officer and non-com alike, to try to escape and no one has any authority to order anyone not to escape.

"Drop dead!", we all retorted in unison, feeling free to disregard them. "We don't have to obey such orders."

For some unknown reason — those two Majors — were the most disliked persons in that prison compound, despised, too, by most of their fellow officers. Always unable to "prove"" anything, we questioned their wearing clean shirts, and wearing new shoes as well as their well fed appearances. (All other P.O.W's looked exactly like the post war movies portrayed us.) Though we no more intended disrespect to our military superiors than to our parents, we all felt that these two majors "got under our skins". So having put them in their place, we proceeded helping Pete and Joe finish their getaway attempt. Needless to say, we used extreme caution to assure that — those two Majors — knew nothing of our plans at any time.

On the assumption that Pete and Joe had broken out, the taunting of the guards at our end of the building gradually tapered off. Grave like silence fell on all the non-com dormitories. After midnight, though, when everyone seemed to be asleep or there abouts, the ungodly bark of a fierce dog came into the windows of the dorm nearest the center courtyard and that fence location. By the time I reached it, nearly a dozen guards were hovering about with search lights. Another guard immediately ran up with a ladder and propped it against the fence. One guard climbed the ladder and, for a minute, simply stood there, on the ladder top, looking down. Meanwhile, that dog would not stop barking - something which only added to the commotion. The guard on the ladder top then said something to a fellow guard and signaled him what to do. The guard did leave and, about five minutes later, we noticed that the dog had stopped barking and flash lights were glowing on the other side of the fence. That fence being high and far enough from our second floor window, we could not see what transpired on the other side.

It seemed like an eternity waiting for some clue as to what was taking place. Finally, we knew, Pete Beyerle was brought in through the front door. We could only gasp at the sight of him. His clothes were torn; scratches were all over his face; blood splattered all over him and his clothes and he had the appearance of being put through a wine press. Those Roumanians were no dullards, for they had set thickets of barbed wire six feet high and six feet thick on the other side of all fences in anticipation of catching one or more of us unfenceable Americans. Actually Pete was not hurt badly, he only looked horrible. He later related his tale of woe. He went through the door at the bottom of the stairs, made a mad dash for the fence and vaulted over it, clearing the top barbed wire and landed in the middle of that clump of barbed wire. In doing so he scared the hell out of that little dog on the far side of the fence. And that dog was more a little mutt than a watchdog. We could only surmise Pete's sanguinary surprise as he landed in that sharp steel bed!

Just then, those two majors intruded again.

"I told you so," one of them cynically stated. They were booed back into their own rooms.

We could not help wondering what happened to Joe. We could not approach Pete to learn anything, for the guards kept him apart from us and we didn't want them to start thinking about what really was going to take place. They had evidently called for an ambulance to take Pete to the hospital for treatment. When, after a few minutes, the ambulance did arrive and Pete was escorted to it. Having decided that we had done and seen enough for one day, we agreed to find out about Joe in the morning.

Morning came, and with it, the realization that that day would be different from those repetitious days previously experienced. No one would be allowed breakfast until the Colonel, who was already standing in the hallway, blood seemed to be in his eyes, and he is trying the best he could to hide and contain his anger. Before him stood his usual table and, on it, the equally usual list of inmates in his charge. Through his aide, Captain Christescu, he served notice that we would have roll call before breakfast unless he was told how many men escaped last night. With no one volunteering information, he hurled his huge frame into the chair and started his systematic count. Seeing that he was furious and would tolerate no nonsense, we offered none but complied with his wishes.

After counting his heads, he sent us into the auditorium to avoid any double counting. The first to enter gathered near the stage, some of them going up on the stage, albeit, few knew why. So, with Chunka there, we re-activated our procedure, maneuvering the guard into looking the other way. Since it was unlocked, I opened that door and after Joe had slipped through undetected it was closed. When Chief was counted and entered the auditorium he was ushered to the stage to relock the door. Once secured, everyone stepped down, leaving only the guard on it.

Joe then told us of the plan for Pete to jump the fence first and for him to wait and secure everything before leaping over it to freedom. But, on hearing the dog bark after Pete had vaulted the fence, Joe decided to stay put, especially since it took the guards no more than a few seconds to reach that fence after the dog's alarm. It is puzzling why the guards didn't try to determine how Pete got there in the first place and discover Joe waiting in the wings.

The Colonel, on the other hand, took nearly an hour and a half to count all our heads and dispatch us to the auditorium. But, being shrewd and unwilling to be outdone, he decided to count us again as we left the auditorium. Five hundred and eighty six men went in the auditorium and five hundred and eighty seven came out and the Colonel went berserk. To our exasperation, another "in" and "out" count was performed. When at last finished, the Colonel tallied five hundred and eighty seven in both directions. Walking away and talking to himself like the late Hungarian character actor S.Z. Sakall, he simply refused to believe that he could have made such a mistake the first time!

Exactly how Pete had surmounted that fence, we never were to learn. We had only learned that another avenue of possible escape had been thwarted by our fast thinking and professional jailers. Begrudgingly, we also learned to respect them, for they had judged us as enterprising young men in constant need of surveillance.

More frequent than our breakout attempts were the air raids on Roumania during our internment. Nearly all day raids were staged by the 15th Air Force against the Ploiesti Oil Complexes, Brasov Air Field and Railroad Yards and those enormous Bucharest Marshalling yards. Night raids, on the other hand, were uniformly a British endeavor. Axis news and propaganda notwithstanding, no bombs were ever deliberately aimed at the civilian sectors, only military targets. True, homes and businesses were damages in those attacks, but only from some timing malfunction in the trigger mechanism of a bomb release system.

This aerial attack alternation provoked many and funny discussions between American and British inmates. Trained for daylight flights, we argued that the Limeys were crazy flying so low at night, when planes could be easily framed by those glaring search lights. Conversely, the British claimed that we were foolish flying by day, with dozens of enemy fighter planes perfectly poised to shoot us down. So, that double-shift destruction of the local Nazi machine would provide not only controversial conversation to pass time, but in retrospect, also offer an analogy between us "think big" daredevil Yanks and our "play it safe" subtler English cousins. Insights on our special styles escaped us then because of our youth and over closeness to the action and each other. Each group simplistically thought that the other was stupid in its strategy. As to our "courage", we probably had little of it, more likely a mix of brass, nervous energy and subconscious resignation to death gleaned from our training and wretched life in that compound. Those constant air raids, however, profiled the progress of the war for us. On the morning of June 10, 1944, for example, we were all scared out of the sack by low flying planes that seemed to be trying to rip the roofs off the buildings. Sleeping near a window, I looked up and glimpsed what looked like an American P-38 fighter plane. Later that same day, we heard that the American air command had become downright frustrated at its inability to demolish the Ploiesti refineries and was sneaking in P-38 dive bombers in the wee hours of the morning. Ironically, though, we P.O.W.'s were the ones menaced - not the people of Ploiesti.

The master plan devised by the 15th's General Staff called for a force of P-38 fighter-bombers, each to carry one five hundred pound bomb, to leave Italy before dawn and fly at tree top level all the way to Ploiesti. While the P-38s maintained that low level, an escort of other P-38s and P-51s would fly at 20,000 feet to distract the Germans, i e. monopolize their eyes and radar. The plan seemed perfect, except that two P-51s encountered German fighter opposition and inadvertently alerted the Ploiesti defenders that something was amiss and dispatched other fighters to engage the enemy. They, in turn alerted their anti-aircraft gun batteries and successfully repulsed the P-38s and prevented any bombs being dropped at Ploiesti. In the ensuing battle the first P-51 to be shot down, the pilot bailing out to safety. Following him down, his wingman saw that he landed in an open field and landed to rescue him. With both men in the plane, the take off begun, only to have the rescue pilot pick the tail up too far and drive the propeller into the ground. Within ten minutes both were captured.

(Post briefing reports that this attack was another disaster due to the aggressiveness of the defenders and in particular Colonel Gerstenberg's insidious smoke screens. Of the Planes that flew on this mission, thirty eight were P-38 fighter-bombers and nine were shot down. Of the twenty eight escorting P-38s and P-51s fourteen, just half, were shot down. Many years later in speaking to a pilot of one of those fighter planes I was told that many more were shot down than was reported at the post mission briefings. Why the erroneous reports — it's still a mystery.)

From that fiasco, however, came some updated news long awaited: The Allies had landed on the northern French coast, were soon to land on the southern French coast and the Russians were starting a summer offensive. That news contributed to our conviction that we would not be interned much longer - that World War II was moving toward a climax and an end - soon!

In popular parlance, that bubble of joy burst, within hours. For our delight over D-Day and the new Russian thrust into the hinderland of Hitlerland was abruptly converted into another ordeal of anxiety. The Colonel would order all non-coms at breakfast the next morning to collect our meager belongings for transfer that very day to a new prison camp! So sudden a move could not but visibly shake us. On a few occasions, we had heard the guards say that a new prison compound was being prepared near the military hospital and that we would shortly occupy it. But, that somehow seemed no more than "scuttlebutt". How we wished such "scuttlebutt" was not true! Our destination would prove to be no "new prison" but hell revisited!

About noon, then, all non-coms were led outside that ex-schoolhouse and, as could be expected, again we would be guarded by no nonsense front line battle tested troops. We were then marched, with machine guns mounted on trucks daring us to try to escape, such a thought never entered our minds. We marched in almost the same direction that we had come and, eventually found ourselves back at the garrison! This march was different though, the citizenry of Bucharest did not seem as revengeful toward us. In fact the women we passed had a more compassionate look on their faces, Perhaps it was because of the youthful appearance of most of us.

Though helpless prisoners, we had our senses and sensed to a man that this move was hardly an improvement. Food wise, (and survival is nature's first law), it proved a deliberate degradation. Our rations of brown bread were taken away at "dinner" that first evening and replaced with the worst quality Roumanian sour bread. Terrible as it tasted, we ate it as one of the few remaining barriers between survival and starvation. Every loaf of it, however, was first scrutinized that black cockroaches, bits of stone, glass particles and assorted dirt might be removed! We had only heard of such precautions being taken, but refused to believe the stories. Even when subjected to a non fictionalized ordeal, we found it an incomprehensible problem and experience. To aggravate that bad bread staple, the soup served was more watery! Needless to say, precious little talk transpired that first evening. That first night was worse, the occasion of another British air raid, keeping us awake and edgy. Fortunately, (or was it), they were targeting the railroad - not us.

By the end of three days and nights in that garrison, each of us had become resigned to whatever fate had in store. We were simply enervated - like Mahatma Ghandi on his bed of nails. Yet, every one of us willed to survive. Though resenting the old location and the down graded food, every prisoner managed to rule out discouragement or despair.

(In later years I was fortunate to meet with a Roumanian Intelligence Officer, Corneliu ValJon, who frequented our camps in 1944. I was surprised to learn why we were treated so badly as compared to the airmen who flew on the tree top attack on Ploiesti on August 1, 1943. The men who flew on that first attack were considered hero's and extremely brave men by General Ion Antonescu, Roumania's Dictator in those war years, and ordered them to be treated well being housed in a mountain ski resort near Brasov. Antonescu made this decision since they did not bomb civilians, only military targets. Conversely, he considered the high level airmen that were shot down as "gangsters" and we should be treated as such. Accordingly he imprisoned us as near to military targets as possible, namely the sprawling Bucharest Marshalling yards, as punishment for our inhumane deeds.)

About 11 AM on the fourth day an air raid siren sounded. As usual we were herded into the first floor rooms. Returning there brought to the surface in most of us the fears which we thought we had outgrown. Anxiety over that droning of high altitude bombers was, of course, ritualistic. When it reached our ears, we instinctively looked westward and, when the glittering dots appeared in the sky, we did not like what we saw. The bombers were heading our way in perfect formation. The closer they came, the more our stomachs churned. Once again we saw

Mother Natures pure elements in revolt: Rippling air waves moved by bombs falling at terminal velocity; The sound of falling bombs reminiscent of an eight by four tin sheet held at the top and shaken to produce an ever increasing thunderous crescendo, synonymous with Ravel's Balero. We could see one bomber burst into flames and as they came closer to the ground several parachutes. And once again we had to watch a sad sight, one fellow in his parachute was dropping in on an oil fire in those railroad yards, the heat started to propel him upward until the excessive heat had collapsed his life saving canopy and he fell to his death. We all seemed frozen in our tracks, watching those giant four engine bombers pass overhead like metallic stars, feeling the air waves vibrate, listening to the distant droning of more approaching bombers and visualizing earth and concrete erupt from contact with their bombs.

No one sought our conventional cover under the beds for we were hypnotized by the sights and sounds. That is, not until we were jolted by the first bomb to explode nearby. Like a huge snapping finger, it sent us all scrambling madly for that sanctuary under the beds. There was no doubt about it, we were really scared this time. That first close in explosion shook all hell out of the garrison's very foundation. Nobody spoke and nobody moved for the next half hour or another eternity. Our suffering as prisoners was not finished, after all. (General Ion Antonescu's goal of placing us on the receiving end of our own bombs was being realized.) We were suffering once again, hearing those bombs explode and feeling them shake what little lay in our stomachs, which in turn, lay on that vibrating floor. Like that recurrent theme of Beethoven's Fifth Symphony, a powerful premonition kept nagging each of us: When would "our" bomb find its target and end all this misery? Almost certainly, many guys had persuaded themselves their time had come and, just as reluctantly, accepted death as a foregone fact. Then just as quickly as the blitz had begun, it ceased. Yet, another eternity seemed to pass before the first of us ventured from his bed bottom cover. No sooner, though, did one emerge when all crawled out, each P.O.W. managing a relieved facial expression which he had deemed impossible minutes earlier. Once more in hindsight, that stand up scene seemed figurative of the general resurrection on doomsday.

Later that afternoon, we were told that the bombers had struck that same arsenal less than a half mile away. Thanking God for our safety, we also learned that most of the bombs had found their target. As for the continual convulsion of the floor, it had resulted from the chain reaction of bombs landing and explosives erupting in the arsenal. Thankful again to the almighty, we lastly learned that we faced our final night in that garrison. We would be moved to our new prison camp the next morning.

THIRTEEN

Our third prison compound was prepared on the grounds of the General Military Hospital, where some of our wounded buddies still lay. Knowing that hospital stood only blocks from the massive Bucharest railroad marshalling yards and American bombardiers and their infamous Norden bomb sights had at times proven to be inaccurate at targeting, we became a little apprehensive for our safety and the safety of the entire hospital itself. I, for one, became obsessed with the thought that, if another stray bomb hit any part of the hospital, the citizenry of Bucharest might turn to reprisals against us P.O.W.'s. Worse yet, I pondered, the stray bomb could land on us! Needless to say, then, we kept hoping for no more air raids on those rail yards.

Morning came and, without ado, we prepared to move. Surprises of surprises, when several busses pulled into the courtyard to transport us prisoners to the hospital ground! The distance did not bother our captors, only the time period a marching line would expose us to the wrath of some of Bucharest's inhabitants. No one could fault any of those inhabitants who had suffered personal loss in the lives of family members and property loss from the constant bombings. Within twenty minutes all buses were loaded and were wending through beautiful downtown Bucharest, whose boulevards were lined with well manicured bushy trees circled at the bases with flowers. Center City Bucharest, their metropolis, was as singularly clean and devoid of litter as one of those Pennsylvania Dutch Cities like Paradise, Bird-In-Hand and Intercourse. Apparently the Roumanians had been educated against litter at least two generations before we Americans would enact unenforceable laws to prevent it.

Arriving at the Hospital prison compound, we found conditions far better than anticipated. Not only was everything tidy but a sizable yard was available for our unrestricted recreation at any time of the day or night. Foresighted enough to appreciate our concern over the proximity of the railyards, our captors had dug two air raid shelters with earth covering for anyone wishing to use them. (though many prisoners felt safer in such shelters, just as many contracted claustrophobia from their compactness). As could be expected further specifications of our new "home" included a highwire fence topped with barbed wire and, outside it, guards for the obvious reasons. The clear uncluttered spaciousness of the prison yard provided those guards unobstructed scanning power, guard towers on the corners being superfluous. Encompassed by the barbed wire were two buildings intended for our housings. It wouldn't be too long before they were filled to capacity and another, third building, at the far end would be added. With the persistent bombings of railroad yards and the Ploiesti refineries a ripple effect was the persistent shooting down of bombers which meant more prisoners to house and feed.

The main building in the camp stood two stories tall. It had a center hall entrance from both the front and rear and four huge rooms on each floor - two on each side of the center hall. Both right side rooms on the first floor contained about thirty beds; both left side rooms contained about forty beds; the entire second floor contained about one hundred and fifty beds. One small first floor room was to be assigned to Pop Culver for his duties as the senior nom-com. Once again Pop was unanimously elected our camp leader. His hard earned experiences in life were advantageous over the youthful average age of twenty one years of the other inmates. The other building was one story, could house about forty men and served chiefly as a medical dispensary for the sick and wounded prisoners. When they required major medical attention or surgery, however, we would carry them, under guard, over to the hospital dispensary outside our compound. In general location, our space lay on one corner of the hospital grounds. On its right side ran a narrow dirt road and, across that road, stood a long narrow one story building, also enclosed with barbed wire, prepared to serve as our mess hall and kitchen. In front of this mess hall stretched a fair sized yard. In time we would talk our captors into using it as an exercise area and would then construct a basketball backboard, that some of us might play basketball to idle time away and more important to exercise to keep our bodies in tune.

Such were the features of our third internment center - with features which nearly persuaded us that, somehow, our incarcerated life was going to get better. However, flies in the ointment persisted, viz., the continued absence of adequate sanitary facilities.

In each large room was one basin, with cold water only, primarily used for cleansing our teeth! In the yard stood a horse trough like tub to be used for washing clothes or to take a bath. In the main building were merely two, yes just two, of those stupid floor type toilets for all prisoners in that camp to use. Fortunate as it was that we rarely overate, for those two toilets were usually full as matters stood - literally stuffed on a daily basis, their water boxes not being as serviceable as those back home. You can imagine for yourself how unique a problem that posed when the air raid siren sounded and the line up to excrete and help relieve our intestinal activity.

Nevertheless, our days in that hospital area were spent as pleasantly as possible under the circumstances. With spacious grounds at our disposal, we enjoyed greater freedom and, with trees surrounding us, we breathed cleaner and fresher air. For the non basketball players there were always bridge tournaments. I entered these. And, despite my total ignorance of the game before arriving in Bucharest, I learned to play so skillfully my partner Saul Goodman and I were the pair to beat. Still other guys preferred to sit around a lot, talking to buddies about anything that came into their minds.

We were even to receive visits from the pilots of the Roumanian Air Force, who strolled by and discoursed with us through the fence, John Chunka and Pete Beryerle served as interpreters. Interestingly, those enemy pilots were not different from us. For the most part, they reasoned as we did, our sole difference seemed to be the language barrier.

We were in luck this day in that we are going to get an answer to a provocative question. We wanted to know why they fought us through their own flak on the April fifth air raid on Ploiesti. Their spokesman, a captain and squadron commander, related to us his version of that air battle. He said, "when we knew you were coming to bomb Ploiesti we were extremely excited for that was the first time the Germans allowed us to do battle. We were so excited that we forgot where we were until we saw you drop your bombs. Then we high tailed it out of that flak area." He added. "We know how those flak bursts could scare the shit out of you but believe me they just as much scared the shit out of us. You probably thought we were either extremely brave or would even die for our cause or we were plain stupid. We were none of these, we were just excited to finally get to fly in this war to get it over quickly just as much as you want it to end so you can go home." Just as he finished the Captain of the guard came over and asked them to leave. We all saluted them as they left. Even in that heated war there still was mutual respect for all airmen, friend or foe.

Indeed, I learned a lesson remembered to this day, viz., that all people are basically alike, they love alike, laugh alike, cry alike, are all capable of compassion and all share an unshakable hatred of war. Even the average Roumanian citizens, who managed a few words with us through that barbed wire fence, were as sincerely sorry to see us confined as we were to have visited our hienous destruction on their homeland.

Anyhow, we endured those stupid asinine clogged toilets and another irritant of lice infested straw mattresses and we survived a near epidemic of diphtheria. The first two of these have been sufficiently stated. However, a mid-June incident relating to the third was to become unforgettable.

When time came for the last of our three anti-diphtheria inoculations we all lined up in the yard. A very charming and attractive, rather on the younger side, Orthodox Nun (Mica, as they are called), started administering the shots. Now, medical facilities in war torn Europe being neither as plentiful nor as sanitary as those in the States, a single needle was employed for this service. Having removed the syringe from her needle, the Mica would lay it on a clean tablecloth, take the conventional cotton swab. clean the recipient's arm, clean the needle, then jab the needle into the arm of the patient. Next the Mica would screw the syringe to the needle injecting a portion of the serum. She would then unscrew the syringe and remove the needle and calling for the next recipient. I stood halfway in that line and, as my turn neared, the routine described was hardly becoming prettier. Though my skin was not tough, she had a problem in getting the needle to penetrate my flesh. Indeed, I winced at the two times she jabbed me without piercing the skin. What did the pretty Mica then do? She clutched that needle with her right hand and turned my head away with her left hand. As I turned my head back, I saw her drive that needle into my arm with the heel of her left hand! Believe me, I felt it. After injecting the serum into my arm she pulled the needle out with the syringe still attached to the needle. Somehow, the extraction hurt more that the insertion. So, glancing at the needle, I learned why. It was Bent! She and I exchanged embarrassed glances; She looked at the needle, placed a cotton swab between her thumb and forefinger, straightened the needle as she said, "next". The fellow behind me saw what took place and casually walked to the end of the line. Apparently he was hoping that by the time he again is next she will have gotten a new needle. (I didn't tarry to find out).

All things considered, the Roumanian medical corps did an excellent job of attending our sick and wounded men, notwithstanding their limited supplies and scarcity of technicians and nurses. One day found me volunteering as a stretcher bearer for a wounded buddy destined for the hospital dispensary. Though always confident about my fairly strong stomach, I broke into my first cold sweat, which I resisted, looking at a hole in his right shin through which a cue ball might roll. The appropriate piece of skin and shin bone was missing, leaving an open meat-red wound in the calf of his leg. The harder I fought my revulsion at the poor fellows misfortune, however, the more profusely I did perspire. Seeing this, the doctor on duty directed the guard to escort me outside for some fresh air. That Doctor later told me the reason for my near fainting spell. It is normal for a person to feel this way, but it is not normal for you to stop breathing and that is the reason for the cold sweat and bringing on the feeling of fainting. So, the next time I find myself in that position I will breathe.

While in that hospital prison compound it was nothing less than a miracle that only one of our buddies died of wounds received in combat. On the other hand, our American healthy bodies enabled us to recover from severe burns, some covering entire heads, and from the loss of arms and legs. Those brave men, too, rarely complained, being quite grateful to be alive, to have opportunities for survival of their ordeals and, most hopefully of all, to await seeing their loved ones once again.

As expected, the day and night bombing attacks on Ploiesti not only continued but intensified with the constant strengthening of defense resistance. The commanders of the Allied 15th Air Force were becoming increasingly frustrated. Their frustration was compounded after the abortive surprise attack by P-38 dive bombers that inflicted only scratches of damage on any of the refineries on the morning of June 10, 1944. The German defenders of those oil refineries and railroad marshalling yards, determined that more raids by the Allies were imminent, increased their most sophisticated anti bombing weapon, "Smoke Screens." What bomber commander would not be frustrated in the face of the huge artificial air mass, a man made cloud, effectively concealing the target of targets?

Yes, history has verified that Germany's Commander, Colonel Alfred Gerstenberg, was very capable and calculating. Those smoke generators he had at his disposal were increased in numbers ten fold. Depending on the direction of the wind, he began posturing them in such a way as to emit "his" cloud of smoke more than ten miles in diameter. He decided that one time the cloud would be centered squarely over the complexes. The next raid he would place his cloud over the western end of those facilities and so the cloud would never be in the same geographical location, thus foiling the bomb aiming and dropping point. Invariably, though, his synthetic cloud proved more than successful at muddling the attempts of the bombardiers to locate the oil supply. For despite all those raids on Ploiesti, allowing hardly a brick of the City unturned, the refineries were still capable of producing a number of petroleum products. (in the center of this book are dramatic photographs of Gerstenberg's cloud and details of the engineering data and how his cloud was accomplished with such little effort.

Needles to say, those stepped up air raids by day and some by night hardly helped our nervous systems. In hindsight, we doubt if it would make any difference to the planners of those raids on Ploiesti if they knew how we on the ground were being effected. But as the bombers approached their targets they caused the sounding of the air raid sirens and these sirens served as a sonar laxative, driving us prisoners into long lines outside the execrable toilets. They also drove us to the air raid shelters in overflowing numbers. We had no idea where or when a stray bomb might fall or that a bomber being blown apart in the sky might let go it's bombs before reaching the assigned target. There is no shame for anyone to want to have head cover during those attacks if just to escape going out of their minds. Some of us, who were there, still remember that first night in the garrison. For this reason we persuaded our captors to let us use the main building cellar as an additional air raid shelter.

Beyond providing physical and psychological sanctuary, however, that cellar suggested reactivation of our escape instincts, which, like Bob Hope's sense of humor, refused to be dampened. Before mid June, we had given no thought of fleeing this hospital prison camp. The obvious method would be over or under the barbered wire fence and the problem of sneaking past guards with loaded rifles. It was only a few days after we received permission to use the cellar did we actually need it. When the siren sounded a guard was sent into the camp to unlock the door he then proceeded down the steps first and took his station in front of a huge steel door. Of course Chief and I had to go to this cellar to satisfy our youthful curiosity. The sight of the guard in front of the steel door naturally teased our desire to find out what was behind it. We simply had to set the wheels in motion to go on another exploratory safari.

When our first cellar incursion ended with the all clear siren, we were ushered upstairs by that guard. The last one to leave, he snapped it's padlock shut and resumed his position at the gate outside the fence. Thereupon, Chief and I began smiling at each other again which signaled a resumption of our old lock picking act. And, once again, Chief had no trouble picking the upstairs lock. We volunteered Randy to be our lookout and entered the cellar, proceeding directly to that huge steel door. We examined it's huge lock that was so big I had to hold it with two hands while Chief began his examination. This padlock resembled one that might have been used by the pirate Captain Kidd to seal his golden treasures before he buried them on some sandy beach in the Caribbean Sea. Chief had a small piece of steel wire that he bent into a grotesque form and started to place it into the key slot. A few little twists in both directions and "voila" it popped open. Puzzled I asked, "Chief, how do you do that," He just smiled.

Although the door was extremely heavy, had rusty hinges and had a eerie intersanctum squeak, we managed to get it opened. At first glance the room behind seemed just like any other boiler room. Off to the left stood a large cast iron steam boiler. My training as a steamfitter's apprentice surfaced when I spotted those steam pipes spanning the ceiling, going in several directions to the radiators on the floors above. Then I noticed one steam pipe stretching across the ceiling, turning down toward the floor and behind some wooden boards. We removed the boards and found what appeared to be a tunnel where the steam pipe turned into it's opening. My first impulse was to enter it now while we are here.

"Let's think about this for a minute", Chief urged, and he was right. We decided to reset the boards, leave the boiler room, to relock those big steel doors, go upstairs and lock the upper door so no one would be the wiser. We told Randy what we found and that we would investigate further probably tomorrow.

We three went to the front of "our" building, after pacing off on the floor just where the tunnel began, to try to visualize the location of the tunnel. We determined the tunnel led to the next building across the small courtyard facing our building outside the barbed wire fence. We guessed that it must be at least one hundred and fifty feet away, the distance we would have to travel in the dark.

Impatient Americans that we were, we assumed we had discovered an escape route but we should keep it under wraps, at least temporarily, until fully investigated. Temporarily, too, Chief and I were ecstatic thinking that the Roumanians had finally left a "hole in the dike", we could easily widen with good old yankee ingenuity. Only Pop Culver was to share our discovery. The following day Chief and I asked Randy to join us but he declined and opted to be our lookout on the main floor as we explored the "downstairs, backroom outlet."

Shortly after 10 A.M. on June 23rd, Chief and I re-entered the basement and its adjacent boiler room. Taking the lead into that crawl space, I suddenly developed doubts about what we were undertaking and stopped a moment to ask chief, in the wartime idiom of American Railroads, "Chief is this trip really necessary?" He nudged me onward and bade me stop clowning. Silenced for the time being, I resumed leading him into our abyss not knowing what was in store for us. The going was tougher than we anticipated since the tunnel was only about three feet wide and a little more than three feet high and was compounded by the darkness. There were spots of stinking stagnant water on the floor, disinclining us from getting noticeably wet. Inching forward, I used my hands as a guide, fingering the walls, ceiling following the steam pipe and the filthy floor. At one point while feeling the floor I swear to this day that, at one moment, my right hand touched some small, furry animal most likely a rat. In any event it was hard to determine which moved away faster, my hand or the furry animal. All that time, we could see nothing not even, as Israel Putnam writes, the whites of our eyes. The very slow progress soon became downright fatiguing, for we had no idea how far we had gone or how far we have yet to go. On the verge of turning back I spotted a speck of light forward and at the top of the tunnel. literally Inching forward, as we had been doing, to the source of that light we saw two holes in the ceiling. We had to find out where the light was coming from. Using my fingers I determined that the holes were the access holes in a manhole cover and that they would serve as a good measuring point.

    Chief suggested that we had enough for one day, I agreed and we turned back. Just turning around was a difficult task, making the return trip much more arduous and very slow. When we emerged from the tunnel, we looked at each other and had a hearty laugh at the dirt and grim we accumulated on our clothes, face and hands. As Chief would tell it, "we were as filthy as baby pigs slooshing in a mud hole," Unable at our best to wipe off the grim, we could only succeed at blending it with the so called conventional dirt on our clothes. Re-setting those boards in front of the crawl space, we decided that was enough for one day. So we left the boiler room, locked the door, mounted the stairs and locked the upper door.

    When lookout Randy saw us he had a belly laugh at our expense, insisting that we looked like a couple of poll kittys (Virginia hillbilly lingo for skunk) that forgot they were sloshing in the swamp. Our first imperative was to stop at the basin to wash up as best we could before being seen by a guard or one of our inquisitive buddies, for we simply had no likely story for anyone.

Cleaned after a fashion, Chief and I went to the front of "our" building to determine just where that manhole was located. Looking toward the building on the far side of that courtyard we saw that the manhole was just about halfway between the two buildings. We also noticed that the manhole was between two benches, one on each side of the walkway. I said, "Chief, it's lucky we turned back when we did without disturbing that manhole cover or making any noise while we were under it. Look, there's two Roumanian soldiers sitting on one of the benches." Not sure whether they had been there while we were in the tunnel, we resolved to be extremely quiet when passing under that walkway in the future.

That night, my back, my arms and legs ached like they never ached before. Unable to understand it at first, I suddenly realized that I had not exercised the muscles of those parts in more than three months. They had become dormant from the lack of use. But, my immediate imperative was getting some rest. I put those aches and pains out of my mind and, with little effort, managed more than just a few winks of sleep.

Morning followed routinely. We dashed water on our faces and used our forefingers as tooth brushes, hoping to detach at least some of the food film. It occured to me that morning that we prisoners should have acquired more cavities but, on more fuller reflection, it was realized that tooth decay must be proportionate to food intake, precious little in our case. After "breakfast", if that's what sour bread and watered down tea could be called, Chief and I headed for the cellar door, Randy was already there waiting for us. In discussing our latest adventure, while descending down the stairs, Chief said, "Boy, do I ache all over. This is worse than chasing and trying to grab those little pigs back on the farm. Bill, I don't think I can make another tour of the tunnel today. I'll open the locks and stand watch in the boiler room for you." I entered that crawlspace again, determined to inch my way to it's end. (I wanted Chief to think that I had more endurance than he.) Without reaching even the manhole, though, I had to turn back because of those aches and pains. On surfacing, I unburdened my plight to Chief, "I guess I'm not as hearty as I would want you to believe, boy, am I sore all over." Chief had a good laugh at my misery. So, we decided we had enough for that day, closed up shop so to speak, and left that cellar and we both headed straight for our bunks for that much needed horizontal therapy. That "arthritic" interlude was to prove providential, however, teaching us an important lesson about attempting to escape. An escapee would have to be healthy, and physically fit for the risk assumed, or see his attempt doomed to failure. A few days exercise to tone up tired muscles and improve endurance became a requirement prior to escaping.

Somewhat more rested by afternoon, I walked out to the rear of "our" building and found Cisco sitting there alone. As I joined him, he inquired about our progress on the tunnel project? With a startled stare, I asked him how he knew. Cisco replied, "just about everyone in this building knows what you two lock picking sneak thiefs are doing but we're also aware that we have to respect your desire to keep it under wraps as long as possible." Satisfied, I then informed Cisco of our progress and what we discovered. When, however, I mentioned our sore and aching joints he was forced to laugh. Not hesitating, I informed Cisco that the tunnel was quite small but I still asked him to join our little adventure to determine just what is at the other end. Cisco agreed to help in anyway he could.

I went looking for Randy and Chief and found them in our room and notified them we would try once more for the far end of the tunnel and that, this time, we would use a fresh pair of legs, Cisco is joining us. So, Chief led the way by picking the locks, Randy posted himself as the upstairs lookout and I showed Cisco the crawlspace and urged him to be quiet as he passed the manhole area. As Cisco started to crawl into the opening I said, "Cisco, one more thing," I facetiously remarked to him as he stopped moving forward, "Try not to utter a sound if you accidently put your hand on a furry little rat and it escapes you! They won't hurt you, they're nice little guys."

"Thanks a lot!" he rejoined, staring wide eyed at me.

It seemed like an eternity before Cisco returned, as it turned out he only needed a little more than a half hour to make the round trip. Coming out, he seemed quite exhausted, even somewhat breathless. He paused to regain his breath.

"Now I know why you had sore legs," Cisco acknowledged. and added, "what a waste of time."

As it turned out those Roumanians did plug the dike as the other end of the tunnel was closed off by a set of steel bars set in concrete. Cisco added, "It would take a jack hammer to dislodge those bars." How naive we were to think our captors would overlook anything. When Chief and I found the tunnel we were positive that they didn't know of it's existence. Now, I have to surmise that they are watching us at this very moment and be the ones laughing at us, not vice versa. In the face of that "little" set back we withdrew, locked the doors and went quietly to our rooms to ponder the next move. I kept telling myself that we should not be deterred by mere concrete and steel rod and scratched my head for a new solution. Then it dawned on me that one of our new inmates, shot down only three days ago, had managed to keep his escape kit and voila! just maybe he still has his hack saw blade!

The following morning, I shared with Chief, Randy and Cisco my high hopes of getting that hack saw blade. Cisco volunteered to try to fetch it and, within ten minutes, had done just that. Then, like the marx brothers in their never say die escapades, we all repaired once more to that basement boiler room. This time I led the way into the tunnel with Cisco following me. After passing under the manhole, I began to hear people talking at the far end. The closer we got the more careful we had to be as their voices were getting louder with each step. Being ever vigilant of our movements, to avoid detection, we would take one step at a time and those executed movements were like the blind leading the blind to no where. When we reached the steel bars we guessed that there was only four or five feet between the steel bars and that draped curtain at the end. It was fortunate that the curtain was resilient enough to emit some light for us. Just as suddenly the talking stopped. Apparently those in the room had left for we heard a door close. Luck was with us, they left the light on.

The hack saw blade was about seven inches long and was supposedly made of the finest steel available. The three vertical bars were set about eight inches apart with the two horizontal bars spaced about twelve inches from the floor and the ceiling. The project would require the removal of at least two bars, one vertical and one horizontal providing enough space for a man to crawl through. We started the task at once, as a test, and quickly learned that it would not be easy, patience being the required basic ingredient. Indeed Cisco and I spent at least an hour and a half on those bars that first day but managed no more progress than a score line on one bar. A major draw back was that we had to stop sawing and freeze any body movements each time someone entered the room. It was quite fatiguing that first day and decided we had enough and began our arduous squatting crawl out of the tunnel. At our exit, Chief proceeded to reset all locks. Walking to the wash basins we again pondered how tired one becomes when unconditioned to manual labor. We had better check this out before we go home or we might starve to death for not being able to work.

The next morning, Cisco and I were rigid, really held motionless, caused by our aches and pains. So as we three, Cisco, Randy and I were posted as lookouts Chief ventured to the far end of "our" tunnel for a session at sawing the steel bars. Cisco and I did not venture there again for three days, the time required to regain out mobility. All together, nearly two weeks of sawing and recuperating were spent cutting that first horizontal bar. The work was performed in shifts, one pair of guys toiling in the morning and the singleton working the afternoon shift. It became obvious that a third week would be required for removing the second vertical bar. We decided to try for one cut and try to bend it upward to enjoy escape clearance.

Meanwhile, Joe Baz and Mel Openshaw were planning their own private evacuation. The plan was to hide in the ceiling rafters of the dining room until dark. Then to make their way to the roof, leap over to the next building and down to freedom. When their time arrived, about midnight, Joe and Mel found success in the deserted streets and stumbled their way out of the City. They said stumbled their way because they had no idea where they were heading or what they would run into. The only concrete information they had was, according to the moon, they were heading west toward the Danube River. As those two were threading their way progress on the tunnel continued at a snails pace. Just three days after those two escaped they were escorted back into captivity with us prisoners. Joe and Mel related their tales of escape pitfalls.

It appeared they had no trouble leaving the City except for one altercation with two Roumanian soldiers. They were challenged for their identity and simply hollered to those soldiers "Nimps", Roumanian slang for German soldiers, and the Roumanians promptly turned the other way, wanting no further dialogue. They traveled by night and sleeping in a wooded area that first day.

As they started to walk that second night a funny feeling was felt in their bodily midsections. It was empty and required a fill-up of energy producing food if they were to proceed and succeed getting back to Allied control. They decided to ask for some food at a farmhouse they saw in the distance. So, that's where they trudged and, finding some people outside basking in the moonlight, rubbing their stomachs and pointing to their mouths asked for something to eat. The farmer, his wife and two teenage daughters seemed delighted to help them and invited them inside. The two daughters put on some older American records while the mother prepared some food. For a period of time both Joe and Mel were quite ecstatic and enjoyed the fruits, cheese and cookies. Trying as best they could with sign language to speak to each other and enjoying this repass they did not notice the farmer was out of sight. Joe and Mel gave no thought of these nice people being anything but friendly to us Americans. Just as suddenly, their mouths dropped open when they saw, standing in the doorway, two gendarmes, their arms folded on their chests and twinkling smiles on their faces. These policemen said nothing but one lifted his left hand and waved his index finger, in naughty boy fashion, at these two surprised Americans. The other policeman bowed politely beckoned Joe & Mel to join them outside the house to be led down the road for about a mile and a night in the town lockup. Joe & Mel felt no regrets in their failure to succeed. They were more delighted to have a chance at some decent food for a change and that made it worth while. Their conclusion paralleled Chief's and my opinion that living three months in prison camps on a substandard diet had sapped the strength needed to sustain a human body through physical and psychological perils of escaping those confines.

It was the thirty first day of July, Cisco and I were just cleaning up from a session in the tunnel when a new member of our fraternity was brought in by some German soldiers. He was an Englishman, named Teddy Lancaster, who sported an astounding physique and an equally astounding personality. It was like reading a good book or listening to Orsen Welles relating a tale when in the company of Teddy while he told of his exploits. He could have easily been mistaken for the American Actor Burt Lancaster in his younger days. From our first meeting, I considered it an honor to be associated with Teddy for, If a man's man really existed Teddy would fill that bill of particulars.

Teddy had first been captured at the Dunkirk debacle in June of 1941 and slammed into a Nazi prison camp. He next escaped from no fewer than seven prison camps in Germany, Poland, Hungary and Yugoslavia. He is now in his eighth P.O.W. center. Four years of fending and foraging all over Europe had nearly debilitated Teddy, although it was not visible. He was now disposed to wait it out with us until the war's end. A statement once made by our captors that we Americans might wear native street clothes or uniforms but our mannerisms betrayed us seemed incredible. But, when Teddy made that same observation, we finally accepted its truth. A man of his experience just had to know. We told him of our tunnel caper. Teddy suggested that we forget it, doubting the hostilities would last much longer. Though we respected his judgment, the fellows and I nevertheless told him it would at least occupy our minds and tease our captors.

Several more days of sawing passed when, with only a fraction of an inch to be severed, our blade turned dull and would cut no more. So little sawing still undone, I looked around for a substitute tool. Alone in that tunnel, I tried pulling the bar, hoping that I could snap it apart, but it would not budge. Having started to return to my room, I suddenly put my hand where the floor met the right side wall and felt some kind of a steel bar, picked it up, and decided it might make a good pry bar. I went back, slipped the bar behind the partially cut bar with the end against the side wall and found that, just maybe, one good pull might snap the uncut portion. Gleefully I found that it would do the job perfectly. But, aside from knowing one good pull would break the partially cut bar, I also realized that the pry might slip and make a loud noise attracting some sort of an investigation by persons in the outer hallway. So, having waited until I was certain no one was in hearing range for a while, I braced myself for one final pull to be followed by a mad dash from the tunnel in case any noise I made was heard. The bar did break, and noisily. No one, however, heard me drop the pry bar. When I had withdrawn from that confining hole, Chief promptly secured all the locks and I rushed to my bed of straw with my heart perceptibly pounding like a jack hammer.

Later that afternoon, I informed Pop and Cisco the cutting was completed and we were ready to find our way out of the other building. Cisco replied that a new inmate, tall and slender, named Bud Lewis, would make an excellent choice to go down and checkout that room, that is if we can talk him into it. Having arrived only three days ago Bud still enjoyed his physical strength and Cisco had no trouble convincing him to join our little charade. Cisco then briefed Bud on the do's and don'ts and in particular the manhole in the middle. Bud seemed quite excited about being a member of our little group and planned to enter sometime before midnight.

I didn't enter the cellar after "lights out", (we were still in a war zone with nightly blackouts), leaving Cisco to coach Bud as he knew as much about it as I did. Besides I was aching all over my body from the crawling and the tension caused by fear of being caught in the act. Instead, I sat on one of the window sills at the rear of our building with Randy. We were ruminating about the prospects of draining the prison camp without the guards ever being the wiser. Then, in his attractive southern drawl, Randy asked me not to leave the compound because he felt that something beneficial would happen to us very soon. I Asked, "Randy how could you reasonably feel that way." He replied prosaically, "I just have another one of my hillbilly hunches." Having always admired Randy since we met in Basic training in Atlantic City I knew he was neither a day dreamer nor one prone to wishful thinking. I warily told him I would consider his invitation to stay put.

After scouting the basement beyond the broken steel bars Bud and Cisco reported that the room was the hospital pharmacy with a corridor on the other side of the entry door. Bud reported that he examined several storage rooms and found the one directly across the hall to be the best as it had an outside window large enough for anyone to crawl through. That being all the intelligence needed, we decided to prepare plans for evacuating this Prisoner of War camp. Being late, however, we postponed all planning in favor of some needed sleep. With a sigh of relief that my work had been completed without detection, I did get a good night's sleep.

Morning gently came after a rare sound sleep for which I was thankful. Approaching my bunk, Chief told me of two new inmates that are going to use "our" tunnel this night in an escape attempt. I almost hit the ceiling, but blowing my top would be counter productive and sure to alert the guards to investigate the commotion. Restraint was the order of the morning so Chief, Cisco and I sought out these two upstarts who knew nothing about what they were going to do. We found them in the rear yard and asked them of the particulars of their planned escape. As would be expected they would tell us nothing except to say that they knew what they were doing. They obviously had no plan, did not know what direction they would travel, did not have any food and did not have the slightest idea of how to get out of the City of Bucharest, They couldn't even speak a word of the local language.

All appeals at patience fell on deft ears. We even tried to help them and our help was refused. We tried to tell them of the conditions in the tunnel and again they refused to listen We then considered hog tying them but that was out of the question. They did accept a half loaf of bread and we wished them luck. It was extremely difficult for me to bite my lip as I envisioned a months hard work about to be destroyed by two obnoxious nitwits. (a soldiers duty is to try to escape if at all possible and any of his fellow prisoners, regardless of rank, who try to prevent such an escape could be court marshalled when returned to active duty and be subjected to a long prison term).

About 10:00 PM the newcomers were ready to depart via the tunnel. I tried once more to convince them of the stupidity of their attempt at escaping and that they stand a good chance of uncovering our escape route to the enemy. To say nothing of the hard work we put into it. Again, they would not listen. So I said, "Chief, "go ahead, open the locks for them, and you two fellows must realize that when you enter that tunnel the only way out is at the other end as Chief is going to lock both doors and come upstairs. He is not going to get caught anywhere near you two." They said they understood.

Making it through that crawlspace would alone have been an accomplishment but it was compounded for not knowing where or what they would encounter. As fate would have it, though, when the two reached the manhole area and saw two tiny spots of light overhead, they believed it to be the moon or a few bright stars and slowly began to lifting the cover! Chief, Cisco, Randy and I were sitting on the front step and, looking toward the other building, wondering just how far they had gone or whether some hungry rat had eaten them when suddenly any question we conjured up would be answered. Immediately, then, we observed a flashlight shining down in the manhole area. A few shouts by someone there calling for the guards and a rush of three guards to the area of the manhole. All had flashlights shining down and then two men climbing out of the manhole. When those two zealots started to lift the manhole cover two guards were on break sitting on one of the benches and merely picked the cover off their hands. The light they saw was from a match as one guard was lighting his cigarette. It was easy to imagine the look of curiosity on the guards face as that manhole cover started to rise at their feet. Thus, all our hard work and another getaway avenue was closed, this time by blind stupidity! When the two were returned inside the compound they kept their distance from us three as it would be easy to succumb to justifiable homicide.

With the thwarted breakout attempt reported to the captain of the guard several more guards entered the building and were stationed at the entrance to the cellar. The Captain made it clear that they have orders to shoot to kill.

The following day workman arrived to seal off "our" tunnel entrance with concrete. I went over to Randy, who was standing near the rear entrance watching the workman, and I said, "Well, Randy, it looks like I have no choice but to stay around a little longer as you suggested a few days ago." Randy simply smiled.

All of our attempted escapes had ended in dismal failure some in unpredictable and comical disaster. By the 10th of August we were definitely dissuaded from further attempts. We were the first to admit to it's futility. The Roumanian people were not that aggressive to defeat us but rather we defeated ourselves by shear stupidity. Again in hind sight I think they were having fun with us to detract from their future fears of a Russian occupation of their country and once again being enslaved. Time and solitude had been on the side of Alexandre Dumas' prisoner-hero Edmond Dantes, the Count of Monte Cristo. We had too little time and no solitude. The escape book had to be closed, and it was.

With the tunnel sealed, we relaxed from our avid but abortive efforts. The food improved decidedly, too, when the Roumanians stopped the sour bread. No longer was it necessary for us to examine the bread for roaches, nails and bits of glass before eating it. They replaced it with a sweet bread similar to American rye bread in taste, color and texture. Being mid summer and their crops being plentiful, we were served various salads instead of that sour bean soup. How could we do otherwise than to appreciate those changes?

Similarly, on or about the 10th of August, our first red cross packages arrived. They contained various "C" rations, candy, cigarettes, medicines and concentrated foods. Ironically, though, those dietary improvements, while appreciated, nearly overpowered our shrunken and abused stomachs. They would not have done so three months earlier when badly needed to dovetail with the American meals served on both home and foreign bases. Still, we were grateful for the "C" rations, all stories about them attributed to the American infantrymen in their Pacific foxholes being wholly discredited by us inmates of that hospital-prison. Compared to what we had been eating, they were like home cooking. Along with the food we received a supply of uniforms and blankets. Incidentally, we later learned that these packages were received in Roumania by the International Red Cross about June 1, 1944 but were confiscated and guarded by the Germans who were adamant in their reluctance to let us have them.

The afternoon that those Red Cross boxes arrived, Pop Culver showed some long overdue leadership by calling a meeting of all us inmates. He insisted, first, that one package suffice for one man, who might do what he wanted with the contents. However, Pop then requested that each of us turn over all the food stuffs in his box to Bill Simon, who was doing one hell of a job in preparing tasty and nourishing meals once a day. (All of us were taking turns at K-P to help Bill in the kitchen). Bill wanted to accumulate the Red Cross food for two reasons; to prepare a meal which, under P.O.W. conditions, would be delectable to all and to prepare it on such a large scale that its leftovers might be stored and served at a later sitting. Knowing and using what the Red Cross had sent, Bill intended to put it with the Roumanian supplied food and formulate plans for decent, American type meals. This made so much sense that no one refused. So, no further words being spoken, all the boxed food was placed by the gate to be taken to the kitchen. Needless to note, however, no one surrendered his chocolate bars, chewing gum, cigarettes and the sorely needed tooth brush and tooth paste.

During the many air raids on Bucharest and Ploiesti, the citizens of "our" City had been allowed to pass the camp enroute to the air raid shelter. That structure about two city blocks away had a steel and concrete skeleton and rose about ten stories from the ground. Destined to be the new general hospital, its construction had been halted because of the Allied blitz. But, some of the civilians walking by spoke good English and would encourage us to perseverance.

"It won't be long now," they exhorted. Then we inmates wanted to know more, in particular, what did they know that we didn't know? All kinds of conjectures and claims would then float around the camp.

Having no idea just who these people were and what they were saying we half heartily believed them. An after thought, maybe they do know something. Suddenly, we were given better food from our captors, followed by the long overdue Red Cross packages. And now with those passing civilians becoming more cordial and jovial toward us. For obvious reasons, though, we had learned to believe half of what is seen and nothing heard - an expedient which dulled our insights on those English speakers. Only later did we learn that they were interned British Nationals working in the Ploiesti complexes at the war's outbreak and who were interned for over four years! Their captive life was, however, a decided improvement on ours for, being civilians, they had been housed in guarded apartment buildings.

FOURTEEN

One of the most memorable nights of my young life came on August 23, 1944. Then only twenty years old, I felt more experienced and inured to hardships than men twice my age. Yet, my experience and hardening were with the extraordinary - with the realities of war. I saw myself unversed in the ordinary ways of adult life - ways like working for a living, being faithful to a wife, providing for a family and old age, patiently contributing to civic betterment of my community and the expenses of my government.

I could not refrain from priding myself - as the rest of the guys must have done - for having the fortitude to endure everything inflicted on us during those miserable months. On second thought, had real fortitude sustained us? Had it not been more or less a first fervor, an experimental curiosity, an athletic-academic zeal temporarily channeled into military madness for surviving rather than thriving? Most likely, that was the answer to my soul-searching. Like saccharin substituting for sugar and penicillin standing in for extra white corpuscles, those educated youthful tensions had done the job - nature's first job - of survival.

Unable to sleep, I sat on a window sill next to the rear entrance to our main building. I sat there, looking up at a clear, starlit night and turned my thoughts from myself to deeper truths. I marveled at the vastness and beauty of the universe. I wondered whether many humans on our planet were really ignorant for not envisioning life on other planets. Had the supreme being been so thoughtless, so unimaginative that he had not considered creating other life forms comparable to earth's man but located elsewhere in those stupendous solar systems? I continued speculating about life on other planets. I looked around those heavens for Alpha Centauri, the nearest star system to planet earth, and wondered when will earthman be able to travel the required two years at the speed of light (186,000 miles per second) to reach Alpha Centauri just to find out if life does exist there. If so, would those lives be worth saving? Would they be sufficiently sophisticated to erase war and greed? On second thought, maybe those comic books are right in speculating on the never ending good guy — bad guy odyssey for all life forms where ever they may be.

Looking deeper into space I realized that each one of those stars in the universe is a self contained solar system. Each one, no doubt, has planets revolving around it and with a planet the same distance from it's star as our Planet Earth and that is where life could logically be found. If this is so then mankind had better get on with space exploration to expend excess energies and forget these warlike exercises.

Reality to my predicament surfaced and not being able to prove my theory I came back to earth to once again survey my meager existence in the small confines of a window sill of captivity. And reality was looking around the grounds to see my fellow inmates coping as best they know how. Some were sitting on the ground star gazing as I was, others were sleeping and no doubt dreaming of home. My star gazing done, I left the window sill and sauntered to my room, sat on the edge of my bunk and began removing those electric heated slippers used as shoes since I was captured. No sooner had I reached for the first slipper when the sergeant of the guard burst in excitedly, seized my arm and stared at me with the widest eyes I could remember.

"Pace! Pace! Pace!" he spoke in a quiet but excited tone of a man both crying and happy. That was all he said as he continued to stare into my eyes. I simply stared back at the sergeant timelessly. As a Roumanian for four months and as a four month dweller in the Italian heal I knew that "Pace" meant "Peace". Shedding my stupor, I took full cognizance of what the sergeant had said and asked how much he had drunk. Then, gently and disbelieving, I pushed him away. But, he only became more excited and, trying to convince me, he bent down on one knee, folded his hands as if in prayer and stubbornly repeated "Pace, Pace", He then added "Ma Duce Casa" — "Da Duce Casa" which meant "I'm going home" — "You're going home". That guard was pleading with his prisoner to believe him! Assuming that he was sincere, I took his arm and eased him to a standing position. I held the sergeant's arm for the longest moment and, looking into his eyes, I faintly saw a few tears developing, tears of joy and a happy man. He kept repeating in a low compassionate tone "Pace, Pace" ! "Ma Duce Casa — Da Duce Casa"! Again, we looked into each others eyes for the longest time and instinctively clasped our hands in fantastic fraternity. My gaze traveled to our clasped hands and once again I saw the vision of our hands becoming the golden link of sincere friendship.

That final gesture alerted me to something that had to be done immediately. But what was it, what should be done? As he continued with "Pace" I placed my right forefinger on my lips, asking him to be quiet and pulled him onto my bunk. I knew! His news had to be suppressed until verified, if the entire camp was not too go "ape" with joy prematurely.

I tugged at Randy's shoulder, who slept in the next bunk, and told him what the sergeant was saying. Half awake and half stupefied, Randy glanced at him with one eye and then at me with the other eye and rolled over to try for more sleep. The sergeant and I then rolled him over and made sure he was awake. "Randy, get up", I insisted. "We have to check this thing out to be sure it's true".

We finally convinced Randy and he pulled on his pants all three of us went over to Pop Culver's room. It took the same amount of convincing on our part to get Pop on our side to check this out. Pop was skeptical and was about to ask the sergeant to leave when the captain of the guard entered, his shoes were unlaced, his pants were unzipped and his undershirt was not fully on his back. The captain then confirmed his sergeant's "Pace" plea. I quickly asked Randy to go get Chunka who appeared out of no where with an unusual look of excitement on his face. Chunka later told us that he overheard the guards say the same thing. Chunka interpreted the captain, who explained in official terms just what was taking place. The captain stated that he just heard on the Bucharest radio station a speech by young King Michael. The young king has requested the Germans to leave their country. If they left immediately the King would guarantee that the Roumanian army would not hinder any of their units in the withdrawal. In essence the captain said, "the Roumanian government had revolted against Germany and the German occupation of Roumania and that their first imperative was to protect us prisoners from the Germans". To prove his point, the captain said, "Any or all of us could walk through the gate without being stopped. Nevertheless, he pleaded that we remain, since a general from the Roumanian general staff was on his way to confirm the news". The captain again pleaded, "please do not leave, at least not until daylight". The captain and the sergeant then departed Pop's room. As the sergeant passed me he paused and once again put his hands in a praying fashion and whispered to me, "Nui Ruskie Bucharesti Roumanesqe". His plea meant, "please do not let the Russians take over Bucharest and Roumania".

Though all this had transpired in no more than eight or ten minutes, the whole camp was agog with excitement. Pop advised all who were standing near the captain to pass the word about peace and requested everyone remain in the camp at least until final verification came and reminded all of us that we still need information about the proper procedure to follow. While no one, to my knowledge, left the camp area, no one really slept for the rest of the night. And, while one loud cheer that could be heard miles away was in order, no cheers were raised. We merely spoke to each other about this wonderful blessing of "Freedom" as we were walking around our compound. We felt that we had reached the unitive stage of life, having been purged by imprisonment and illuminated by coming to terms with ourselves - we survived. In any event, our feeling that night closely resembled the heavenly peace of "Silent Night". Less than an hour earlier, I had bade a guard "good Night" addressing him by his title, "sentinela" and he returned that greeting in kind. Now, as I passed the same guard I said, "Hello sentinela". And his rejoinder was quick, and accompanied by a pounding on his chest he said, "Nui sentinela", "Comrade". How ironic and ideal! We were no longer guarded prisoners but all comrades-in-arms against the a common enemy, the Nazis.

It was an unusual feeling walking around that camp and the joy of seeing so many smiling faces was an unparalleled aurora of excitement. I must have walked for more than an hour and decided to talk to Pop. As I entered the building the General's car pulled up to the gate and I quickly went in to advise Pop. I waited with Pop till the General came to his room. The General had with him Captain Christescu to interpret his message.

The General was a huge man. I stood directly in front of him, as close as that Senegali sentry in Dakar. And, as before, I had to tilt my head back to look up into his face. In a strong commanding voice the General explained to us that the Roumanian Government had ended the rule of Marshal Ion Antonescu and with the aid of young King Michael, Mr. Maniu and several other leaders had decided to oust the Germans from Roumanian soil. In a very happy tone he shouted,

"Now, we are on the right side"!

We all cheered heartily. Then, the General raised his hands to calm us and continued with his message. We were told that the new Roumanian regime had met with the German commander, Colonel Gerstenberg, who gave his word as a German officer and a gentleman that he would order a complete and total evacuation of all German forces from Roumanian soil. The General further advised that, while King Michael believed the German commander, he was skeptical and ordered maximum security for the American and Allied prisoners of war that were held in the city of Bucharest. The possibility existed that the Germans might try to abduct us during their evacuation from Bucharest and our protection was extremely high on the King's priority. He informed us that, within eight blocks of our prison camp in all directions, Roumanian tanks are stationed for our protection and implored us not to leave the area - at least not until daylight when we could see where we were going and whom we might encounter. He further advised that, if any of us did wonder and got lost, we should simply ask anyone for directions to the "Marle Stat Majur", Roumanian for the General Military Headquarters. Again, the General repeated in his booming voice:

"Finally, We, are on the right side". The smile on his face was a realization of an awesome burden suddenly being lifted from his shoulders.

He began shaking hands and he reached out for my hand first. Indeed, my hand was nearly lost in his massive paw. The General's clasp was incredibly strong and I winced at his strength. It was a feeling that my hand was receiving the first sign not of surrender but of a new Ally against a common enemy. I had quickly developed some admiration for him and once again our handshake seemed like the only way to achieve universal friendship, the Golden Link. Wasting no time, he took leave of us, saying that he had to go to the school house to inform the other American and Allied men of their freedom. As the General's car pulled away from the gate everyone let out a loud cheer accompanied by much applause. I guessed that every patient in that vast hospital complex was awakened by our thunderous roar of excitement, it being only 2:30 A.M.

Needless to say, most guys spent the balance of that night in private mediation. I, for one, had plenty to ponder. My thoughts returned to that kind elderly lady who stopped a man from planting an axe in my skull and then to the compassion which she showed by wiping the blood from my face. After which the man with the axe came over to me and taking my hand in a sincere handshake expressed his apology for wanting to kill me. My thoughts recaptured that fellow prisoner who had awakened me to save me from being splattered with glass when a bomb exploded outside the garrison. My thoughts noted the facts that the sergeant of the guard first told me about the imminent peace and that the general first shook my hand in his new alliance with us Americans. Paradoxically, I felt humbly proud of those firsts, though, to this day, I do not know why they happened to me. I only know that in Pop's room on the night of August 23, 1944 that General's warm sincere handshake will clutch me for the rest of my life. Cat naps were in order for the rest of that night as the aurora of freedom enraptured all of us in shear joy. I later was informed that when the Russians occupied the City of Bucharest on August 28, 1944 that General was stood against a wall and shot by the Russians without so much as a trial. As the morning sun crossed the horizon, an increasing number of us began milling around the main gate, adjusting to the "feel" of freedom by simply walking in and out without the challenge of a guard. By 10 A.M. a group of us had decided to stroll down the lane outside the barbed wire enclosure and away from that tall skeleton of a building commonly used as an air raid shelter. Our party included Cisco, R.O.White, Randy Joe Rendleman, Nunzio Tripaldi, Duke laughing boy Brioli and myself. (The other men are but a shadow in my mind due to the ravages of time). We covered a distance of about two American city blocks and emerged from that lane onto a wide boulevard type street.

We looked in all directions just surveying where we were and what could we do. Bucharest's citizenry walking by were very friendly, nodding good morning with genuine smiles. They seemed to know who we were which gave us the feeling that their acknowledgments were sincere. Kindness and good will being universally contagious, a wonderful human trait that leaps over the language barrier.

Looking to the right, we were almost magnetically attracted to the sign of a beer mug. Smiling and quickening our pace, we approached the corner tavern, then hesitated to enter it. Instantly, the twelve of us were noticed by the proprietor who rushed outside and signaled us to enter. We did. He quickly preceded us to the tavern center and motioned us into chairs at one large table. in looking around I could not help but notice all the other patrons and the smiles on their faces indicating their delight in our presence. The proprietor snapped his fingers in the universal sign of his trade, ordering a round of drinks for this table. Meanwhile, we all gaily cackled like hens at hatching time, finally releasing that "feel" for freedom restrained during those precious previous hours. Two barmaids fetched a dozen mugs of beer, frosted on their outside and frothing on top. The mere sight of them so excited us that we all stood up and raised our mugs over the center of the table to toast our sweet liberation. And how sweet is was for that mini-second as our mugs approached.

Fate had ordained, however, that we should not drink that toast to freedom. As our raised steins met high in celebration, machine gun fire erupted all over the area. Our beer mugs, tapped together solidly in the same second that bullets blasted windows and walls, were instantly dropped onto that table and floor and fragmented into a thousand pieces, wasting so much of that beautiful beer. In another mini second, our eyes met. We all spoke at once, "let's get the fuck out of here." We dashed madly from that saloon and ran as fast as our weak legs would carry us to safety within our old barbed wire enclosure! Meanwhile, local Bucharest pedestrians wasted no time entering any available shelter.

It took only a few minutes to arrive at the camp and we found it to be lifeless, everyone left for the security of that ten story building at the opposite end of the lane about two city blocks away. Several of us just stood there, for a time, how long, I forget. It was long enough, however, to realize that the word of a German officer and gentlemen isn't worth the energy it takes to speak it. Apparently Colonel Gerstenberg had no intentions of withdrawing from Roumania at least not without a fight. And it was long enough to learn that the retreating German army and the Luftwaffe would not accept expulsion in stride and had embarked on machine gun harassment and indiscriminate bombing to terrorize the people.

Standing in the center of the camp yard, I heard what sounded like two small planes flying at slow speed. In scanning the sky, I saw one ME-109 fighter turn toward our camp and start a slight dive aimed directly for the high air raid shelter. I could see very clearly that he had a small bomb under each wing. I could not help but think to myself "what the hell is this idiot trying to do". It was inconceivable to believe that he would purposely drop those bombs on helpless civilians. My wartime experience was limited to airman against airman, man against man or machine against machine. My first experience of ground warfare and the war against civilians in wartime Europe was a revelation that was hard for me to accept. But there it was in front of my eyes and I found it an abomination, my first real experience of man's inhumanity to man.

Still bewildered at the pilot's tactics, I nevertheless sensed his intentions. As he approached our camp, his height was less than five hundred feet, he dropped one bomb that fell short of our yard by about fifty feet and exploded. When he released it I instinctively hit the dirt and when he flew overhead I rolled on my back to follow him. He flew extremely close to the high rise building and after making a sharp left turn he released the last bomb and fielded it into an open window on the sixth floor. I saw that his timing was right but the bomb went straight through the building and out the other side and exploded when it hit the ground. It was fortunate that the people were inside of the building seeking safety. The other ME-109 tried fielding his bombs into other buildings a few blocks away and out of my line of sight. Air raid sirens were blasting their warnings and the citizens of Bucharest were scurring for protection wherever they could find it. If the

Germans were trying to terrorize the general public they were succeeding in keeping them breathless

After the planes left we all got to our feet and looked around for possible casualties, there were none. We then saw a few men coming out of the earth covered slit trenches in our camp yard. Most of them then left for the high rise air raid shelter. It dawned on all of us that we had sick and wounded men in another building and possibly these same planes might return to drop bombs on them. It was decided to find Pop. We headed to the high rise and on the way met with Pop who was organizing a party to carry our sick and wounded to shelter while others were preparing a safe place in the building. I volunteered to help and in between ducking bombs and strafing attacks we managed to transfer all of the sick and wounded to a room deep inside that building. We also managed to get some food and medicine for these men.

Joe Baz was returning to the hospital for more supplies and stopped to pick something up from the ground. It was a paper packet with a skull and cross bones printed on it. he was examining it when a young girl of maybe sixteen years of age stopped to help him. With sign language and the little each knew of the others language Joe determined that she was telling him that the Germans may have poisoned the water supply and that packet was to be put into the water before drinking. As they both understood each other another Me-109 started diving in their direction. The young girl pushed Joe against a wall and placed her body over his to protect him. Words couldn't describe the felling Joe had for this young girl. She managed to tell him that she was a nurses aid in the maternity ward, and that's where she was heading. Joe just looked after her till she was out of sight.

How nerve racking on us, and more so on the helpless sick and wounded, airmen turned foot soldiers to learn by experience what it is like to be on the receiving end of bombings and sniper attacks. The street at the end of our camp lane was a wide boulevard and once while helping to carry a wounded airman across we had to duck behind some trees as another fighter was diving and shooting at anything that moved. People were running in every direction to get out of the path of the bullets or laying prone on the ground, how many were hit or had heart attacks was unknown. The citizenry of Bucharest had a lot of company in being scared almost to death's door.

With the approach of night, the sun sagged below the horizon and all Bucharest expected a lull in the bomb-bullet outrage. As the city gradually darkened, people started emerging for fresh air. No sooner, though, had the night darkened completely when another round of bombings began. The Germans were flying over the city, dropping their deadly cargoes at random and for no purpose other than terrorization of the people. Again, a mad scramble for the supposed safety of the air raid shelters ensued. Cisco later told me of a horrifying sight. While running across the street to the shelter and away from a strafing fighter he saw two Roumanian soldiers jump into a manhole, they apparently considered it the safest place to be, and that, just as the second man's head disappeared underground, a small bomb from the fighter followed him in and exploded! (Having heard that story, I could not help but to speculate about the gambler's odds on such a fluke of fate). Anyhow, as night fell I went back to our camp to see if anyone needed help. Except for a few other men the camp was deserted. I went inside and found my bunk still in tack and this time with no glass imbedded in the straw mattress. I just sat there deliberating whether to return to the shelter or to just "sit tight". The constant night long droning of German planes distracted me to distress, preventing any conjectures on where the next bomb would land. It seemed these German pilots had devised an incidious way to cause more agonizing pain on the peace loving people of Bucharest. That was to climb to a few thousand feet and then idle the engine and glide somewhere over the city to drop the bombs. This fact alone finalized my decision to stay put in the old camp when one of the gliding planes dropped a bomb about two hundred feet from "my building" killing several of the sick patients and adding additional wounds to others. That bomb shook my bed and convinced me there will be no safe haven this night and decided that even this two story building was unsafe. I retreated with several other fellows to the basement. Fortunately for us, all those locks had been removed from the doors, I remembered the basement's floor plan, a fact that enabled us to descend. That knowledge kept tripping in the pitch black darkness to a minimum.

Incredibly, we had been informed not quite twenty four hours earlier that we were free men - no longer prisoners of war - and that we would be guarded and protected as such. Just as incredibly, we now had to reconcile ourselves to being prisoners of another kind. To paraphrase the song we P.O.W.'s wrote about our predicament, "The Bucharest Connonball", we thought the war was over for us, but the bombers were still flying and the bombs were still whistling. Nor could we feel differently about bombs dropped by the enemy - as opposed to bombs dropped by our fellow Americans. For, when someone is on the receiving end of a bomb, he fears equally from friend or foe. A bomb is a bomb and both kill with equal force. We who have been exposed to even one of them know its destructive power.

Everytime I dozed off from sheer exhaustion, another bomb would explode nearby, shaking the entire building, awakening me and reminding me of my first night in the garrison. During one of my waking periods, I recalled the rats encountered in the tunnel and wondered whether any remained in that boiler room. My mind recaptured those rodents for only a moment when, suddenly, one crawled from my right side up onto my chest. Frightened out of my wits, I could only lie still, thankful for not being able to see it. Though the vermin left via my left side, I was too "nerved" to sleep for the rest of that night.

As morning neared, the bombings lessened to the rate of an explosion every half hour or so. When morning did arrive, we emerged from a frying pan to a fire. From an unprotective rat infested dungeon to a scene of near total devastation. The building to the right of our old confined area and where only eighteen hours earlier housed our sick and wounded was almost completely crumbled. I noticed Joe Baz at that building and went over to him. He was standing there with tears in his eyes looking down at a lifeless body of a teenage girl. It was some time before Joe could compose himself to tell me about that young lady.

While at the far end of our camp a one story building was completely leveled. Two additional bombs had fallen inside our fenced area as attested by the craters. Needless to say, had we known the closeness of those explosions while in the boiler room, our fear would have magnified and remagnified into some geometric progression.

Within four short months, we had been wounded in an air battle, parachuted to safety of sorts, been placed in an internment camp, been bombed out of it by our own planes, gone through a diphtheria epidemic, been transferred back to the original garrison only to be routed from it by British night bombers, been placed into a third camp, been set free, been forced to use the camp as the sole available sanctuary and then be forced to endure the German blastings there too.

How paradoxical that, after these five months as war prisoners and one abortive escape for each of the three internment centers, the first feeling of freedom plunged us into meditation rather then merriment! Or, was it paradoxical, ironic, enigmatic, whatever? That lengthy interlude from April to late August of 1944 had made us airman-prisoners run a round trip gauntlet: the "going" trip to experience such varied emotions as enthusiasm, frustration fear, despondency, aggravation, mischievousness, apathy and disappointment; the "coming" trip to experience the need for emotional control and self illumination. We were young and had been conditioned to fight - to shoulder a global war against totalitarian rule based on militarism. Soon, that war would end. We would return home to the peaceful pursuits of family and business. How were we to adjust, to revert from the Mr. Hyde of soldiers to the Dr. Jekyll of civilians? By medication? By Drinking? By illicit sex? By aggressive hobbies like gambling and auto racing? No! Such "therapies" might destroy our nervous systems and make life intolerable for our loved ones. Capture and imprisonment by a half hearted Nazi satellite, harsh and disillusioning though it was, had "dried us out" and made us accept restraints, taught us patience in suffering, taught us to settle for half a loaf in the great game of life and ruthlessly reoriented us by making us find peace within ourselves that we might impart peace to the world of future decades. Would that those lessons had been learned more gently - not by means of the P.O.W. stockade! But, late 1941 to mid 1945 were war years. And, war is hell! Those unexpected agonies of April to August 1944 had "Grown us up", had been our college of human knowledge. By the wee hours of the morning of August 25, 1944 we were in the unitive stage - unitive and true to ourselves. That in retrospect, can explain our silence and sobriety. I wondered what else might happen to us. My wonderment was soon to be satisfied. And, we wouldn't like that kind of satisfaction either.

Above - The author Bill Fili being decorated at the Dover Air Force Base, Delaware, with the Bronze Star medal for meritorious action in Bucharest, Roumania. Below - The Author Bill Fili standing beside the B-26 Martin Marauder bomber that was being used to drag target for student P-47 pilots at the Dover Air Force Base. Fili was the airplanes engineer and co-pilot.

FIFTEEN

After surveying our ruined prison camp and not finding anyone who really needed any help I decided to go to the high rise air raid shelter where I knew help was needed. On the way I could not help but to let my mind wonder about the real meaning of the word "FREEDOM". I wondered about my family and the people back home in America. Do they really know how lucky they are to have all the freedom they want? Do they ever think about how they would cope if they ever lost that precious commodity? The one lesson I did learn in that prison camp was the value of freedom, for no one knows the real value of it until it is taken away from you.

Most of my group spent the second day of freedom (?) setting up quarters on the second floor of the air raid shelter, particularly for the sick and wounded. All the food and what little medicine we had were wisely stored with the infirmed for safe keeping. Then, the Roumanians stationed an around the clock security guard to prevent any one from entering other than us former P.O.W.'s. While those German bombings and sniper fire continued throughout the second day they did so with somewhat less intensity. We were hoping that this was an indication of some success of the Roumanian Army in driving the Nazis from Bucharest and the Luftwaffe was running out of fuel and bombs. (Perhaps it was a combination of both). The sick and wounded were being cared for with tender loving care by some of our men who had medical knowledge I began to relax. At dusk I took a walk out on the plaza in front of that building. That second evening brought near normalcy for us and the people of Bucharest. The citizens began emerging from their confines, slowly at first, to converse with us Americans. Through interpreters, we culled from those conversations that the local people were generally pleased by our presence and were significantly happy that we were there rather than the communist Russians. They seemed puzzled when they were informed of a

Russian destruction of Ploiesti and they were now marching on Bucharest. Being so close, too, we could not understand why the Soviets had not accelerated their advance to assist those brave, outclassed Roumanian soldiers, whose sole asset was their will to win - something proven by outlasting the demoralized Germans. History did record that the Russians had a game plan of their own that was unalterable and that game plan was the enslavement of all Eastern Europe.

The people of Bucharest wanted to talk about America and why did we travel all that distance just to bomb their small country? They wanted to know how they could go to America to work and live. They asked us to take them with us when we leave. They were asking us for help in saving their freedom - to save their small country from Stalin and his communist domination. We were soldiers who were trained to liberate not dominate and we sincerely wanted to help in any way we could but it was impossible for us to give them any of the answers they were so desperately seeking. It was with a heavy heart that I had to leave those people and their pleas.

That second night was spent at the high rise shelter and more pleasantly with at least two lovely Roumanian girls who wanted nothing more than to be near an American Soldier! I soon found out that flirtation and smiles will also leap over the language barrier. Being young and having an eye for beauty, I refused neither their attentions nor their closeness, holding one in each arm. During all these warm interludes we needed to, periodically, duck into the building when a few Nazis planes came close on their bombing and strafing missions. This seemed to add to the closeness as well as lessen the trauma of being bombed and strafed.

When night finally did come the two lasses did not want to go home. Going to our guarded area after a few hours of togetherness, I borrowed some blankets to be spread on the floor of the plaza for these two Bucharest damsels. Did we enjoy fornication that night? I honestly cannot answer "yes" for their combined "come-on" proved too powerful for me alone. On second thought, too, I am glad that my passions cooled into such pleasant, platonic pastimes as chit-chat, jokes and teasing. I never did determine whether those two sweet young things were ladies of the street. All three of us laid on that plaza under the warm summer star filled sky. When they finally were asleep I left them and went into our area in that building. At sunrise and after helping to pass out coffee and breakfast to our wounded I went out on the plaza to see the ladies but they were gone and so were the blankets. I left them that night never to see them again. Still I was happy to have the opportunity to be gracious to other human beings and so thankful to be able to share what little I had.

Returning to our area I helped myself to some tea - this time with sugar - and pastry and performed a few chores for the bed-ridden fellows. I left those confines and headed for the plaza where I found Cisco, Ike, R.O. and several others in a discussion with an officer from the school house, a second lieutenant bombardier, who had a pistol on his hip, cowboy style. Approaching, I picked up the conversation's trend. It seems this lieutenant was trying to recruit his own mini army to pursue Germans. In fact, he was so intent on retaliation and taking the offensive, he tried ordering some of us to accompany him! So what else could we do but to roar with laughter? Becoming angrier by the second, the junior officer then departed disgustedly.

As he left our group he turned and yelled, "I'll have you all court marshalled when we return to Italy"! That was the first and last time I ever saw the young bombardier. I didn't even learn whether he made it back to Allied H.Q.

When our laughter subsided I asked Cisco and R.O. whether they had ever compensated themselves for that first mug of beer we dropped two days ago. They stared at me as if I were a comedian or a clown. Cisco, replied that, aside from dodging bombs and ducking everytime he heard rifle or machine gun fire, the only spare time he had was to discharge some urine - though where or when remained a mystery! For his part R.O. thanked me for reminding him that he has a discharge to make and said, "don't go away I'll be right back".

No sooner had that hot headed second lieutenant departed when a Roumanian man, in his early thirties, approached and addressed us in broken but fluent English. He had overheard us discussing that we should secure guns for our protection in case the Germans initiated a counter-offensive. His suggestion directed our thoughts to protecting our sick and wounded, some were bed-ridden. We agreed with this approach and began listening to what he had in mind. The man offered to find guns for us but pointed out that, to do so, we would have to accompany him to the opposite side of Bucharest. He would, of course, lead us around much of the fighting in the center of the city. He mentioned that as he came here he had to pass through pockets of German snipers in downtown buildings. We all discussed it and particularly with R.O. since he is a former foot soldier and was trained in this type of scouting maneuver. We all agreed to go with this Roumanian. Our group numbered about eight, Myself, Cisco, R.O. White, Joe Rendelman, Nunzio Tripoldi, Duke Brioli and two others who, today, are but shadows in my aged memory. For more than two hours we trudged the narrow streets of Bucharest and as expected, they were deserted. Nearly all windows were closed with shutters or black drapes as most of the citizens were still hiding and fearful for their safety, the primary concern of all mankind. We too were fearful of the unknown. Calling up the soldier experience of R.O. we walked these streets as scouts. Half on one side and half on the other side and forever vigilant in scanning the surrounding buildings for a gun that may be pointed at us. Quickening our pace, our eyes forever and constantly looking for anything suggestive of harm. We were fortunate, though, as we stayed out of harm's way. The further we walked from our contrived home base at the air raid shelter, the less gunfire we heard and the less destruction of any kind could be found from American, British or German bombardments. We seemed, indeed, to be heading for a residential suburban type community.

With all sights and sounds of fighting stilled, we were beckoned by our guide to the steps of an immaculate and attractive house with scrubbed white marble stone steps. After mounting about ten steps to it's entrance, we were ushered into a lavishly furnished living room. Warmly welcomed in fluent English by someone we assumed to be the owner who directed us to make ourselves at home. Suddenly many people joined us, and our guide began introducing us as the conquering Americans! When he said this we all looked at each other, the question marks on our faces read,

"Just what the hell is going on here"? I changed the tempo of these introductions and asked our guide about the guns we came here for. His reply, " We just sent someone for them and they will return shortly. So, please, enjoy your stay with rest and relaxation". It did not take long for this home to overflow with people. Men and women starting to spread enough food and liquor to really whet our appetites too long undernourished. We were then served those fine solid and liquid refreshments. One extremely beautiful young lady put on the latest Bing Crosby records, whereupon Cisco, not at all a bashful boy, seized her around her small and fragile waist and started dancing. We must have eaten and drunk their delicious liquors and wines for more than an hour. Our host became super charged from alcohol and began boasting of his wartime exploits. He even brought out a cash box and showed us about $300,000.00 in American money. Then started showing photographs which he had of Roosevelt and Churchill at the secret Casablanca conference. Things just did not seem to click from where I was standing. I felt I was right in the middle of a fire that was about to blaze. I looked around that living room and suddenly it dawned on me there were Stars of David in every form all around that home. There was one huge six pointed star on the fireplace mantle that had letters that read "IRGUND". (Many years later I learned that these people may have been the advance cadre or similar group poised to establish the nation of Israel.)

It dawned on me that we were in a Jewish community A fact confirmed when an elderly man entered the front door wearing a shamulka, then I noticed most of the other men wearing one also. But, at that instant it seemed we were all hit by lightening at the same time and in unison became aware of the scenario. I pulled Cisco aside and asked if he was getting the same vibes as I was and he said, "funny you should ask, because I was going to ask you the same thing".

We perceived that we had been lured there on false pretenses, that we were not going to be given any guns or ammunition. On the contrary, we had been brought there, rather, to stimulate the morale of the Jewish community. How had these people obtained all the latest Bing Crosby records, including White Christmas? Where had they gotten those American green backs? Top secret photographs? How had they escaped the Jewish purge started by, as I was led to believe, Marshall Ion Antonescu and his Iron Guard in Roumania even before Hitler started his purge? (Indeed, the Fuehrer was supposed to have copied from Antonescu). Unlike millions of Jews who did suffer extreme cruelty, even death, in the ovens and gas chambers at Buchenwald, Auschwitz and other infamous depositories of man's inhumanity to man, these people were living in the lap of luxury. It seemed a fair bet that they represented some tie in between two warring factions. Were these people the advance guard or cadre to establish the state of Israel? We didn't know the answers to our many queries and did not want to ask as our sole purpose was survival of ourselves and our fellow P.O.W.'s. It was a sure bet that we were not going to be caught in the middle of someone else's war. Politely, I asked our guide, again, about out guns. This time his reply was, "There will be a slight delay until tomorrow morning". As politely as we could we thanked our host for his hospitality and told him and his guests we had to leave. They tried to persuade us to stay but we left post haste. Once outside we walked briskly to the corner , then turned and ran as fast as we could for a few blocks in the direction of the sounds of gunfire. We had been used as pawns to satisfy someone's ego. We didn't like it one bit.

Deciding against returning by the same route, we tried to sense a straight line course back to the shelter even if we had to run the crossfire of snipers and some bombs. The gun fire heard was not continuous but more or less sporadic as though snipers were being located and flushed out or killed. Occasional airplanes, too, were heard flying at moderate altitudes.

As we neared the center of Bucharest we heard the dreaded drone of fleets of bombers from Italy, the drone that put fear into our intestines when we were in the garrison or the school house. Then we could see them, what appeared to be several groups of B-24 Liberators passing over the city heading west. Again we heard the thunderous roar of falling five hundred pound bombs, a roar that would make even the Egyptian mummies cringe with fear. We later found out that the Roumanian Military with the help of Paul, (Destiny Deb's radio operator) built a transmitter in a down town bank vault and managed to contact Allied radio in Cairo. Their radio message, relayed to Allied Headquarters in Bari, Italy, of the plight of the Roumanian people and their desperate need for military assistance and the need for a bomb run to eliminate the terrorization by the German Luftwaffe. The bomb run requested was to eliminate the two German held airfields to the northwest of Bucharest. The Germans had a division of troops to the west of one field and they too saw the bombers approach and one of those unfortunate situations of war occurred on the perimeter of that airfield. When the German commander realized where those bombs were going to be dropped he pulled his men back and the Roumanians thought they had a rout going and proceeded after the retreating Germans. The bombs rendered the airfield ineffective for airplanes but in the process killed hundreds of Roumanian soldiers with hundreds of German soldiers. The Roumanian commander was not advised of this bombing effort to eliminate the indiscriminate bombings by the Germans.

Those bombers were a beautiful sight but did they know about our situation? Did they know that we were waiting to be rescued? Apparently not! Anyhow, we decided to split up and myself with two other nameless buddies, the others went another way, we chose a route that took us through the business district of Bucharest. There, we saw countless buildings damaged by recently exploding bombs, dust was still in the air. We were on one side of a park like square when an air raid siren sounded. Spotting a doorway we ducked into it and into the company of Bucharest Citizens who looked at us strangely, knowing that we were not from of their community. All our heads turned to the door as the plane dropped another bomb in the empty center of the square, sped away and never returned. That was the last German plane I saw, obviously it was a last ditch effort.

Again, all of us in that doorway started looking at each other. Noticing their wondering, I said pointing to myself and the others, "Americans". One of the citizens, a man, nodded his head, repeating, "Americans". When he told the others our nationality, their inquisitive looking faces transformed into smiles, and then into sheer delight. No sooner did the all clear siren sound when several men started yelling, "Americans! Americans"!, prompting a sizable crowd to gather about rapidly.

Adults and children approached us, patting our backs and repeating, "Americans"! The joy on the faces of the children was something to behold. It told us that even the little children in that small country realized the value of freedom.

We could not help but wonder at their happiness in seeing us. Indeed, the phenomenon experienced was equally new and incomprehensible. Just then a man and a woman approached me, asking in English, " when will the rest of the American army come to Bucharest"? I replied, "I don't think they will be coming because they are too far away". I added, "we were just released from a prisoner of war camp at the Hospital and we are trying to find help to protect our sick and wounded from the Germans". Then the woman turned and shouted to the other people in that square, "we must have the American army come to Bucharest to protect us from the Communists." She was almost hysterical and turning back to me both she and the man (I assumed the man was her husband) fell on their knees and, with hands joined as if in prayer, begged us not to let the Communists enter their country! It was a tormenting gesture, one that I have never seen before, a gesture that was repeated, with the kneeling in prayer, in unison by so many other citizens of Bucharest. Like the lepers seeking a permanent cure they went down on knees en masse to us, a small group of American flyers in tattered clothes, begging us to help save their freedom and keep Stalin's Communists out of Roumania!

I am neither a politician nor a historian, not even an educated man. But, when rank and file people like myself are as afraid of an ideology as those Roumanians were of Communism, I know something must be wrong. How badly they wanted to enjoy our way of life instead of that soon to be forced upon them. How I wished with all my being that I could somehow, in someway, might help those lovely peaceful folks in Bucharest! I couldn't, though, and suffered sheer torment at having to leave them so totally disadvantaged and dependent. Harder yet, was to leave the children who were pulling at our clothes in an effort to have us stay.

We finally made it back to the air raid shelter and found that things were much calmer. The medics were more relaxed because they obtained some medicine and morphine to ease the pain and suffering of those who needed it. Food was plentiful and the general morale of everyone was greatly improved. Night came easy for me just the sight of a cot, even though it had the same strawfilled and lice infested mattress, brought a few well deserved gapping yawns. Sleep did not come easy. My mind would not get into step with my body, as I kept remembering the events of that day. One community of Bucharest had been spared any destruction, not even at the hands of the Nazis, it's inhabitants being obviously in constant contact with the Allies had offered no help to anyone, no help to the prisoners of war while they were incarcerated. Conversely, the average Bucharest citizen was suffering mortal fear that his or her country would end up in the clutches of Communist Russia. The former spared inhabitants of Bucharest were not afraid of the eventual Red Communist Regime and, in fact, they appeared to be waiting for them. I can only hope that I was wrong in judging them so harshly.

Sleep finally won out over sheer exhaustion. It proved to be the first sound sleep I experienced since landing in Roumania on April 24, 1944.

Three full days had passed since that morning when we raised our steins of beer to toast our new freedom, only to drop them smashingly to the sadistic strains of machine gun fire before we could savor a single sip. During those days of terror we luckily lost only one man to bombs and bullets. The one unlucky airman remained back at our former prison camp inside one of the earth topped slit trenches used as an air raid shelter. That first incident of bombing where I lay prone on the ground, I didn't notice the pilot of the second plane also dropped one of his bombs and apparently it landed just beyond the trench but did not explode. That sole airman must have stayed below ground for sometime after I had left. He then decided to have a look above ground and as he exposed his head the bomb exploded severing the top half of head completely off. Apparently the bomb had a delayed action or malfunctioning fuse. To repeat the oft-repeated, such happenings so frightened and agonized us that it remains a wonder, we were not immobilized and demoralized, that so many of us did survive.

We were advised through the Roumanian military that late in the afternoon the Russian Army is going to make a triumphal entry into Bucharest not as liberators but as conquerors. The advisory further stated it would be best if we kept our distance as their intentions were not clear and at best unpredictable.

At the plaza, and after duty in the infirmary, I wandered outside and spotted Cisco, R.O. Ike and Randy. Once again I asked Cisco about the mug of beer. Cisco, said, "let's go, that rain check is long over due". (I had developed a mini-fetish about missing it). Approaching our former camp, that old feeling of deja vu came over me. Being on the outside looking in was a feeling I was not used to. The guards were still there, there were prisoners inside, nothing has changed, or has it. With a closer look I saw the change. We Americans were on the outside looking in and the Germans were on the inside looking out. I could only chuckle to myself at a sight befitting the reversible fortunes of war. Inside the barbed wire fence were German officers and their wives! I had thought such ironic twists of fate happened only in fiction novels, not in real life, and not in life and death struggles as we have been exposed to. There we stood, amused at the sight of a German General washing his socks in the horse trough like tub we had so often used. Their women, wearing only skirts and brassieres and waiting for their blouses to dry, were trying to wash as many of their outer garments as possible. One guard, recognized me and allowed us to come still closer. Following retaliatory instincts, we began jeering the general in a way I was not used to. We hollered:

"Hitler, Kaput! All Heines Kaput"! I felt like a little brat getting even and I suddenly didn't like me.

The general merely glanced at us, not changing his facial expression. Then, recalling how I felt when called a murderer and gangster, somehow I sensed that this man should not be jeered at and I immediately ceased doing so.

Cisco grabbed me by the arm and tugged saying, "come on Bill, forget this jerk, we have some sudsy beer waiting for us". I replied, "no you guys go ahead, I'll be right with you".

When they left my attention returned to the General, I asked, "do you speak English"?

"Perfectly well", was his reply.

Almost staring at each other, we tried to determine the best subject of conversation. lacking any imagination I inquired about his health, which, he said, was just fine.

For not being able to think of something to say, I did say, "It looks like the war is over for you"?

He shrugged his shoulders.

General, I continued, "I would like talk, but if you would rather that I didn't bother you, I'll oblige".

He interrupted me saying, "I also would like to talk".

That German General, equal in rank to our one star brigadier general, was in his early forties and seemed to be well educated. I asked him about his time in Roumania. His reply, "I only arrived here in Bucharest about two months ago. I was on the Normandy front in France and tried to persuade Hitler to take a logical stand against the Allied invasion. But he wouldn't listen. I guess he would have had me shot for questioning him but his need for officers was too great, so here I am serving under a Colonel". I then asked him about the German "Super-race" soldiers. This man was very open minded and without hesitation he replied,

"You're too young of a man to ask such questions and it may be hard for you to understand about propaganda. The "Super-Race" propaganda was used to instill fear in the minds of all German enemies.

He continued, "It worked well in countries where the people were fed that sort of propaganda before we invaded them. The "Super-race" theme served it's function". I just had to add my candid opinion and I said, "But the American soldiers are kicking the hell out of them all the way from North Africa heading to the suburbs of Berlin"!

His eyes lit up as though I hit a soft vulnerable spot on his ego. His reply, "Acht! The Americans are not soldiers, and they will never be soldiers. They don't know how to take orders, they don't know that the officer is the only one who knows how to fight a battle". Suddenly his eyes softened. He said "let me tell you what I learned about the American soldier on the beaches in Normandy".

The General began, "First, a soldier has to be taught to take orders without question, to be obedient to his superiors. The Americans were not taught this and to us, therefore, became totally unpredictable. The Americans were taught a buddy system, they fought in pairs. And if anything happened to one buddy the other buddy would become so enraged that nothing would stop him until he retaliated on the person(s) who did hurt his buddy. Now when you magnify this by hundreds or thousands we found we were running out of bullets to try to stop them. You Americans have something that we Germans should have had and that is self determination to achieve your objective at all costs and not to just take orders. The so called American Soldier was taught to think for himself particularly when his superiors became ineffective. That is why you are winning this war".

He continued, "In the German mind it is inconceivable that the officer would be wounded and incapacitated and that is why we did not train our soldiers to think for themselves. But let me add, "With the German Generals with their military history and the so called American Soldier we could lick the world". I said, "General, I hope that day never comes and this is the last war the world will ever see". He agreed.

It was a hopeless cause to try to fight the war through barbed wire fences so we just talked about more mundane things, like music and how I liked their song, Lilly Marlene, and was looking forward to some good German beer. Talking with that captive General for almost an hour, I became a very enlightened young man. In boyhood, I had been convinced that all war was political and caused by the pagan few. That conversation confirmed my viewpoint, that no intelligent man of any nationality would intentionally inflict harm on other persons but does so only when conditioned and compelled to do so. Without that conditioning in boot camps, in military colleges and that compulsion for survival on the battle scenes, the consciences of individual servicemen would revolt. Not "Brainwashed, about their country's goals or righteousness, how could they obey orders to do the ultimate evil, "Destroy Lives." Of militaristic governments, then, what else can be said other than "Theirs is the greater sin." In leaving I could not help but to salute that general, in a single movement of his body he quickly came to attention, clicked his heels in typical German fashion and returned my salute with a sincere smile of mutual respect. That was the last time I saw the General. In walking back to the air raid shelter, I thought so much about the intellectual food I just received that I had completely forgot about that postponed mug of beer!

When I reached the end of our camp lane I ran into Cisco and R.O. who looked a little tipsy. They never even asked me why I didn't join them in the beer garden. We could hear band music and guessed that the Russians must be in their triumphal march into Bucharest. Cisco said, "let's go see what they look like." We started toward the center of the business district, about ten blocks away, and on the way we passed by several Russian officers and soldiers. Only side glances were encountered from both sides. I for one was not looking for any kind of confrontation. Cisco and R.O. feeling no pain were apparently looking for any mischief to get into.

We stopped at the Victoria Maria Boulevard and caught the tail end of the parade and could not help but to notice the trucks and jeeps with the makers name plate, Ford, Dodge all American made on lend lease to the Russian Government. I asked Cisco, "I wonder if they're going to send those trucks back to the U.S.A. when the war is over." Cisco looked at me like I was nuts. I added, "I can dream can't I because they're only being lent to them." It seemed the only Russian weapon they had was their handheld machine guns.

Cisco beckoned us to walk to the next corner and possibly another tavern. Reaching the corner I noticed a Russian officer standing there watching the parade. He was well dressed in a clean uniform and doing just what everyone else was doing, watching. I went closer to him, saluted with a smile which was returned in kind. Once again I used the motion of pointing to my chest and to my friends saying, "we're American". He responded that he could speak some English. I suddenly felt subconsciously hostile, like the brat or bully in grade school, and wanted to act impish. But R.O., feeling no pain from that beer hall, beat me to the punch and started to ask questions. R.O. asked the young Russian officer, "how do you like those Americans trucks and artillery pieces". That maladroit move really changed the facial expression of that lieutenant. The lieutenant gruffly insisted that they were Russian machines and made in Russia. We went along with R.O. who wanted to take this scenario to it's limit. Laughing at him R.O. said, "how stupid can you be to think they are Russian since Ford and Dodge decals were visible on the hood's of all those vehicles given to your government under lend-lease"!

Yet, the young lieutenant, a man not yet thirty years old, indignantly and stolidly stated loudly, "those trucks and guns are Russian made"! In fact, while sticking to his absurd claim, he began reaching for his American made 45-caliber pistol! Viola, how quick can one come to his senses and I grabbed R.O. at the same time Cisco grabbed him and we all started to walk away. In this instance discretion was the better part of valor. We had been through too much to let some hot headed Rusky stop our tour of sightseeing by threats, even bloodshed. Politely agreeing with him, we took our leave, with drawing to the safety of our shelter, arriving there just as darkness was falling on the city.

I arrived just in time to relieve someone in our makeshift infirmary and spent some time doing chores and just helping to make life more comfortable for those who could not do for themselves. Later that evening, with most of the patients asleep, I wondered out onto the plaza. I must have just strolled for a period of time when I noticed two Russian soldiers approaching the entrance to the shelter. One was helping the other across my path. The second man, very young, possibly no more than seventeen or eighteen years old, and rather short in height was limping and using a heavy tree branch for a crutch. As it turned out the younger man was a lieutenant and the other a private. As they neared me they began speaking in Russian. I couldn't understand them but it wasn't hard to guess that they were looking for some medical aid for the private kept pointing to the young lieutenant's broken leg. One look at it told me that he had to be in extreme pain as it appeared to held together with just his flesh and tied with pieces of his trousers.

I guided the young man over to our door and asked the Roumanian guard if he could speak Russian, fortunately he could. We managed a three language translation and found that the man was wounded three days ago but could not see the Russian doctor for two more days despite his piercing pain.

How Pathetic it was to see another human being going in search for medical attention or for someone who cares. And, notwithstanding my desire to admit him inside our area, the guard had been strictly enjoined against admitting anyone but us Americans. Just then, an alternative dawned on me and I had to use my persuasive powers to let these two Russians in to stay in those cots within eyesight of the guard post and with the promise that I would stay with them. He agreed. I escorted both of them to the bunks, urged them to rest as I would get some blankets to spread on the straw mattresses. In the infirmary I asked the medic if he had a little bit of sulfa for the young Russian. He did and went out with me to help put it on the man's leg and then wrapped it with some gauze. The Medic went back while I helped the lieutenant get into bed. I gently spread his broken leg on it noticing throughout how sorely he must be suffering. After giving both of them the blankets, I was "blanketed" with endless gratitude.

Once more I fell into a deep restful sleep and don't remember stirring the slightest other than opening my eyes to daylight in the morning. I went to our makeshift latrine to brush my teeth and throw some water on my face. Then to the makeshift kitchen for some tea and a sweet roll and remembered the two Russians. I gathered two servings of tea and bread and took them to my new friends who were sitting up by the time I arrived. Additional thanks were expressed by faces beautiful to behold. Instinctively, I joined them in drinking and eating. (in those war time days I learned manners by intuition-not instruction). Finished, the three of us rose to our feet. And, what did the lame lieutenant do? He took my right hand, leaned from his hips even though he was in shocking pain, and kissed it. Sensing that his aid would repeat that gesture of gratitude, I tried to restrain him. I clasped the lieutenant's hand and shook it firmly indicating my preference. The protracted pleasure on the faces of these two men told me that, once more, I had done well by other human beings. Again in my young life it had been demonstrated that acts of kindness toward others costs nothing and tends to make the doers better persons. How I wished, that moment, that gestures of generosity, concern and involvement might replace complacency and apathy- not to mention hatred and violence. As the soviet officer and his aide departed the air raid shelter, I could see that my little courtesies had added meaning and motivation- however small- to their lives and hopefully to their futures.

Above and Below - The Russian Army marches into Bucharest as Conquerors and not as Liberators.

SIXTEEN

I awoke just after sunrise on the 28th of August and after tending to personal hygiene, gorging myself with tea and some of the most delicious pastries I have had in a long time and taking my turn at infirmary duties I went out to the plaza. Coming from the darkened confines of our protective quarters inside the air raid shelter I had to squint my eyes from the brightness of the morning sun. I could not help, but enjoyed, the feeling of a certain inner peace from the pleasure of experiencing a peaceful morning without the danger and the need to dodge bullets and bombs. It would be hard to find in any dictionary the proper adjectives to describe such a feeling other than to say, "I'm alive, thank God." In walking around that plaza I could not help but to ask myself some appropriate questions. Questions that had to answered. Where did all those medical supplies and delicious food come from? Who sent them to us? One thing I was sure of, they didn't come from anyone in that selfish fashionable suburb we were lured into. Then forgetting about my full belly my mind reverted to more important issues and needs of that very moment. Mundane issues and needs like, "where the hell do we go from here."

With the ending of all the bombings and sniper fire, our infirmed buddies were being cared for physically, medically and mentally, as good as could be expected under our present conditions, I had time to stop and think about our immediate future. What is going to happen to us now? How and where do we stand with the Russian army? How the hell are we going to get back across the battle lines, across the wide Adriatic Sea and to our home base, Manduria, in southern Italy? What is being done and who is doing it? Who will take the initiative? These queries and many more were soon to be answered, and answered in a way that surfaced the needed confidence in our ourselves and in our leaders. However, with all the confidence we had in anyone we all knew that we were not yet out of the woods

Unknown to anyone in the two camps, The school house camp for the officers and the hospital grounds camp for the enlisted men, a Parallel effort was taking place. Our efforts to secure shelter, food, medicines and safety for all our buddies were combined with the efforts of a few officers at the school house who did realize the precarious situation we found ourselves. These same officers decided to take some action to effect a rescue of all American and Allied P.O.W.'s from Roumania. And everyone was still quietly asking the same questions. How the hell are we going to pull this off? More than eleven hundred bodies, four hundred miles behind the battle lines! Who's kidding who? Such an air rescue or evacuation or what ever anyone wants to call it has all the ingredients to present to the world another Dunkirk! Yet, everyone knew something had to be done and we all were willing to tempt fate this one more time.

It was early morning on August 25, 1944 when Dana Varvil, Destiny Deb's captain, was walking around in one of the court yards of the school house just savoring the air of freedom. Walking up to Len Bahti, Destiny Deb's co-pilot, Dana started asking the same questions that everyone else was asking. He said, "Len, we have to get something started, let's go talk to Colonel Gunn since he's now the ranking officer." "Dana," said Len, "He can't do any more than we tried and besides he only got here six or seven days ago and that's not long enough to know where the latrines are. For a moment Len hesitated then added, "well, Son of a buck, what the hell we got nothing to lose anyway, let's try." Dana and Len went back into the school house to seek out the Colonel and after treading the halls and looking into every room they finally found him on the side walk outside the front entrance.

Dana took the initiative. "Colonel Gunn we have to do something as quickly as possible before we end up with men scattered all over this country." Colonel Gunn asked, "That's easier said than done, what do you propose we do?" Dana took the leadership and presented his proposal. "Colonel, since the Roumanian's apparently are now our Allies, why can't you, as the senior Allied officer, talk them out of a plane to fly to Italy to get the help we need?"

Dana then added, "this would be the quickest way for all of us to get the hell out of this country and back where we belong.

Most any kind of plane would do, have the American flag painted on both sides, skip the waves over the Adriatic Sea, slip into the Bari air strip with your wheels down, rocking your wings and hope those bloody Limey anti aircraft gunners see the flag before they think you're just another crazy pilot who drank too much Italian vino and shoot you out of the air as they would a clay pigeon. If you need a pilot or two Len and I are available." With his eyes wide open and a gaping mouth Len interrupted Dana saying, "Hold one minute Dana, who said I would do such a crazy thing like flying a German airplane into any Allied airfield, I don't remember volunteering. Dana said, "yes you will, you're my co-pilot and where I go you go. Besides I just volunteered you." Then Len's favorite expression, "son of a buck, here I go again."

Colonel Gunn looked at both of them like they just got out off the looney farm or they were smoking too many Roumanian cigarettes. But, Colonel Gunn just stared at them and began thinking out loud. "You know we have manuals for just about anything that can happen in a war time situation. A manual to fly four engine bombers that are not supposed to fly; manuals on how to load bombs on the bomber and how to drop them on cities and people; manuals on how to conduct yourself in a prisoner of war camp and manuals on how to harass the enemy guards and how to escape from a prison camp. We even have a manual on how to wipe our asses without toilet paper. But, gentlemen, and Colonel Gunn's voice grew louder only from frustration, we do not have a manual on how to rescue more than eleven hundred men four hundred miles behind the enemy lines." The more Gunn ranted and raved about the manuals for everything but no manual for our immediate needs the more agonizingly helpless he felt. After being quiet for a period of time, seconds that seemed an eternity, Gunn realized they were right and said, "Dana and Len, maybe we could make something happen, you're both right, let's do something. Standing here talking about it is just too counter productive. I'm going to find a Roumanian that has some authority."

Colonel James Gunn, shot down over Ploiesti on August 17, 1944, only six days before the Roumanians decided to rout the Germans from their small country, became the senior ranking

Allied officer in Roumania, an awesome responsibility for anyone to assume. It did not take long for all of us in either camp to gain the respect and admiration for this man Gunn. He appeared to be a quiet reserved individual, a deep thinking man blessed with an analytical mind and a man who had the rare instinct of knowing what need to be done and never would hesitate to take action even to the extent of placing his own life in jeopardy. There is an age old cliche, "the boss says do it, the leader says let's do it." Time has proven to us, to his peers and to his superiors that Colonel Gunn was a natural leader.

Colonel Gunn left Dana and Len and immediately sought any Roumanian that could take him to a person of authority. This seemed to be an easy task at first but soon became an unexpected stumbling block. It was now late morning of the 25th of August and street fighting was still taking place. When the German commander, Colonel Gerstenberg, left King Michael he set the wheels in motion to destroy all forms of communications in the city of Bucharest and this left the Roumanian General Staff in a state of chaos depending on individuals to hand carry orders to where they were needed. Finally Colonel Gunn ran into sergeant Daley, a Roumanian of questionable allegiance who seemed to be a member of some elite aristocratic circle and while traveling on his motorcycle spent much time visiting the non-coms at various intervals. Sergeant Daley (how he got that name is still a mystery) took Gunn to a temporary command post near the bombed out war department building in downtown Bucharest. Sergeant Daley introduced Gunn to a Captain as the senior Allied officer and then acted as an interpreter. Gunn told the Captain of the horrible conditions of his men at which point the captain interrupted Gunn and asked him to accompany him to his superiors. Gunn agreed and was taken to a temporary War Department Headquarters in a recreational building in a wooded area several miles outside Bucharest. Colonel Gunn was then introduced to the Roumanian Secretary of War General Racovita. Again Gunn related the deplorable conditions of his men. General Racovita understood what was happening and agreed to all of Gunn's requests. Food and medical supplies were immediately sent to the air raid shelter near the hospital and it was general Racovita that ordered the security guard in our area of the building. The question of where did all that food come from was finally answered. General Racovita summoned a Roumanian Major from the adjacent office and issued orders to have all the P.O.W.'s in Bucharest evacuated out of the city and to the south to prevent any German attempt to recapture them.

Just as General Rocovita was completing his orders to the Major a rather important looking man in a neatly tailored double breasted suit entered the room. Gunn was introduced and advised that he was Mr. Rico Georgescu, Roumania's Secretary of State and Minister of the National Economy. Rocovita began telling Mr. Georgescu of his intentions concerning all Allied P.O.W.'s. Smiles appeared on Mr. Georgescu's face and he nodded his head in approval as he shook hands with Gunn. (The text between Colonel Gunn and all Roumanian officials will be told in English with the understanding that an interpreter was present at all times and to preclude any redundancy).

The true leadership of Colonel Gunn surfaced with his first request. Gunn knew his first responsibility was for the well being and safety of all his men, regardless of rank, and that they were being properly housed and feed. Only when he was assured of their needs did he embark on his next primary objective, rescue. No doubt Gunn looked to the majestic blue heavens for divine guidance, or assistance because he knew in his heart that we would need all the help we could get.

After spending all day in his quest for help, the sun was now disappearing under the horizon, Gunn, too, had smiles on his face for he had finally found a Roumanian official with some clout and one that was able to get things done in a hurry. Gunn began relating to Mr. Georgescu of his plan to fly to Italy.

"Mr. Georgescu", said Gunn, "If you could find me an airplane I could fly to Allied Headquarters in Italy where I might be able to arrange for an air strike to put a stop to the terrorizing bombings by the Germans. I could also put into effect a plan to relocate all the Allied P.O.W.'s that were recently held captive in your country. We know that the Germans have control of one or more airfields to the north of Bucharest and one of them is the Banasea airfield only fifteen miles from here. With your help and permission I would like to get started right away on this project and prepare to leave at first light in the morning."

"Colonel Gunn", said Georgescu, "how can you be sure that you will be able to convince your superiors of the need for a bomber or fighter air strike against the Germans?" Gunn responded, "Mr. Georgescu, surely you know that the goal of the Allies is to defeat the Nazis regardless of the cost or danger to the fighting Allied Armies. You, yourself, have experienced the determination of the aircrews, and particularly the American aircrews, that were shot out or blown out of their airplanes in an effort to deny the Germans the much needed petroleum products. Life expectancy for those airmen was not very high and yet they did come and were never turned back from ferocity of battle. The German must be defeated and I am asking your help to continue this fight for your liberty and the liberty of the world."

Mr. Georgescu stood in that office after Gunn had spoken and just looked him squarely in the eyes for what seemed like an eternity. Georgescu was without a doubt thinking about what Gunn had just said and had to digest it's implications. Georgescu said, "Colonel Gunn you make it awfully hard for me to refuse your request, evidently you have given it a lot of thought. and I appreciate your sincerity. But, I cannot alone make this decision as it is not a simple one. We here in Roumania have hopes of installing a democratic form of government when this war is over. We must start right now and present your request to other high level officials who have joined together, risked their lives, to rid our country of the German occupation for the second and hopefully for the final time in less than thirty years. We Roumanians also want peace and most of all our Freedom." "Colonel Gunn," Georgescu continued, "I would appreciate if you would be my guest for this evening at my home where we can try to relax and discuss the merits of your plan in detail. "Gunn answered, " I would be delighted and honored Mr. Secretary."

It was about an hour's drive from the command post in the woods to Mr. Georgescu's home only because the driver had to use extreme caution and not draw attention to the fact that high ranking officials might be in the car. German sympathizers were still in existence in and around Bucharest. When they arrived Mr. Georgescu sent an assistant to prepare a dinner for them. Gunn related later that it was one of the most succulent dinners he had ever eaten. (considering the circumstances anything other than our usual sour bread and sour bean soup would surely be succulent). Though the dinner was enjoyed it was punctuated by an occasional wail of air raid sirens, sniper fire and bombings.

After dinner both Gunn and Georgescu began their discussions not on the Gunn's plan to fly to Italy but the Roumanian Secretary of State wanted to talk about the United States and how it maintains a free society. Georgescu admitted that Democracy was completely new to him. He related that in his life time his country has been invaded on several occasions, had a monarchy, and never had known what it would be like to live in a peaceful and harmonious society to do what you want to do when you want to do it. Gunn was at a loss for words of wisdom because his life time was just the opposite, Gunn never knew what it would be like to live a life under totalitarian rules and didn't care to find out.

Throughout their conversations, that were constantly being interrupted by field telephone calls that required the immediate attention of Mr. Georgescu, a keen sense of awareness of the two different societies was accepted by both men. Weariness overtook Gunn at about 4:00 AM and both retired for some needed rest. Gunn later related that he didn't believe Georgescu ever went to bed or even rested.

Gunn was awakened early by Mr. Georgescu and after throwing some water on his face and becoming cognizant of it only being 7:00 AM joined the Secretary for a light breakfast of tea and pastry. Mr. Georgescu said, "Colonel I've got good news for you. You Americans will never cease to amaze me. It seems that since we have no long range communications system one of your men was taken with our radios experts to a bank vault in down town Bucharest where he built a radio transmitter powerful enough to contact the Allies in Cairo. I'm told that this young man of yours was so young that he had yet to grow a full beard on his face and where did he get so much knowledge at such a young age?"

At hearing this, Colonel Gunn could do nothing but smile and say, "that's an American for you, that's what we do best, we help other people."

(Paul Swearingen the youthful radio operator and a Beau of Destiny Deb was the man Mr. Georgescu was talking about. Paul stayed in the Air Force after the war and after several tours of duty in Vietnam retired as a Colonel. He now makes his home in Benton, Illinois.)

Mr. Georgescu continued, "Colonel, we were able to convince your headquarters of the need for a bomb strike and one is being prepared at this time to eliminate all three airfields north of Bucharest this afternoon. This action convinced myself and other officials to grant your request for an airplane to fly you to Italy. It is being prepared at this time and you will leave late this afternoon." (this bomb strike was sighted and reported during the return to the air raid shelter after the aborted attempt to obtain guns for the protection of the infirmed P.O.W.'s.)

Around noon of August 26, 1944 Mr. Georgescu accompanied Gunn to the temporary office of the Secretary of the Air Force Mr. Chanescu. After proper introductions Gunn was told that an air crew had been assembled to fly him to Italy in a Savola Marchetti (an ancient model of an Italian twin engine aircraft). Gunn was advised that the flight plan has been kept secret for security reasons, the pilot was aware of the dangers and experienced in the air route to Italy. Gunn was then driven to Popesti airfield for the eventful flight that could be compared to the return of the Phoenix, " Out of the Fires of Hell, Hell being the Fires of Ploiesti."

When Gunn arrived at Popesti airfield he was introduced to the air crew, a Roumanian major and two sergeants, who could speak no English. This was a serious concern for Gunn as he had no way of telling the major how to fly into Bari without being shot down. He told this to his interpreter but it was shrugged off by the major who pointed to his chest saying that he knows how to fly his plane into any airfield safely. Gunn could only say to himself, "I sure hope he knows what he is about to fly into." Gunn noticed that the sergeants were carrying side arms and stayed a noticeable distance from him. It appeared that the lower the chain of command the less trust anyone had in anyone. Gunn was sure that he had no intentions of commandeering the airplane after it was in the air, the sergeants were not so sure. The major entered the plane first and sat alone in the pilot's cabin. Gunn was motioned by the sergeants to enter next and then the gun toting sergeants who sat on one side of the plane toward the rear with Gunn toward the front. Gunn tried to shake off those leering eyes without success and just settled back as the engines were started. Taxing out for take off was uneventful except for the bumps in the grass taxi-ways and runway. Take-off was to the west so there was no need to circle the airfield and a direct course into the setting sun was set for Bari.

After about twenty minutes into the flight and not yet in sight of the Danube River the pilot started a slow turn to the left and returned to the Popesti airfield. Upon landing the same interpreter came up to the airplane and after a discussion with the major, Gunn was advised that the left engine was acting up making it too dangerous to cross the Adriatic Sea. Gunn detected no engine trouble, in fact he thought the engines were running quite smoothly. Gunn also detected no conversation on any radio and could only guess that this major didn't have the guts for such a flight. Gunn wondered who the major feared the most the Germans in Yugoslavia or the Americans in Italy. The major and the two sergeants quickly disappeared in the small crowd that gathered around the airplane.

Just as Gunn started to wonder, what the hell he is to do next someone tapped him on the shoulder and speaking in excellent English said, "Colonel, if you will crawl into the belly of a Messerschmidt 109 I will fly you to Italy." Gunn slowly turned around and found an extremely handsome man, a little younger than himself, a man who had a dashing appearance to want to do the risky, an adventurous sort of swashbuckling pilot that we only read about. His name was Constantine Cantacuzino, a captain and commander of an elite Roumanian fighter squadron who, as Gunn learned later, had many combat victories to his credit. He appeared to be a well educated man and one who seemed to be a member of the aristocracy in Roumania. Needless to say Gunn was dumb founded considering what he just experienced and was some what hesitant. But Gunn's leadership again surfaced and without asking about the danger he would be placing himself in said, "let's go now."

Captain Cantacuzino said, "no we can't leave now, it would be too dangerous to try to enter Italy at night. It would be better for us to plan the flight tonight and to take off sometime tomorrow morning." Reluctantly, Gunn agreed to delay a few more hours.

Gunn had an enjoyable evening talking pilot talk with a former adversary and that made the time pass without notice. When both were talked out from a friendly argument of who had the best tactics in aerial dog fighting or who bested who in the greatest display of airmanship the world has ever seen or ever will be seen again they found a couple of cots in one of the buildings at Popesti airfield to rest their weary heads. Colonel Gunn still remembers how peaceful he slept that night.

Three days of total weariness, Gunn was exhausted and the few extra hours of sleep was well earned. It was now 7:30 AM on August 27, 1944 with Gunn and Cantacuzino making plans for their historic flight. Cantacuzino was getting quite perturbed because he could not find a single map of Italy that could be helpful in their flight to Bari. In turn Gunn was getting perturbed at Cantacuzino for being so meticulous in planning the flight. Gunn was told that he would be buckled into the fuselage of that tiny fighter plane and in the event of being shot down by either side his lot for a continued life would not be too good. Gunn was told how cold it was going to be and that they might have to go to altitude and he could suffer hypoxia from the lack of oxygen. Gunn never flinched an eye other than to say, "let's get on with this planning."

As Gunn and Cantacuzino continued with their planning Mr. Georgescu entered the room and addressing Gunn requested him to accompany him for a meeting with the interim President of the new Roumanian government, Mr. Maniu. Upon arriving at the government office in down town Bucharest and being introduced to Mr. Maniu Gunn listened to the most impassioned plea he will ever hear in his lifetime. Mr. Maniu, did everything but get down on his knees, Pleaded with Colonel Gunn that when he arrives in Italy make the recommendation in the name of the Roumanian government that his country be occupied by either American or British forces. Mr. Maniu continued, "since you are an American representative and since you were here before the Russians I make this plea to save our small country and it's people from another form of dictatorship." Gunn stretched out his hand saying, "Mr. Maniu I will carry your message and try my best to see that it reaches the proper authorities." With that promise Gunn was driven back to the airfield to continue with the necessary preparations. Ever since his release from the prison camp Gunn sensed something was not right with the people he met, now he knew. Every where he went, every person he met, on every street corner there was overwhelming evidence of terror, on the faces of the average citizenry, at the prospects of a Russian occupation of Roumania and President Maniu was no exception.

At the Popesti airfield Gunn found Cantacuzino hard at work. He had the American flag painted on both sides of the fuselage with quick drying paint. Gunn also found the captain in a rather arrogant mood because he could not locate any usable maps. Gunn went over to Cantacuzino and put his arm on his shoulder to try to calm him a little and told him that he can draw a suitable map that will get them into an Allied airfield. So Gunn sat down with pen and ink and drew a detailed map of Italy on a piece of cardboard. From that map Gunn briefed the captain. Then on a smaller piece of cardboard Gunn sketched a smaller and more detailed map. On this smaller map were noted barrage balloon locations and the anti aircraft gun positions together with any outstanding landmarks which could be used for pilotage after crossing the Adriatic Sea. Captain Cantacuzino was an intelligent man and he realized the significant importance of following only Gunn's directions because he has been there many times.

Gunn further advised that crossing the Adriatic should be at minimum altitude, skipping the waves so to speak. But Cantacuzino objected because of the many speed boats the Allies were running between Yugoslavia and Italy and if they spotted us could radio a warning. After considerable and heated discussions Gunn reluctantly went along with Cantacuzino's plan to cross the sea at maximum altitude.

The plan agreed on was to leave Popesti airfield at minimum altitude to a point thirty to forty miles from the Adriatic Sea and then climb to 19,000 feet to the center of the sea and then a shallow dive to the Italian coast with enough power to make the last portion of the flight as fast as possible reducing the possibility of interception by American fighter planes. This plan would also have Gunn at altitude without oxygen for the shortest period of time.

On the reverse side of the small map Gunn drew in the necessary details to effect a safe and healthy landing at the San

Giovani airfield near Cerignola, Italy, Gunn's home base. It was fortunate Gunn made good use of his training to memorize certain headings and land marks in case he lost his radios or navigation instruments from flak or from fighter's bullets.

While the ground crew was putting the finishing touches on the Messerschmidt 109 fighter plane and removing the radios in the fuselage to make room for Gunn Cantacuzino came over and put his hand on his shoulder and took him side. "Colonel Gunn", said Cantacuzino with a worried look on his face, "I am very concerned, in fact I am alarmed, about the fact that our plans are so widely known. We are in the heart of an area where Allies and Enemies intermingle and on most occasions it is extremely difficult to tell one from the other. Colonel, I am concerned that we might be shot down soon after take off and I need your approval for a change in our plans for a dawn take-off tomorrow."

"Captain," Gunn said, "I've learned to judge men early in life and I know I can trust your judgment, what do you propose." Cantacuzino cleverly suggested that the news be spread around that take-off would be dawn tomorrow morning, August 28th. We will, however be leaving this afternoon as soon as everything fits together and with you in the fuselage and sealed in. Without hesitating a second Gunn agreed. Cantacuzino added, "the only other persons who are aware of these changes are Mr,. Rico Georgescu, the Secretary of War, Mr Chanescu, the Secretary of the Air Force and, of course, the interim President Mr. Maniu. I took the liberty to advise them as I felt you would approve."

Gunn was outfitted with heavy leather flying clothes and at first he thought it would be impossible for him to squeeze through that eighteen inch square hole and lay down in such a small space. Everything was ready and Cantacuzino was trying to throw everyone off guard by making a joke about how much weight Gunn had gained and said, "Colonel, no wonder you want to go home, you put on too much weight from our good Roumanian food." None of the ground crew was aware of what was about to take place. Cantacuzino continued, "Colonel, let's see how you fit inside and how comfortable you will be." Gunn started in head first with all that flying gear getting caught on the inspection hole sides. With help of the ground crew who used flat pieces of metal using them like shoe horns, Gunn finally made it inside. Cantacuzino yelled, "how do you feel, Colonel." just fine was Gunn's response. Without hesitation The Captain grabbed the inspection plate laying on the ground and with a small screw driver he had in his pocket fastened the four dzus fasteners to hold the plate in place. Cantacuzino then jumped in the cockpit, started the engine and in less than two minutes they were airborne headed once again into the setting sun on their way to Italy. It was the beginning of a journey and rescue mission unparalleled in the history of Mankind.

Author Bill Fili and Colonel Gunn meet after forty-six years at a farewell banquet for Princess Catherine Caradja on May 18, 1991 in San Antonio, Texas.

SEVENTEEN

The modern day Phoenix in the two forms of Captain Constantine Cantacuzino and Lt. Colonel James Gunn, two human beings of unsurpassed excellence, were on their way in the death defying service of others. The initial leg of the flight from Popesti Airfield to near the Adriatic Sea was at tree top levels and caused some uncomfortable vibrations to the body of the Colonel. Fortunately the heavy flying suit provided some cushioning effect to Gunn's anatomy and limbs. Low altitude flying usually does not provide any smooth flying air and this day was no exception. However, nothing could stop Gunn from sweating profusely from the bumpy air and the heavy flying suit. Gunn's immediate concerns turned to how cold it could get when they climbed to altitude. Would his sweat dry up or would it freeze making his prone position that much worse. But Gunn knew he had to put this out of his mind for the moment as there was nothing he could do to add to his comfort. He also knew he had to accept the inevitable heat and cold for the short period of time needed to cross the Adriatic Sea.

Upper most in both men's minds was a silent question, soon to answered. Were they going to be recognized as friends or would they be shot out of the sky as an enemy? A ventured guess would be that most men in that position would opt for finding a sandy beach, make a wheels up belly landing and walk the rest of the way, that is if they survived the crash landing. But, both the Colonel and the Captain knew too well the urgency of their mission.

Other than personal discomfort the flight to Italy was uneventful and according to plan. In trying to seek some comfort Gunn accidently found an access plate in the fuselage just opposite his head, a kickplate (foot stirrup) that was used by the pilot when climbing into the cockpit. He discovered that by pulling a spring he could open it to get a limited view of the terrain below. At the same time he was blowing into his hands for some warmth as they were now at their crossing altitude of 19,000 feet. When he finally opened the plate he found that they were just crossing the Yugoslavia coast and he knew it would be only a few more minutes for them to start their screaming dive for the Italian coastline. And Gunn began to smile to himself as the decent was initiated he felt the increase in temperature and wishing for some sweat to warm his body. Gunn thought to himself, "the easy part is over, now for some nail biting and plain old fashion being scared shitless."

Gunn had to admire the Captain for his superb navigation and smooth flying ability. In opening the kickplate he got a glimpse of the Italian coast and the land spur he earlier instructed the Captain to cross on a certain heading, which he did. Apparently Cantacuzino was following Gunn's map with great precision even to following the stream Gunn drew on the cardboard. Arriving at the precise landmark the Captain took a heading of 340 degrees that would take him directly over the San Giovanni Airfield, home base of the 454th and 455th B-24 bomb groups. (Colonel Gunn was the Commanding Officer of the 454th Bomb Group and is the reason he knew so much about the location and landmarks in the area to direct Captain Cantacuzino.)

Gunn warned Cantacuzino that the perimeter was protected with British Manned forty MM anti aircraft guns. Both the gunners and guns had a reputation of not losing a target anywhere from Rommel's planes in the North African Desert to central Italy and they are quite anxious to maintain their seniority in that respect. "So Captain," Gunn said before they took off at Popesti, "let's not do anything to test their aiming ability." The Captain was instructed that when in sight of the airfield he should drop his landing gear and wing flaps and make a slow approach while rocking his wings. Gunn was positive that no one would shoot at a plane in such slow flight. In looking through the kickplate Gunn knew how close they were and began to enjoy a big sigh of relief. Suddenly the Captain started a slow turn to the right and Gunn almost shit his pants as he did not know what the Captain was doing and tried to scream to him not to make any false moves but the noise of the low engine power setting and the air stream drowned out his yells. Gunn could not know and could not see that the wind was blowing downwind making it too dangerous to land in that direction. Cantacuzino decided to go around and land in the opposite direction.

Gunn was beside himself not being able to do anything and not knowing what the hell his pilot was doing. In a calmer sense he opened the kickplate again and saw that the Captain was still rocking his wings while making a slow and deliberate 180 turn around the airfield. A sense of relief came over Gunn as he felt the plane turn on final approach to his home airfield. A dollar to a donut says that Gunn had white knuckles when they crossed the field perimeter then heard the familiar sound of rubber tires hitting the runway and then the gradual slowing of that small but respected fighter plane. Another dollar to a donut says that those white knuckles quickly turned into watering eyes. Gunn looked up as best he could, symbolic of looking at the heavens, while saying, "Thank You."

Cantacuzino was puzzled at Gunn's instructions when he was told that if and when they do land at an American airfield a jeep would come in front of your plane. with a large sign saying "Follow me". He never experienced such instructions. Sure enough the jeep did show up at the end of the runway and it was followed as precisely as all of Gunn's other instructions. They stopped at what Cantacuzino guessed was a field headquarters building and he was right. The Messerschmidt plane was immediately surrounded by four other jeeps each with machine guns in turrets and ready for action. Base military police officers came up to the plane as Cantacuzino was opening the canopy. The first motion of Cantacuzino was to raise his hands with palms open signifying the absence of any weapons. As he stepped off the planes wing he was grabbed by two MP's by the arm but the Captain again raised his hands and spoke in such perfect English, it surprised everyone there, "Gentlemen, I have a wonderful gift for you, will some one quickly get me a screw driver." A nearby mechanic heard the request and offered one. Cantacuzino removed the inspection plate and all anyone could see was a pair of GI shoes. Everyone without exception was astonished. Cantacuzino added, "please, gentlemen, help me get this man out of this plane." Helping hands were in abundance that afternoon as Colonel Gunn emerged through the inspection access door a lot easier than when he got into it.

When Gunn emerged from that fuselage he wasn't immediately recognized by anyone. The heavy flying suit was wrapped around his neck, his face was flushed from the ordeal he experienced and he was anything but steady on his feet. The ordeal did take it's toll on Gunn. The real trauma of not knowing if you are going to make the airfield, not knowing if the gunners will read you as a friendly and the final trauma of knowing that you are really home safe and sound. Gunn's nervous system was like the over stretched rubber band that had to be returned to normal very slowly. All Gunn needed was a few minutes to compose himself. This he did by leaning his head in his folded forearms against the fuselage, waiting for his equilibrium to return to normal and by taking deep breaths of oxygenated air to overcome the dizziness and hypoxia. Cantacuzino helped to hold Gunn erect and told the MP's to be patient, the Colonel will be alright in a few minutes. The silence was deafening as all waited for Gunn to come to life.

Someone had sent for an ambulance that arrived just as Gunn withdrew his head from his arms and, with his back to that small planes fuselage, lowered the collar of his flying suit removed the heavy jacket and britches, then stood erect and brushed his hair back with his hand. With the biggest broadest smile ever seen on anyone's face Colonel Gunn said, "Gentlemen, it's so good to be home again." Back in the crowd someone apparently recognized Gunn and shouted, "it's Colonel Gunn." Then a deafening roar and applause that would drown out any noise or sounds coming from any where. Those happy smiles on the many faces were indescribable. There leader, their commanding officer had returned alive and well and ready to answer any and all questions. Though no one gave any orders all the men, officers and enlisted men, alike popped to attention and saluted both the Colonel and the Captain.

Gunn advised the MP's that Captain Cantacuzino is a command pilot in the Roumanian Air Force and is now on our side and is to be treated as an Ally and added, "We would like to stay here and talk to you but we have much work to do as there are more than a thousand men we have to rescue from the clutches of the retreating German Army and bring them back here. We must go to headquarters and get started." The MP's escorted them into the building. As they entered Gunn turned and looked to the west at the setting sun that was causing elongated shadows of planes trucks and guns reminding him of the war that is still in progress and yet another perilous mission he might participate in.

Passing through the doorway both Gunn and Cantacuzino spied the water bag hanging from the ceiling and both increased their pace to savor that life saving liquid. The trauma and nervousness of their escapade drained what little moisture they had in their bodies and it was imperative that it be replenished. It was then they realized that the last bite to eat or to drink was at seven thirty AM that morning.

Gunn's first objective was to call Fifteenth Air Force Headquarters in Bari to advise General Twining of his return and the urgency of his mission to rescue the American and Allied airmen. General Twining was absent and Gunn spoke to his second in command Brigadier General Charles Born, Chief of Operations. Gunn also called Colonel Fay Upthegrove, 304 Wing Commander to advise him of his return. The wheels were in motion to convene a top level strategy conference before the end of the night. With his calls completed Gunn asked for some food to be brought to them as they were famished. As soon as they finished eating they were on their way to Bari and General Twining's headquarters, about an hours drive from San Giovanni air base arriving a little after 2100 hours.

Immediately high level intelligence officers started to interrogate both Gunn and Cantacuzino, separately and then together to determine the military and civilian situation in Roumania. It was imperative to have as much knowledge of the air targets, the location of the ground forces of the Roumanian Army, the retreating German army and most important the location of the Russian advance ground forces. The Allies had to be extremely cautious not to drop bombs on any Russian forces and possibly start World War III before World War II is over. Both Gunn and Cantacuzino were invited into the secret strategy conference for their valued input. The strategy conference lasted from 2230 hours to 2400 hours and resulted in three recommendations to be made to Supreme Allied headquarters.

A - The Roumanian Air Force pilot to fly a P-51 type aircraft to Popesti airfield, to land alone and clear the way for a Fifteenth Air Force advance rescue party to land.

B - Two B-17's escorted to land at Popesti airfield with the advance rescue party.

C - The airborne evacuation or rescue to be carried out when favorable conditions are reported from the advance rescue party.

General Twining was about to excuse Gunn and Cantacuzino from that meeting when Gunn addressed the General. Gunn said, "General, I have an urgent message from the new President of Roumania, Mr. Maniu. Sir, I was requested to ask that the American or British forces occupy the Country of Roumania. The outclassed Roumanian soldiers fought valiantly to defeat the German Army and Marshall Antonescu's Iron Guard to finally free their country of dictatorships. Now they want to live in a democracy. General, I implore you to send this message to the highest authority as I have seen mass hysteria on the faces of the people of Bucharest at the mere thought of a Russian occupation and more years of slavery under totalitarian rule. All I heard in the short time I was there was "the Americans are here" and "we are free at last." Sir, the people were referring to the freed American P.O.W.'s." Gunn's final words to the General were, "General please send this message."

In replying General Twining said, "Colonel, the sincerity of your message and the compassionate plea of the new Roumanian President is well taken and recorded. But this is out of the realm of a military decision, However, when Captain Cantacuzino returns to Bucharest he will take the message to Mr. Maniu that I personally sent his request to my superiors at Supreme Allied Headquarters and to General Eisenhower. I personally hope that this can be achieved for the Roumanian people."

(The compassionate plea of the interim President of Roumania Mr. Maniu was written into the congressional record in a speech in the House of Representatives by the Honorable Henry B. Gonzales of Texas on Wednesday May 3, 1967. No reason was ever presented why this plea was not acknowledged or why the freedom of the people of Roumania was not preserved).

Gunn and Cantacuzino were finally excused from that meeting just after midnight and were escorted to well deserved much needed and appropriate sleeping quarters. The shower and the toilet kit they were given must have been received like manna from heaven. For it doesn't take very many days in a prison camp to know the value of a small thing like a tooth brush or a piece of soap, things that we Americans always take for granted. It also goes without saying, they slept like new born babies nestled lovingly in their mothers arms.

Gunn awoke about 0700 hours and his first thoughts were about Cantacuzino. He thought, "I hope he didn't wonder off some where and get lost or thrown into the brig by the MP's as a spy?" But there he was in the latrine taking care of personal hygiene and Gunn joined him. Both men went to breakfast and enjoyed a leisurely and well deserved relaxing meal. After that Gunn said, "let's get busy we have a lot of work to do for the guys we left behind."

They went over to the headquarters building and were given an unexpected memorable greeting and went directly to the intelligence office. They were greeted by Colonel Donovan, (not related to Wild Bill Donovan, Director of the Office of Strategic Services, OSS, during World War 11), and were informed that everything is going as planned. Colonel Donovan was a big man, about 6'6", had a strong commanding voice, broad square shoulders, and extremely intelligent appearance and was the Chief of Air Corps Intelligence in Italy. The type of a man who would be expected to head up such an office. Gunn asked the Colonel, "Sir, we want to help, what can we do," Donovan took them into a private office and briefed them on the procedure that they have to follow. They were told the three recommendations were sent to the Director of Operations and Intelligence, MAAF, to the Commander in Chief, MAAF, and to the Supreme Allied Commander SHAEF. "Gentlemen," he said, "this decision has to be made by General Eisenhower and his staff. We hope to have his approval within the hour."

Again, Gunn asked, "what can we do?" "There is so little time to help those men in Bucharest." Colonel Donovan said, "Colonel you and the Captain have done your part and I must say that there are not very many men who would have placed their lives in jeopardy as you have. It was a very courageous and dangerous thing you have done. Now just let us take it from here and in only a matter of hours, I assure you, those men will be back here with you. Right now we are making preparations to airlift those men from Bucharest because we know General Ike would want it that way." Then Colonel Donovan added, "right now we are preparing more than thirty B-17's to airlift your men still in Bucharest. We know that the B-24 can fly faster and carry more of a pay load but we cannot trust the nose wheel on the B-24 to hold up on a grass runway. Surely you will admit that the B-17 and the tail wheel type landing gear is more suited for this type of an operation. Wooden platforms are now being installed in the bomb bays and guns are being removed. So, Colonel just relax and we will finish the job that you started. Be assured, Colonel, we will bring them home."

Then Donovan suddenly became deep in thought and after a few minutes he spoke. "Colonel Gunn, we are so certain that our three point rescue plan will be approved we do have something for you to do and right now. Captain Cantacuzino will have to lead the advance rescue party to Bucharest. Since it is not possible for him to go back in the German Messerschmidt we have decided to have him return in a P-51." Hearing that, Cantacuzino's eyes lit up brighter than a child's eye's when coming down the stairs at Christmas time and seeing all those presents under the tree. It was very hard for the Captain to compose himself. Cantacuzino knew the Mustang was a pilot's dream airplane and he was going to fly one. So, Colonel Gunn I may be jumping the Gun, (no funny pun intended) why don't you take the Captain over to operations. There is a P-51 parked on the ramp and it would be advantageous to use this time to indoctrinate Captain Cantacuzino in the planes operations. There is also a pilot standing by to check him out in it. Good luck to both of you." With that order Colonel Donovan asked to be excused. With a childish and excited grin on his face Cantacuzino grabbed Gunn's arm and said, "C'mon, let's go."

Gunn, Cantacuzino and the checkout pilot spent most of the day learning about the P-51 Mustang and simply enjoyed flying it. At dinner that evening Colonel Donovan entered the mess hall came over to inform them that the plan was approved. He told them to come to the briefing room at 2000 hours that evening for further details.

Upon entering the briefing room Gunn and Cantacuzino were motioned to their seats by Colonel Donovan who was presiding at this briefing. After introducing everyone the procedure was outlined in detail.

Captain Cantacuzino is to lead the way back to Bucharest in a P-51 airplane with escorts of three other P-51's. The flight formation will be a four plane right echelon meaning that each plane will fly to right and just behind the forward plane. The flight will be at 24,000 feet which is high enough to deter any flak opposition. When over the city of Slatina, about one hundred miles from Bucharest you will descend to 3000 feet. Arriving at 3000 feet and within sight of Popesti airfield the three escorting P-51's will break formation, stay within safe sight of the airfield and allow Captain Cantacuzino to circle the field to determine if it is still clear of German resistance and then land. Upon landing Cantacuzino will advise the escorts the airfield is safe by shooting one red flare, then a green flare and followed by another red flare. The three escorts will radio the all clear signal to Bari Headquarters and immediately climb to 25,000 feet and return to base. Colonel Donovan asked Cantacuzino if there were any questions and none were asked. Donovan said, "Then Captain Cantacuzino and Colonel Gunn you are excused to get some needed rest. Take off is scheduled for 0700 hours and the weather is finally cooperating with clear skies all the way. Gentlemen, the morning will bring with it a turning point in this war and, hopefully, also will bring it to a speedy conclusion."

Gunn and Cantacuzino went instead to the mess hall where over a couple of cups of coffee they sat and talked for a long time. Somehow they knew, after tomorrow morning, they would never see each other again. They just wanted to savor the memories and to remember the ordeal they shared. As was stated by Colonel Donovan very few men would have volunteered to do what they did. They had a right to be proud of their accomplishments and soon retired for the night.

Meanwhile back in the briefing room business as usual but more secretative. Colonel Donovan was speaking. "Gentlemen, we have no idea of what is going to take place tomorrow morning. Are we being lured into a trap? Had the Roumanian Government really capitulated against the German occupation? Is the Russian

Army already in the City of Bucharest? We must have answers to these and many other questions so we must proceed with extreme caution. To this extent General Twining has ordered maximum security and protection for our men still in Bucharest and the men that will be literally plucking them out of the hands of the retreating German Army."

Colonel Donovan continued, "Although Captain Cantacuzino appears to be an honorable man we must not forget that he is from a different culture. However, for the sake of those men in Bucharest, we must take him at his word but with caution. It has been decided to follow the Captain with yet another escort as insurance against any foul play. All fighter pilots are now being briefed on this mission. In addition to the secondary escort there will be two photo reconnaissance P-38 airplanes flying high above them to radio immediately any deviation from the flight plan. Should Captain Cantacuzino pull any funny stuff he will be the first to suffer retaliation. In conclusion, gentlemen we are planning for an evacuation of our boys from Bucharest in accordance with what we were told by Colonel Gunn and Captain Cantacuzino. Within forty eight hours we should see the results of our planning on a lot of exuberant and smiling faces. Now let's all get some rest, it may be the last chance we get for the next few days."

Six Am August 29, 1944 found Gunn and Cantacuzino leaving the mess hall and heading straight to the flight line and the P-51 Cantacuzino was to fly. At the mustang the two men stood there face to face looking each other squarely in the eye and in unison saluted each other. That salute quickly turned into a bear hug with a mutual "good luck and God speed." It was an emotional sight to see, two warriors saying good-bye for the last time. Gunn wouldn't leave him until he was safe inside that cockpit. The Tower shot the green flare signaling the start of the engines. The "FOLLOW ME" jeep was already alongside Cantacuzino's plane and with a bon voyage salute from Gunn the P-51 carrying the Roumanian pilot home was on it's way.

Gunn watched for the longest time until the planes were out of sight and then slowly walked back to the operations office. There he was advised that a B-24 was standing by to take him back to San Giovanni and his 454th bomb group. (Colonel James Gunn stayed in the Air Force until he retired in 1967. He makes his home in San Antonio, Texas).

The flight to Popesti Airfield was uneventful and in complete accordance with the plan. Cantacuzino landed and gave the all clear signals. The escorts then radioed to the P-38 reconnaissance plane of the all clear situation and to dispatch the advance party in two B-17's. The three escorting P-51's were joined by the other six P-51's and together all nine airplanes buzzed Popesti airfield in a display of airmanship never before seen in Roumania then took up a westerly direction, rocking their wings, climbed almost straight up into the sun and headed for Bari. When Captain Cantacuzino saw the other airplanes he just smiled, saluted and no doubt said to himself, "I would have done the same thing myself if I were in their shoes."

But Captain Cantacuzino's job was not complete. He hastened to the new government center in downtown Bucharest to see the new President Mr. Maniu. There he advised the President that his message to have either British or American forces occupy Roumania was being sent to the highest Allied authority. A letter was then prepared for General Twining from Mr. Maniu to have the Allies proceed with the evacuation of their airmen. Cantacuzino rushed back to Popesti and returned to Bari to deliver the letter. Once there he looked around for Gunn but was advised that he had returned to his bomb group. Cantacuzino returned before nightfall to Popesti and continued to fight the Germans in his P-51. That is until the Russians took it away from him and grounded him. This was devastating to a man like Constantine Cantacuzino who loved flying so much.

(Captain Constantine Cantacuzino was a professional stunt flyer before the outbreak of World War II and was drafted into the Roumanian Air Force. He escaped from Russian Rule in early 1955. Arriving in France he applied for a visa to the United States but for some unknown reason was constantly denied entry into America. He was reported to have died on the operating table while being administered emergency medical treatment for a severe intestinal ailment while in Spain in 1969.)

Above - Left is Colonel James Gunn, right is his Roumanian Pilot Captain Constantine Cantacuzino.
Below - The German Messerschmidt 109 that brought Colonel Gunn to Italy to begin the greatest aerial rescue mission ever attempted.

EIGHTEEN

With sounds of exploding bombs and ricocheting bullets absent from our environs the peace, quiet and serenity on the plaza that morning of August 29, 1944 was a prayer answered.

Knowing we could walk around without being ever vigilant of what is behind us or what is overhead or wondering whether we would be alive the next minute gave us the assurance that our lives were in the protective hands of someone somewhere. There were no crowds in the air raid shelter or on the plaza that morning except for our wounded men and about thirty of us healthy bodies to care for them. It seemed the citizenry of Bucharest felt safe enough to return to their homes. I realized it was about nine o'clock and we still have not had any word if Colonel Gunn had made it safely to Italy.

The morning passed quickly by being busy in the infirmary and just chit chatting with the people of Bucharest as they passed by. Their smiling faces again conveyed the happiness they felt now the fiery ordeal has passed.

It was a little after the noon hour when two doctors and two orderlies came from the hospital to help with our sick and wounded. This was the first real medical assistance we were offered since the bombing had started. It was not that they were ignoring us but because of the awesome numbers of people that were being brought to the hospital were wounded from the bombings, airplane strafings and snipers bullets. These doctors suggested we move our infirmed men back into the hospital where they could receive better care, better sanitation and a cleaner bed than the straw filled mattresses they were laying on. In hind sight it was nothing more than a miracle these men did not have their wounds further infected from those lice infested mattresses. It was agreed this would be a good move and preparations were initiated to start moving these men later in the day.

The calmness we experienced was enjoyed to it's fullest. We could easily enjoy the moments of relaxation and a life worthy of human beings. We were at liberty to talk to anyone, walk anywhere and rediscover the pleasures of being free and not looking through barbed wire fences with guards on the other side ready to shoot if you dared to go through. Freedom rediscovered! It is easy to image a question that I would remember all of my life and ask my fellow Americans. When did you last appreciate your Freedom?

It must have been just after the doctors left the building when three sedans drove up to the plaza and to my astonishment out jumped several American officers in spit polished uniforms who very briskly walked up onto the plaza and introduced themselves. Several of us were standing by and with unbelievable smiles we all saluted those men. One was a bird Colonel, two majors and four master sergeants. The Colonel introduced himself as Colonel Kraiger, Army Intelligence, the two majors were doctors to examine the wounded and the Sergeants were medical technicians. I escorted them into the infirmary and their first impression was a revolting condemnation of the area we had to house these sick and wounded men. Colonel Kraiger, whose very presence and commands left no doubt of his authority, told the doctors to examine each and every airman. Colonel Kraiger was then briefed on the adverse circumstances we had to survive under and that everyone was doing their best under such trying conditions. He was advised all the wounded were going to be moved back into the hospital this afternoon. He was also advised that the buildings in the hospital grounds that housed these men prior to being set free were now a shambles and this was the closest and safest shelter we could find. Colonel Kraiger was more at ease and understanding when he was told that these men were removed from those buildings only hours before they were destroyed by German bombs.

I couldn't contain myself any longer and just had to have answers to some questions which I addressed to the Colonel. "Colonel Kraiger, did Colonel Gunn make it to Italy? Is he all right?" Kraiger responded with a smiling face, "Yes, Colonel Gunn did make it to Italy and that is why I am here." Kraiger then briefed us on just what is being planned right now and ended with, "all you men will be back in Italy and on your way home in an matter of a few days." Yells of joy were in order and a lot of back slapping ensued on such joyous news.

A lot of questions were asked by the Colonel with reference to our stay in the prison camp and about our treatment. I later found out that he was a high ranking officer in the OSS (the Office of Strategic Services and the forerunner of the present day CIA). The fact that he was only a bird Colonel was only symbolic. His true rank was commensurate with his ability to get things done in a hurry.

With a more relaxed attitude Colonel Kraiger told us of the rescue plan. "The two B-17's that landed at Popesti airfield today carried the advance party to make preparations for the massive airlift of all you men. The plane I was on carried the medical team and the second plane had the intelligence team. I sent the intelligence team directly to the City of Ploiesti and to the oil refineries to inspect the damage inflicted by our bombs. They have orders to take extensive photographs of all refineries, and railroad yards for evaluation and effectiveness of the efforts of the bomber crews. They were told to inspect the defenses against aerial bombardment; to pay particular attention to the anti aircraft batteries; to find out why they were so much more effective and accurate over the Ploiesti targets than any other target in Europe at shooting down bombers that flew so high they were almost out of sight. We need this vital information for the protection and effectiveness of all the other bombers crews that still have to fly over Germany."

Kraiger continued, "The intelligence team has orders to work as fast as possible as it is not known if the Russians would object to an American inspection of the refinery and defense complexes since they, the Russians, occupied Roumania first. In order to insure maximum effort I instructed one of the members of the intelligence team to continually travel back and forth from Ploiesti to Popesti airfield with film and place it on one of the B-17's for safe keeping. It was believed that the Russians would not attempt to search an American military plane."

We discovered later the work pace of the intelligence team was frantic and proceeded efficiently only because of the volunteered help of the Roumanian people who provided transportation and directed the team members to the any location they desired to inspect. They were able to photograph the oil complexes, inspect the radar station, examine antiaircraft batteries and even found the defense headquarters which contained a complete layout map of the Ploiesti gun emplacements. In only five days the American intelligence team landed at noon on August 29, 1944, succeeded in their mission of unprecedented intelligence gathering and left on September 3, 1944. The success of their mission is attested to by the dramatic photographs in the center of this book.

One of the Doctors came out to the plaza where these discussion were taking place and told Kraiger that none of the men had a fever and this lead them to feel they were in no immediate danger from infections. The doctor also recommended that the wounded not be moved to the Hospital for such a move could be traumatic for some of the patients. He advised that these wounded men could be best cared for here and that their next move will be to a bus and the airfield to be airlifted back to Italy where they will be assured of the best of medical care possible at the 26th Army General Hospital in Bari. Of the wounded in that air raid shelter ten were litter patients, seventeen were on crutches and twenty three walking wounded. It would have been extremely difficult to find a more happier group of intrepid airmen considering all of the misery they went through. Some may say it was fate and others may say it was not ordained but in reality it was just not their time to enter Valhalla.

That evening on the plaza was passed with non descriptive conversation with Cisco, R.O. White, Nunzio Tripoldi, Duke laughing boy Brioli, Joe Rendleman and a few others whose names have long since been erased from my mind. The quiet could almost seem like a let down from being ever vigilant and ready for action at any second. It could have become a problem until we started to talk about home and how good it would be to see an American girl in mini skirts. As always talking about a new life at home was the needed therapy to forget about our recent ordeal. The following day August 30, 1944 was tranquility well deserved and passed without any complications or issues.

When that long awaited morning of August 31, 1944 arrived, it did so in soaring style (if a pun is permitted). The air space over

Bucharest was filled to capacity with B-17's being escorted by P-51 and P-38 fighters. All were flying at low level with the absence of anti aircraft firings and those dreaded black mushroom like clouds. Everyone of us hoped that that sight was symptomatic, for we were a little nervous about flying over German lines to Italy and extremely reluctant to be shot out of the air again.

Our nervousness was compounded when we learned all guns and ammunition were removed from the bombers to make room for us rescuees. On a mature thought, however, we realized that 15th Air Force Commander, General Nathan Twining, was determined not to lose us a second time. Later news substantiated that realization. The airlift evacuation was an all-out effort of the United States Army Air Force. Every available fighter plane in Italy would take part in this unprecedented operation to protect those unarmed bombers making it virtually impossible, even suicidal, for any Nazi fighter to try to penetrate such a protective flank.

At the same time as the bombers and fighters were flying over Bucharest three buses escorted by Roumanian military police drove up to the plaza. An English speaking Lieutenant told us they were to take the wounded and sick personnel to the airport. At last the start of the long awaited return trip was being initiated. No time was wasted in assisting all the wounded out to the buses. The smiling faces at the windows as the buses pulled away was an unforgettable sight. "Tomorrow will be our turn" was the thought on everyone's mind. Once again tranquility was set in place on that plaza.

The rescue/evacuation was planned to assure complete success in every detail. There were three waves of B-17's of twelve planes each and each spaced an hour apart. The first wave landed at ten o'clock and left at ten forty five as the next wave was approaching Popesti airfield due to land at eleven o'clock. The third wave was to land at twelve o'clock. During all this time the skies were filled with fighter planes to assure complete protection. Since the fighters cannot stay in the air as long as a bomber there were constant shuttle runs of fighters to and from Italy. With the relieved fighters returning to their bases in Italy, refueling and taking off immediately again. At no time during the six hour round trip flying time between Italy and Bucharest were any of the bombers without full fighter plane escort.

The mission records show the second wave of B-17's were, on the return trip, intercepted by four German ME-109 Messerschmidt fighters. They were driven off by the escort with one ME-109 and one P-38 being shot down. There was no damage to any of the bombers or their precious cargos. If any of the men had known of this attempt I'm sure there would have been a lot a messy pants to be cleaned.

This first day of evacuation returned to Italy seven hundred and forty seven former prisoners of war including twenty five British personnel. When all were assembled at the Bari airport General Twining personally greeted them and, confidentially, he was over heard quietly saying, with the appearance of tears in his eyes, "Thank God Some of My Boys have returned."

The following day September 1, 1944 was our and my day to return from limbo. Only one bus drove to the plaza this morning as our number dwindled to twenty four. We slowly walked over to it and without exception each one stopped, looked around and in their own way said good bye to the people of Bucharest and expressing a "Thank You" for helping us survive. For some unknown reason there was a huge crowd gathered at the plaza as we were leaving and all waved farewell to us. As the bus pulled away I could not help but to wonder about their future. The sight of those men, women and children who, only a few days ago, were on their knees begging me to help them save their freedom. I'm not a highly educated man but I wonder about one society wanting to be free and that freedom could, without reason, be denied by another society. Something has to be wrong with that second society that has created so much fear in so many people.

This second day of the rescue mission brought only sixteen B-17's as that was all that was needed. Standing next to the plane into which I would climb into within a few moments, I casually looked around and let my mind re-live that time not so many days earlier when I had been paralyzed by a premonition of not seeing deliverance day come. Just then someone snapped my picture, a photograph which I would not see developed until twenty eight years later to the day on September 1, 1972 when it was shown to me at the first national reunion of the survivors of the Roumanian Prison Camps by Harry Harris, now Reverend Harry Harris.

Entering that B-17, I "managed" an enviable place between the pilot and co-pilot, where I could view a panorama almost five months late. Recrossing the muddy Danube River and the wide Adriatic Sea canopied by azure skies, I could restrain neither my incredulous exhilaration nor the silly smile which expressed it. Like Monsieur Manette in Dickens tale of London and Paris, I had been "recalled to life." Childishly I repeated to myself, "I made it! I Made it!"

Excited that the war was over, for me at least, I then tried previewing a long, wonderful life, even if only in glimpses. Having conquered despair I wondered if modern man was ready to come to his senses about his awesome social responsibilities and stop this nonsense of kill or be killed, commonly referred to as man's inhumanity to mankind et al. I knelt silently in that cockpit speculating on the future with only my limited knowledge of history and my wartime experiences to guide me. But, I was too young and naive that day to visualize man's postwar course. I could do no better than "idealize." Accordingly, I let my mind revert to sky gazing and enjoying another flight of the Phoenix.

While still flying over the Adriatic Sea the distant sky started to darken, it dawned on me that we were approaching the Italian coastline. Again, childishly, I decided then that "I had really made it." The pilot looked around at me and asked, "why do you have that particular smile on your face?" My reply, still with that smile was prosaic, —- no, it was colloquial: "If you don't know, I don't think I would be able to explain it to you." The pilot's eyes widened and his face puckered somewhat as he looked at me and said, "Yeh, I know."

Approaching full sight of the Italian Coast the pilot started to chit chat and the co-pilot joined in. We found out later that they were told not to question us too much but to let us offer conversation. They were keenly interested in the events of our imprisonment and the treatment accorded us. Despite time limitations to landing, I condensed for them the contents of this book. The pilot had only two bombing missions to his credit and the co-pilot had but three. Just before landing I said, "Sirs, I wish I had some word of wisdom for both of you but the only thing I have right now is to wish you the best of luck and hope you know how to say a lot of prayers.

It is impossible to forget getting off that plane in Bari! Most of the guys actually knelt down on all fours to kiss the Italian soil, while others were content to laugh wildly and exchange congratulatory handshakes galore. On that second day of ex-P.O.W. arrivals General Twining could not welcome us personally as he was seeing the wounded at the General Hospital. Though disappointed at his absence, we understood and appreciated his joy at our safe return.

The Battles for Black Gold, Oil, began on April 4, 1944 and culminated with the last mission on August 19, 1944. The Roumanian Government ousted the Germans on August 23, 1944. In that span of time 314 bombers, each with ten men, and one hundred and eleven fighters were shot out of the skies over Roumania. The lives of 3251 airmen were in jeopardy. Only 1277 men (39%) returned, Indeed life expectancy for a bomber crew was not very encouraging in those days. Today, in 1989, one plane with one pilot with one bomb could inflict a thousand times more damage. But, in 1944 that was the only way we knew how.

After that jubilant lighting on the Italian soil trucks took us at once to a tent area on the far side of the airfield. Snacks and refreshments were already prepared for us and after filling our guts we were told that all sorts of goodies were waiting for us. After snacking we were called aside en-masse and issued the most singular order of a lifetime. We were to be de-loused before being readmitted into society. In an adjacent olive grove, then, we shed our clothes onto a huge pile and ushered into a makeshift tent-type shower for the first hot soapy shower we had since being shot down more than four months ago. Next, after drying, we were methodically sprayed with a white powder: first , our heads, until we looked like grey headed old airmen instead of young lions; then our arm pits and trunks; lastly our anuses and "jewels", ticklish though that powder felt in such private parts. And would you believe that the whole scenario was being amusingly observed by a squadron of W.A.C.'s, some from behind trees.

Once decontaminated, we were issued clean undershirts, shorts. and brand new khaki uniforms. Nothing felt better than cleanliness, the luxury most missed by all. After delousing we were then allowed to mingle with other members of the human race. My crew members had hoped that I would be on one of the last planes and kept a vigil for me. They were all there, Randy, Chief, Paul, Charlie, Pop, Dana, Len, Glenn and Ed waiting for me to be appropriately attired for society. Hand shakes and no doubt some tears were present on our way to a fantastic dinner of roast turkey, roast beef and just about anything we would want. They even prepared a clean bunk for me, that's why we were the best dam crew ever assembled.

That night was spent filling each other in on our hectic experiences after the bombings started. That clean bed in that tent was overwhelming and inviting. That was a night of deliverance for me for a whole night without being woke up with lice crawling up my ass or in my nose. My very last thought before dozing off into a sound sleep, "We made it! and we made it together."

The first morning of absolute freedom brought to me an indescribable feeling. At breakfast we were advised to go to the operations office for a taxi trip back to our home base in Manduria. Arriving at the Bari flight line we could not help but be drawn to the sight of those white tailed Liberators the fabled "Cottontail Bombers." It was only a thirty minute flight and upon landing and parking we found a very special person was waiting for us, Sam Grybel our crew chief. Approaching me first with a bear hug, he then greeted the entire crew in a similar fashion. So ecstatic with joy was Sam that tears gleamed in his eyes.

The circumstances of a bomber crew chief were never easy. When his plane and crew did not return from a combat mission he would endure long and lasting personal torments. Had his maintenance been adequate? Was it some how his fault that the plane had not brought back it's crew? Sam had hassled with these anxieties which were but melting memories at that reunion. In the next few days Sam would not let us out of his sight, always asking more questions like, "how was it over there?" And always ending with " God, I'm glad you all made it back and together! Sam was from the Detroit area and this would be the last time we would ever see each other.

Walking back to our barracks I ran into our Group PR reporter T/Sgt Jim Campbell. He said, "Fili, boy am I glad you made it back, I have a message for you." "You remember Johnny

Oaks don't you?" "I sure do!" Jim continued; "Well Johnny transferred to another crew and finished his fifty missions and went home. Before he left he told me that if I ever see you again to tell you "Thanks" for getting him the Silver Star for releasing that bomb." I could only say "Great, Johnny deserved it". Jim said, "I have another message for you. Frank Gentile who was thrown out of Lt. Edward's bomber over Yugoslavia to save his life was picked up by some farmers who couldn't do anything for him so they took him to a German garrison. The German's took him to their hospital, fixed up his wounds and he is alive, well and no doubt giving those Heinie's a hard time in a prison camp." In saying thanks and good bye to Jim it was hard to find words to express my feelings at such good news.

In these few days at our squadron camp we were processed to leave by the first available surface transportation to the good ole U.S.A. We were flown to Naples and boarded the French frigate Athos II.

That ocean voyage took us through the Straits of Gibraltar at night. We were not allowed on deck at night and missed the rock itself. We were told that Nazi agents were still counting the Allied ships that passed and relayed that information to their submarines in the Atlantic Ocean.

Two days out of Gibraltar, I was standing with a few other men at the side railing about the middle of the ship just doing some more reminiscing about recent experiences and anticipating my homecoming. My thread of thought was suddenly snipped in the bud by the wailing of a destroyer's siren. It was coming full speed in our direction. Not being a seagoing sailor I could only guess that it was about to engage something that was not a part of our convoy. When I saw it I could only say. "What? My God! That destroyer must be on a collision course with a something!" Glued to my spot at the railing I froze in that position when suddenly a white streak in the ocean became visible. Stupefied by fear once again, grabbing that railing my knuckles became pure white. The upper most, and only, thought in my mind was to be shipwrecked by a torpedo would be the last misfortune necessary for my treading the whole winepress of World War II. With my eyes still glued to that white streak in the water it passed in front of the ship close enough to know that it was there. While I hardly remember how long I held my breath after sighting that missile I can never forget how deeply I exhaled after it missed us. And, as few of us that did see it, we were treated like madmen when we tried to describe our close encounter to the others.

That Naples to New York return trip took thirteen days. Puffing into New York Harbor, we hailed the statue of Liberty with our eyes gleaming at that magnificent sight. We hailed The Lady as enthusiastically as the European immigrants did for the past fifty years. My eyes were glued to her raised hand that carried the torch of eternal freedom. Her words echoed in my mind, "Give me your tired, your poor, your huddled masses yearning to be free"

The words "yearning to be free" reverberated in my mind. I was enchanted at seeing her for the first time. Suddenly I became alone with my thoughts of freedom and unaware of even being on an ocean going vessel or that any other persons were near me. I was once again — alone.

With my eyes glued on her face a shadow slowly passed between us and startled me. It was the stewardess's arm, coming for the breakfast trays, that broke my concentration, and, with her soft compassionate voice, she asked the lady to my right for her tray and this time without any incident. I was back on that jet airplane on my way to Rome. I glanced at both of my seat companions and could see they were relieved I was back to a normal state although they reserved a final opinion.

"Miss," I said, "I would like that cup of coffee now, if you don't mind." She nodded and brought it to me immediately. In grasping the coffee cup I noticed a cold claminess of my hands, my mouth was dry, my face felt ashen and my heart was palpitating to an unusual degree. Only I knew why. I took a few deep breaths of air, drank the coffee and laid my head back on the head rest. I looked out again at those snow covered alpine peaks. Did I relive that whole scenario and in such a short span of time? How was that possible? Did someone guide me to be here this day? The more questions I asked the more frustrated I became. It became apparent that I had to accept this apparition, if that's what it's called and be thankful that I am alive. The next few moments brought a rare feeling of peacefulness unparalleled in my life.

I could not leave those mountains without one more look. I leaned forward and closer to the window to get a better view. The lady in the window seat looked at me and I at her with a smile and "voila" she smiled back and this time she had an understanding look in her eyes. As I looked down I could not help but think about those American and British airmen I knew that are now entombed in the high glaciers of those European mountains. Another monument to man's inhumanity to man. In my final look I could not help but to touch my right hand to my forehead to salute them — to let them know they haven't been forgotten — and that — they did not die in vain.

EPILOG

It is incumbent on me to reflect on the course of events throughout the world since the end of that global war of the forties and those death defying flights over Hitler's Europe.

Yes - we thought the war was over after the surrender of Germany and Japan and there would never be another threat of any new wars, Mustered out of the Air Force, we all began the enormous task of converting from a wartime economy to a peacetime economy. We were happy, for we thought that man had finally learned his lesson - the bitter truth that war, in its sheer stupidity and idiocy, brings nothing but sorrow, pain and misery to all the peoples of the world.

Unfortunately, in the questionable practicality of global politics, war seems to be the end result of two political beliefs with their respective ways of life, and the never ending arguments seem to require the shedding of human blood for a temporary respite.

The closing year's of the 1940's were supposed to bring sunshine. happiness and peace to all on earth. Heaven was supposed to come down for all, and only good things happen. We looked backwards, noting man's great progress in the humanities - progress from the inhuman and barbaric days and customs of the crucifixion to the modern intelligent and sensible approach to problems such as the gas chambers and ovens of Buchenwald, Auschwitz and other infamous repositories of progress. The dark ages of cruelty that resulted in the inquisition have been replaced by the enlightened approach that resulted in the Nuremburg trials. We have indeed progressed from the atrocities of the hundred year wars to such simple exercises as World Wars 1 and 11, Korea, Vietnam and terroristic actions of a few sadistic leaders of developing third world nations. Vietnam, the great war that penalized our young men, for the crime of being so poor that they couldn't go to college, by the unique punishment of forcing them to go, most unwillingly, to the maiming eroding and death dealing service in the Vietnam war. More than 50,000 had died - over 300,000 were wounded, crippled, maimed physically, mentally and spiritually - many for the rest of their lives - in a war they did not make, they did not want, they did not deserve. But they did die, in a war against which their elected leaders refused to hear- refused to listen - to any legal arguments

In looking back on the events of those autumn days in Bucharest, I am aghast at the total disregard our government showed towards the cry for help and compassion brought out by Mr. Maniu, the new head of state of Roumania. He made this compassionate plea, this begging for understanding, sympathy and aid, to the senior officer of a group of interned American soldiers. Princess Catherine Caradja added her voice and prayers to the same officers.

The common citizenry of Bucharest went down on bended knees to a small group of interned Americans begging them to help save their freedom, "don't let the communists enslave us was their plea." Never before has a country shown such a total unity in the common cause of saving their small nation. Three words from America could have saved this small country from forty five years of enslavement behind an iron curtain. "WE OCCUPY ROUMANIA".

Yet, we turned our backs on them. We, the selfsame people who repaid Germany and Japan for their temerity and iron disregard for the safety and well-being of the rest of the world by pouring countless millions of American tax dollars into their economy until today their currency is stronger than ours. We, the self same people who fought and died in Korea and Vietnam under the guise of saving a small nation from communism, but couldn't be bothered with saving a nation such as Roumania, totally united in their common purpose of remaining free.

I am an ordinary citizen and human being, yet I question the rationale that could permit one group of people - begging for help - to be swallowed by the communistic juggernaut, yet pour such a treasury of human lives and dollars into the very same effort where it wasn't called for by anyone there. I would also question the opportunism that would permit such a travesty to occur.

Our elected government leaders, the President, the Senate and the Congress enmasse told the American people that we were in

Vietnam to prevent the spread of communism and that the citadel of communism was in Moscow, Russia. Yet, these same elected leaders allowed the same communist government in Moscow to send their engineers and purchasing agents into mainstream America to buy up American technology, machinery and materials to be sent back to Russia. These same Russians were using American abilities to produce war materials, guns, grenades and bullets, to be sent to the Viet Cong in North Vietnam to kill or wound American servicemen. These Russians set up offices in the Mellon National Bank Building in Pittsburgh, Pennsylvania and in the General Motors building in New York City. If anyone else attempted or approved such an action they would, without the slightest hesitation, be tried for treason. But when promoted by elected leaders it is called something else. I am sure that historians in the near future would not and could not attempt to justify or exculpate these two totally divergent actions taken in Roumania and Vietnam.

The sneak attack on Pearl Harbor accomplished one very positive action - it welded the people of the United States into a single massive block with one objective - to win the war, to protect our homeland and prevent any enemy from invading and degrading us. The day after Pearl Harbor America had no Navy, no Army and no Air Force. It took only four years to build a two ocean navy, assemble and train a ten million man army, build the largest air force in the history of aviation and fight a two ocean war to the final defeat of the enemy.

The war in Vietnam was the exact opposite. Never, since the Civil War had this country been so divided, with literally brother against brother and father against son. Did we learn our lesson? Did we learn from our own history? Did we learn from our own mistakes? Apparently not! It took ten years to lose a war that we should not have been involved and in a land that was less in size than the whole state of North Dakota. Four of those ten years was just to wind down the war as stated by President Nixon in 1969.

We must once again become a united people. We must once again find the heritage, national pride, dedication, patriotism and determination that made America great, a heritage we seem to have lost. We must once again face the common enemy, by whatever name it goes under, war or corruption, and winning the conflict decisively and hopefully for the last time.

Throughout history, every great nation has fallen, and usually through the same causes: Deterioration of the home and the mutual love and respect that was a part of home and family life. The imposition of greater and greater tax burdens until the national economy becomes farcical and mistrusted. Indulgence in greater, more costly and totally useless armaments. The loss of real and dedicated leadership - instead of passing the reins of government into the hands of small, astute and grasping people.

This seems to be a cyclic series of events. But I believe that an intelligent approach, enlightened and unencumbered research and a driving desire to break the repetitive nature of new nations - from building to power structure, corruption asserting itself and the final decay of old, tired third rate countries - will result in a turning of the course of events and a resurgence of the elements that made America the great and enviable land of freedom for all.

We are standing on the threshold of decision as we start a new era for Mankind in the last decade of the twentieth century. Historians of the future will have to record if this was the decade that Mankind had finally found the wisdom to abolish war as a way of life on Planet Earth. Or will they record a dismal failure?

The cold war between the two super powers, America and Russia, has come to a sudden conclusion. The symbolic demarcation line between democratic freedom and totalitarian dictatorship, the Berlin Wall, has come tumbling down. It tumbled not because of political persuasion but because the people of all lands have had enough of bondage and political corruption. And only the people can keep the pressure on to assure peace and harmony for all people of all lands.

In looking back on those days of deprivation in Bucharest I am humbled to tears and thankful for being spared entrance to Valhalla and any cruelty by my captors. Such as the cruelty that was forced upon the P.O.W.'s during the Bataan death march, the experimental laboratories in Manchuria and the cruel and inhuman torture inflicted on the P.O.W.'s by the Viet Cong, (some for the most of nine years), and so many other places.

As for my homeland, America, the citadel of universal freedom and opportunity, I hope to live long enough to see a resurgence of the national pride that made us great. For only we the people can once again wake up this sleeping giant to the total futility and folly of war as a solution to political ethnic or financial differences in the world. Only we the people can, by the intelligent and complete exercise of our most potent weapon - the ballot - eliminate the rampant and out of control corruption in government and market place. And only we the people can, with the ballot, insist on a government that rules only with the consent of the governed.

The long, harsh winter at Valley Forge is over. The early spring brings forth a new inspiration, and George Washington is kneeling at prayer, thankful that most of his brave men have survived the ordeal. The monument below now rests within a few feet of the magnificent bronze statue of General Washington at Freedoms Foundation in Valley Forge. At left is an enlargement of the plaque on the monument.

One of the many lessons the author learned while a POW was that man could live in peace and harmony. This inspired him to create a monument for America. This monument was presented and accepted at the Freedom's Foundation in Valley Forge for perpetual care. It now rests within a few feet of the awesome bronze statue of General George Washington kneeling at prayer.

Above - A 1975 photograph of the author Bill Fili standing beside his airplane that he named DESTINY DEB II. Below - A 1992 photograph of the author Bill Fili as he lectured to high school students on the trauma of aerial warfare and how all wars could be eliminated as a way of life on Planet Earth.